NOËL

NOËL

Charles Castle

W H Allen
A Division of Howard and Wyndham Ltd
1972

Printed in Great Britain by Fletcher & Son Ltd, Norwich, for the publishers W H Allen & Co Ltd 43 Essex Street, London WC2R 3JG. Bound by Richard Clay (The Chaucer Press) Ltd, Bungay, Suffolk.
ISBN 0 491 00534 2

To
SIR NOËL
In admiration and devotion

ACKNOWLEDGEMENTS

I should like to thank Sir Noël for his help and for his permission to publish this book, and to thank him for his generosity and support in the making of the documentary film *This is Noël Coward* on which it is modelled.

To thank, too, all those who helped the book along its way to completion—Cole Lesley, Graham Payn, Joan Hirst and Geoffrey Johnson, as well as so many others including Stanley Hall, Arthur Marshall—and Jeffrey Simmons and Adrian Shire of W. H. Allen; Ken McCormick of Doubledays, Mavis Johnson, and with special thanks to those who gave their time to film tributes to Sir Noël, the transcriptions of which appear in these pages.

The publishers and I are grateful for permission to use photographs, theatre designs, sheet music, cartoons, graphics and news items from Sir Noël's private archives, Sir Cecil Beaton, Angus McBean (The Harvard University Theatre Collection), Osbert Lancaster, Chappell & Co. Ltd, Universal Pictures, The Rank Organisation, The Raymond Mander and Joe Mitchenson Theatre Collection, Gladys Calthrop, Dorothy Wilding, Allan Warren, Lorranne Richards, Joan Williams, Erling Mandelmann (jacket photograph) and Beaverbrook Newspapers Ltd.

Charles Castle

A GREAT EVERYTHING

Maurice Chevalier

'He is a great everything. He is not only a great gentleman, he is a very warm person, very very talented and warm,' said Maurice Chevalier.

He had known Noël Coward for almost fifty years, and we had flown to Paris from London to film him.

'Of course I've seen Noël in Hollywood, and I've seen him in Paris too. In Paris he was very nice to me. He came when they made a big affair of my eightieth birthday.'

A big affair indeed. The *Lido*, the magnificent night-club on the Champs-Elysées, had been taken over for the celebration, and was crammed with two thousand or more celebrities come to drink Chevalier's health in champagne in between acts of a spectacular, specially-produced floor show.

'All I can say is that I hope Noël and I can still be as friendly and successful for another fifty years, and like that you know, for me, it would be absolutely fine and okay!'

I had known Sir Noël Coward for only ten years. With another friend of his, Stanley Hall, I came to his home in Switzerland to film him talking about his life.

In the drawing-room of his pink and white villa stands a large glass screen, covered with signed photographs of many of the stars of today and yesterday who shared his successes—Vivien Leigh, Marlene Dietrich, Laurence Olivier, John Gielgud, Beatrice Lillie, Gertrude Lawrence and dozens of others, and of friends and neighbours— Joan Sutherland, Lilli Palmer, Richard Burton, David Niven. Propped up on the two grand pianos that stand back to back are more photographs, framed and signed— Queen Elizabeth the Queen Mother, Princess Margaret,

Lord Mountbatten, Audrey Hepburn, Merle Oberon, Margot Fonteyn, Rudolph Nureyev . . .

In a corner there is a record-player and tape-recorder, and packed below them dozens of records and tapes of his shows—*Bitter-Sweet*, *Pacific 1860*, *Ace of Clubs*, *Sail Away*—sung by Joan Sutherland, Beatrice Lillie, Gertrude Lawrence, Evelyn Laye, Alice Delysia, Judy Garland—and of course his own recordings by the dozen. At the side of the fireplace stands a huge photo blow-up of Maggie Smith in *Hay Fever*. Shelves climbing to the ceiling are crowded with books on every conceivable subject. His own writings—novels, short stories, autobiography and plays—are in his study upstairs. Here, too, are neatly arranged photograph albums of his plays—*Private Lives*, *Blithe Spirit*, *Tonight at Eight-Thirty*, *Present Laughter*—films

Sir Noël's house in Les Avants in Switzerland.

8

—In Which We Serve, Brief Encounter—and revues—*London Calling!, On with the Dance, This Year of Grace!* and *Words and Music.* There are albums, too, of his world-wide travels and snapshots of friends visiting him at his homes throughout the years, in Kent, London, Bermuda, Jamaica, and here in Switzerland.

Huge picture windows provide magnificent views of the Swiss mountains above, and Lake Geneva below. During the summer he lives and works in these peaceful surroundings, then leaves for his second home in Jamaica to spend the winter months.

As we drove down to the village of Les Avants, on our way to film Richard Burton and David Niven in Monte Carlo, the lone figure of a woman approached us in the distance, struggling up the hill along the narrow lane with

The drawing room.

two enormous shopping bags. It turned out to be Joan Sutherland, looking quite different from the last time I'd seen her, singing in *Norma* at Covent Garden. When she saw us she stopped, dropped her bags and roared with laughter.

'What the hell are you doing here?' she called in her disarming Australian accent.

'We've come to film Noël.'

'Why haven't you been over to see us at our place? I could tell you a thing or two about him. We live right next door to him. Just through a hole in the hedge.'

She had been to the hairdressers and her thick auburn hair was swathed up on her head.

'I have it done this way to draw attention from my enormous jaw! I really do it for my mother-in-law's sake. With a face like mine what else can you do?'

below, Noël at Les Avants.
right, Joan Sutherland.
right below, the Drawing Room.

'I think some of the marvellous things about Noël,' she said later, 'are his human qualities. He's wonderful to our young son Adam. I mean, you wouldn't think that some-one like Noël, who has so much to do, would bother with children, but do you know, he taught Adam to paint—well, I suppose it *is* a painting!

'Noël said to Adam, "Why not come and have tea with me, and perhaps we could paint something together?"

' "But I can't paint," Adam said.

' "All you have to do is put down what you see," Noël replied, and so under his guidance Adam painted the mountains and the lake—he was triumphant!

'At Christmas time, we always troop over to Noël's house to unwrap *our* presents under *his* Christmas tree, and on Christmas Eve, he and his house guests come over to us to unwrap *their* presents in *our* home.'

Lilli Palmer.

Sir Cecil Beaton.

Richard Burton.

'My mother said if you ever bring that naughty boy here again, I'll turn him out.'

Hermione Gingold

'He's kind, he's good, he is of course tremendously talented—but we won't mention that.'

Brian Aherne

'Noël is the supreme master of the art of comedy.'

Lilli Palmer

'He has an incredible talent for friendship.'

Yul Brynner

'He can get into two or three words, just dripped out, such a witty comment on the situation. He doesn't waste words.'

Dame Edith Evans

'He is punctual, polite, precise and elegant; he became as popular and as much talked about as the Prince of Wales.'

Sir John Gielgud

'I've never had a happier experience in the theatre than working with him.'

Sir Cecil Beaton

'I still didn't see why he should be called the Master and perhaps some of the other more towering figures in the theatre should not also be called second Master or third Master and so on.'

Richard Burton

'A great thing about him is that like all men of enormous talent or genius who is also essentially a modern person, he did not merely echo the age he lived in as a youth, or as a very young man, but he helped to create it. If anyone was one of the creators of what we call the 1920s nowadays, Noël was that man.'

Micheál MacLiammóir

Yul Brynner.

Dame Edith Evans.

Sir John Gielgud.

A narrative on
Charles Castle's documentary film,
This is Noël Coward,
in which those who have worked with him
and shared his life talk of him.

THE BOY ACTOR
by
Noël Coward

I can remember, I can remember.
The months of November and December
Were filled for me with peculiar joys
So different from those of other boys
For other boys would be counting the days
Until end of term and holiday times
But I was acting in Christmas plays
While they were taken to pantomimes.
I didn't envy their Eton suits,
Their children's dances and Christmas trees.
My life had wonderful substitutes
For such conventional treats as these.
I didn't envy their country larks,
Their organized games in panelled halls:
While they made snow-men in stately parks
I was counting the curtain calls.

'...A BRAZEN, ODIOUS LITTLE PRODIGY'

NOËL COWARD:

I was born in Teddington, a suburb of London, through which the Thames flowed serenely without paying the faintest attention.

Noël Coward aged five.

The event took place on December 16th 1899, and shortly afterwards Noël was baptised into the Church of England. His father, Arthur Sabin Coward, sang in the choir of St Alban's Church, where in 1890, during choir practice, he fell in love with a Miss Veitch, and subsequently married her.

Violet Veitch's father, a naval captain, had died quite young in Madeira, and she lived in genteel poverty in Teddington with her sister Vida and their mother. Her union with Arthur Coward was a love match, for his circumstances were little better than her family's. Their first child, Russell, died of meningitis at the age of six, and Noël was born eighteen months later. As Teddington became more popular, the Coward family moved to a small rented house in a less expensive part of Surrey. Mr Coward now left his job at Metzler's, the London music publishers, and became a piano salesman. Shortly after their arrival in Sutton Noël's brother Eric was born.

Noël's mother was a little deaf from an early age, and he first developed his characteristically crisp, clipped manner of speaking for her benefit. Unfortunately she never learned to lip-read in all her ninety-one years.

As Noël's parents sang in the choir, and his father sold pianos, it was naturally a family custom to sing at the piano in the evenings. Noël quickly developed a taste for music, and also for the theatre as the result of frequent family outings to Broadstairs, Brighton or Bognor in the summer to see comedy and song-and-dance acts on the sands. Annual birthday treats were trips to theatres in London for performances of *The Dairymaids* and *The Blue Moon*, musicals at the London Hippodrome and pantomime at Croydon. Noël made his first stage appearance at the age of six at an end-of-term prize-giving concert dressed in a white suit and singing 'Coo' from *A Country Girl*, but he failed to win a prize and was led away wailing.

NOËL COWARD:

From Sutton, we finally made London. When I was nine, we moved to 70 Prince of Wales Mansions, Battersea Park, where we had a flat at the top of a building without a lift.

Aged ten.

But lift or no lift, the move to London resulted in a rise in their living expenses. An increase in the family income was therefore accomplished by the appearance of two lodgers, Mr Baker and Mr Denston, who helped keep the wolf from the door and bowed to tradition by joining the family in their sing-songs around the piano.

Noël was obviously talented, and he always delighted in pleasing his mother by showing off. She was inclined to spoil him, and, since she had lost her first child, seemed to shower more than the usual degree of love and attention on her second.

By the time he was nine, Noël had appeared in school concerts and taken ballet classes. He was anxious to join a school choir, which resulted in a second blow to his musical ambitions—his voice was not considered good enough.

When I was young, I was always in Southwark Cathedral or somewhere hooting away 'O for the Wings of a Dove', and was always furious, after finishing an anthem absolutely beautifully, to find everybody in the church crouched on their knees in prayer and not applauding me.

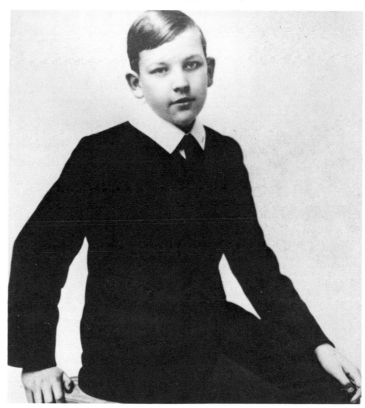

Messrs Baker and Denston now departed—perhaps their voices weren't up to it—and Mrs Coward decided to let the flat for six months and looked for a small rented cottage in the country. Noël and his brother stayed with their grandmother and Aunts Borby and Vida at Southsea until a cottage was found not far from the village of Tichfield. The family stayed there for six months, enjoying the doubtful benefits of a thatched roof and a lavatory at the bottom of the garden.

Meanwhile the children's education was being badly neglected and on returning to school in London, Noël, spoilt as ever, was allowed to take dancing lessons in Hanover Square in his spare time.

NOËL COWARD:

My further education stopped when I was ten, and I began to learn my job, which was theatre. My mother worried about my choice, but I have no regrets about it. The sad thing was that she knew little about the theatre, but she used to take me to it on my birthday, and I knew by the age of ten that I would go on the stage.

Oddly enough I have always had a reputation for high-life, earned no doubt in the twenties with such plays as The Vortex. *But as you see, I was a suburban boy, born and bred in the suburbs of London, which I've always loved and always will. But I've never forgotten the dreariness of those early years when I was earning a living. All those people looking for jobs. You get to know people much better in adversity than you do once you're* 'up there'.

The real secret is concentration. I've always been a hundred per cent concentrated on what I was doing at that moment, and that's terribly important. But I've never concentrated much on games. I played football when I was ten, but I wasn't any good at it, so I gave it up when I could, and concentrated on what I knew about.

Little June Tripp.

My first job in the theatre came as a result of an advertisement in the Daily Mirror *which said, 'Handsome attractive boy wanted for part in Christmas pantomime. Must be talented.'* [There was no question of Noël's talent in either his own eyes, or those of his mother, and since there was no reason on earth why he should not be employed on the spot, an appointment was made for an audition in a small bare rehearsal room near Baker Street.] *I sang and danced briskly to a woman called Miss Lila Field, and she said, 'Very very good. I will engage him. The fee will be a guinea and a half a week.'*

'But we can't afford that,' my mother replied.

'No,' Miss Field said. 'That's what he will **receive.**'

Noël led a number with Princess Sole, played by Little June Tripp (who later, calling herself simply June, became a famous actress and married Lord Inverclyde).

'Mrs Worthington'

Regarding yours, dear Mrs Worthington,
Of Wednesday the 23rd,
Although your baby,
May be,
Keen on a stage career,
How can I make it clear,
That this is not a good idea.
For her to hope,
Dear Mrs Worthington,
Is on the face of it absurd,
Her personality
Is not in reality
Inviting enough,
Exciting enough
For this particular sphere.

Don't put your daughter on the stage,
  Mrs Worthington,
Don't put your daughter on the stage,
The profession is overcrowded
And the struggle's pretty tough,
And admitting the fact
She's burning to act,
That isn't quite enough.
She has nice hands, to give the wretched
  girl her due,
But don't you think her bust is too
Developed for her age,
I repeat
Mrs Worthington,
Sweet
Mrs Worthington,
Don't put your daughter on the stage.

Alfred Willmore, who was the same age as Noël, appeared as King Goldfish in the same all-children production, *The Goldfish*, a fairy play in three acts in which Noël played Prince Mussel. He vividly remembers their first professional engagement together (he later changed his name to Micheál MacLiammóir).

MICHEÁL MACLIAMMÓIR:

I am flattered by being told I am the same age as Noël, but I'm not really, as Noël never fails to remind me whenever we meet. 'Micheál,' he says to me, 'you are seven weeks and two days older than I am and don't attempt to deny it to me or to anyone else.' And that is because I was born on the 26th of October in the same unspeakable year which was I think vaguely connected with the Boer War and a few other world events. But as Noël was born on December 16th we are of the same generation at any rate.

I vividly remember Noël's bowler hat. It wasn't at the first rehearsal that he wore it, but he did create a great sensation once the play had at long last opened in a professional theatre after indescribable vicissitudes. It was produced by Miss Lila Field, who had been educated, as

below, Alfred Willmore (Micheál MacLiammóir) aged ten as King Goldfish.
right, Micheál MacLiammóir.
right below, Noël as Prince Mussel the Jester, amusing the Court in *The Goldfish*.

the papers so rhythmically said, 'in Peru', where she was born, 'educated at the College of Notre Dame in Lima, Peru'. She and her sister were very picturesque ladies with sort of fandango hair and eyes, and the kind of lovely soft pink cheeks and the frilled blouses of the times. They were very kind to us all.

I remember Noël's look of well, scepticism would be saying too much, after all he was only a boy of ten, but he already had an incredulous look of not quite believing everything he heard. And he was wonderfully certain. I recall my first conversation of all with him. I was the soul of uncertainty and could never decide whether I wanted to be a painter, a farmer or a draper's assistant, because of seeing somebody in Cork when I was very small dealing out bales of silk stuff with flaps and claps on the counter and then pushing money into a little wooden ball and sending it across a wire across this big shop called The Arcade. I had never got over that and I always thought that would be lovely. Then I wanted to be a Japanese acrobat, so when I first saw Noël, I said: 'What do you want to be?'

'An actor, of course,' he replied without the slightest

As Slightly.

hesitation. '*Don't you?*'—*he raised a defiant eyebrow.*

'*I don't know,*' *I replied in a voice rather like Mrs Patrick Campbell,* '*I don't know.*'

'*Then why are you here?*' *he demanded. And that was our first conversation.*

He was extraordinarily secure, and I've always admired and loved him for the very limitations that I think are in his nature. He reminds me of a shining, narrow road leading to a theatre with NOËL COWARD *in letters of fire written across it, and he's never lost his way for a moment.*

People sometimes ask me, '*Noël is a genius, isn't he?*' *And I never know the answer, because a word like genius, well, the definition of a word seems to be the basis of every argument. What does one mean exactly by a genius? What does one mean by a man of enormous talent? He is obviously not quite in the class of William Shakespeare or Leonardo da Vinci or what you will, but I think he has genius. To me, a man who has genius is one who knows with uncanny accuracy at a strangely early age precisely what God means him to do in life, and does it. And that, it seems to me, Noël has done. He's always pursued the star he's seen, and it may be a limited, although very bright star, but he's pursued it with amazing brilliance and tact and taste. He's very seldom let himself slide for a moment, and that is one of the things I admire about him.*

As a child he was abominable! As the mother and father of a very famous young lady said to me lately, '*We love her very much, but oh, we dread her!*' *And we loved Noël very much in the early days in* The Goldfish, *but oh, how we dreaded him!*

MacLiammóir wasn't the only one. Even Noël later admitted that when he was a boy he was a 'brazen little prodigy, over-pleased with himself, and precocious to a degree'.

The Goldfish was, by certain standards, a success. It ran at the Little Theatre for a week of matinées at Christmas, and was succeeded by two revivals at the Royal Court in April and then at the Crystal Palace for two matinées in May. Two years later Micheál MacLiammóir and Noël appeared together in *Peter Pan*.

MICHEÁL MACLIAMMÓIR:

Noël was very bad in Peter Pan, *critical faculty not being at its height at twelve (we were both twelve). I had already*

22

Noël's Mother.

ADRIANNE ALLEN:

played it for two years, and Noël was new to the cast. He played Slightly and he was bad, because he was far too intelligent for Slightly, the poor, half-idiot, lost boy, slightly soiled. He played it as though it were Fallen Angels *or* Blithe Spirit. *He played it like one of his own characters, and couldn't have been less like Slightly.*

I remember Noël vividly, with great admiration, and everlasting affection. When we meet now, he's like a different person, and when people say what an unpleasant boy he was, I say what a charming man he has become. In a way it is true, I remember his mother so well, and she was much the same.

She always seemed to me to be immensely tall, very charming, very dignified. I remember her always with a fur hat on. It never came off in summer or winter, whenever I saw her, it was there. And I remember her once in the middle of a furious combat in which Noël was attacking everybody—I don't think me, he had a soft spot for me, or even probably pitied me.

'Noël is not a quarrelsome little boy, he is not a quarrelsome little boy!' she kept saying. And that was that. But we all knew that he was *quarrelsome.*

Noël's mother was a very dear friend of mine and I adored her. Noël gets so much of his character from her. Many years ago Mrs Coward went up for the first flight in a small aeroplane, an open two-seater, from an aerodrome near Goldenhurst in Kent. So off she went, and Noël was waiting at the airfield—very nervous to see what would happen. When she came down, he said, 'Darling, was everything all right? You weren't frightened?'

'Not at all,' she replied with colossal self-assurance, 'I used to swing very high as a girl.'

After *The Goldfish*, Noël had a small part in *The Great Name*, directed by and starring Charles Hawtrey, who was both one of the most delightful comedians in London and an extremely expert director. He belonged to the school of gentlemen actors, and at a first meeting would hardly have been taken for a member of the theatrical profession.

He was stout and moustachio'd, witty and casual, and possessed of irresistible charm. He was also a man of leisure, a spendthrift and a gambler. Although he had made several fortunes as a manager and as an actor, he was always in financial difficulties, due mainly to a love of

With Charles Hawtrey in *The Great Name*.
far right, Charles Hawtrey.

racing. Before he opened in a play in New York once, he drew fifteen thousand dollars from the management at whose theatre he was going to play, as an advance against his salary, went to the races on the Friday and Saturday, played the field, and returned to the theatre without a cent on the Monday. When he finally became a bankrupt and the Official Receiver asked what was the beginning of his financial year, he replied, with a smile that would have charmed a bird from a treetop, 'Oh, my dear fellow, every damn day.'

Late in life he married Katherine Elsie Robinson Clarke, a clergyman's daughter, widow of the Honourable Albert Petre, who became a strong influence on his life. Not only did she manage to steer him clear of his financial disasters but her great wit matched her husband's. She was in a nursing home once after a severe operation; the matron knocked at her door and she called out, 'Come in! Friend or enema?'

Although Noël had only one line in *The Great Name* with Hawtrey, he had the good sense to study Hawtrey's performance, and learned a great deal from him.

NOËL COWARD:

I played the page-boy and Charles Hawtrey was supposed to be a great composer, and I had to come in and say, 'Stop that noise at once, please, they're playing The Master-singers. *Making such a horrible row. We're used to good music here.'*

But I made such a production of the line, put the emphasis on the wrong words, and in general threw the balance of the scene entirely—and walked off to the biggest round of applause that had ever been heard. Afterwards I heard

24

Hawtrey say to the stage manager, 'Never let me see that boy again.' But then later he said to me, 'Listen, boy, I know you've been brought up as a little gentleman, but this is supposed to be a common little boy. Do you think you could speak cockney?'

'Of course I can speak cockney,' I replied.

So he said, 'If you come on very quickly, say your line very very quickly, in cockney, and go off, I'll give you an extra entrance. You can bring on a vase at the beginning of the scene and put it down. And walk off. Quickly.'

So he bribed me with an extra entrance. A perfectly dear thing to do for a clever little boy.

Hawtrey taught me everything I know. Every time now when I'm playing a comedy scene and I'm in trouble, and it's tricky to do, I think, 'What would the Guvnor have done?'

He played another page-boy in the next Hawtrey production, the children's play *Where the Rainbow Ends*. He was inclined to be cheeky and rude, and often made himself unpopular, but he learned how to listen and absorb some of the theatrical lessons which the older man was never too busy to teach him.

NOËL COWARD:

Where the Rainbow Ends was originally produced by Charles Hawtrey in 1911 and I played in it for two years— two Christmasses—and then went back to it four years later and played another part in it. I remember the cast distinctly, but I have a terrible feeling that nobody else would.

There was Esmé Wynne, and Roland Pertwee, who was rather good—he played Dunks—and Brian Aherne played my part in later years. There was an enchanting little creature called Mavis York who played Will-o'-the-Wisp who was really lovely and everybody prophesied a great career for her. But she disappeared. I think she married and retired from the stage.

HERMIONE GINGOLD:

Also in that first production was Hermione Gingold: *We were children together. Very naughty precocious children. Noël used to come to tea sometimes at my home—well, it was my mother's house—and my father's —I was only a child—and my mother used to say, 'If you ask that naughty little boy to tea ever again, I shall just turn him out of the house.' We used to slide down the stairs on tea-trays, which she didn't like. It made an awful clatter, and naturally enough ruined the stair carpet.*

I didn't see a lot of Noël after Where the Rainbow Ends,

With Philip Tonge in *Where The Rainbow Ends*.

because he went his way and I went mine. (Until 1949, when she and Hermione Baddeley appeared in the controversial revival of Fallen Angels.*)*

Hermione Gingold, one of Britain's most eccentric and seasoned comediennes, was born two years earlier than Noël. On a trip to England (she lives in New York these days), when an Immigration Officer at Heathrow Airport asked her the reason for her visit she replied, 'To see my two sons, both of whom are older than I am.'

Brian Aherne went on to become Hollywood's *beau idéal* of the charming English gentleman, but in 1913 he had a very small part in the third annual Christmas production of *Where the Rainbow Ends*.

BRIAN AHERNE:

I don't think Noël remembers me in that production, but then of course he had a speaking part whereas I was just a dancer. I had wings on my back and was the Spirit of the Woods.

Now I admired two actors in this play very much; James Carew and Reginald Owen. James Carew played the Demon King and Reginald Owen St George, and they fought a clashing sword fight in armour. I didn't admire Noël so much, he was a rather fresh youth, a little frightening, with big ears and always a smart retort, which to a shy boy like myself was a little daunting.

I had an autograph book, and James Carew, Reginald Owen and Noël were sharing a dressing-room, and I wanted Carew's and Owen's autographs, so I asked them, and sent them my book. They sent it back to me with their signatures in rather small writing in the bottom corner, but right across the page in very large bold letters was scrawled NOËL COWARD. *I was furious! The autograph book was ruined for me—but I wish I could find it now!*

below, Brian Aherne.
below right, Hermione Gingold.
opposite, Noël aged fifteen.

'BURSTING WITH REMARKABLE TALENT'

By the time he was thirteen Noël had appeared in five productions and his education was again being neglected. Not being a studious child, he often opted for visits to the theatre in preference to school, and after performing in a matinée, instead of returning home to study he would remain in the theatre, drinking in the atmosphere and rehearsing on stage before an empty auditorium, singing loudly and dancing to himself.

In 1912, he appeared as a mushroom in a curtain-raiser ballet entitled *An Autumn Idyll* at the Savoy Theatre. The following October he was at the Coliseum in a sketch called *A Little Fowl Play*, again with Charles Hawtrey. But a magistrate refused to license him for the evening performances, for the law, then as now, was strict about under-fourteen-year-olds appearing on the stage late at night.

After Christmas, and his second appearance in *Where the Rainbow Ends*, he toured with the Liverpool Repertory Company in *Hannele* by Hauptmann, one of Stanislavsky's greatest successes in Moscow twenty years before, and now produced by Basil Dean. This was Noël's first encounter with the director who many years later was to direct some of his first successes—*Easy Virtue*, *The Queen was in the Parlour*—and also the disastrous *Home Chat* and *Sirocco*.

In the *Hannele* company Noël met Gertrude Lawrence, then a young actress of fifteen with ringlets. He took to her immediately and she to him.

On this, his first tour as a child, he was consistently and violently homesick. 'Miss Italia Conti dosed me with Epsom Salts, doubtless in the belief that the root of all evil

Gertrude Lawrence.

lay in the bowels. But this merely succeeded in making rehearsals extremely convulsive.'

By the time he returned to London, Noël's family had moved from their Battersea Park flat to the upper part of a maisonette overlooking Clapham Common.

There his father sailed his model yacht on the pond, but although Noël's brother Eric joined in the fun, Noël even at that age was too sophisticated, preferring instead matinée performances at West End theatres.

NOËL COWARD: *Life is what matters to me, not games.*

He now picked up the threads of his neglected schooling, unwillingly enough, but there were few parts going for thirteen-year-old boys, however talented. On top of this he suffered for three years, until the age of fifteen, from intermittent though fortunately mild attacks of tuberculosis, which prevented him from exerting himself in any direction.

So when Esmé Wynne moved to a house in the neighbourhood she and Noël spent much of their out-of-school time together riding on trains without tickets, exploring the West End and the suburbs and developing their mutual love of the theatre. Young as they were they both became determined to be writers, and together they began composing love songs, and writing poems, short stories and plays. Two of the plays they wrote under the pseudonym Esnomel, *Ida Collaborates* and *Woman and Whisky*, were produced on tour three years later.

Noël spent his first holiday away from his family with a friend, Philip Streatfield, with whom he motored in a borrowed car along the coasts of Cornwall and Devon, stopping long enough in fishing villages for Philip to do watercolour sketches, and Noël to wander for miles along the clifftop. Later he was to develop this ability to be alone for extended periods while he was writing and composing. This habit of solitary concentration and the cast-iron discipline which he learned from the theatre are two of the keys to understanding his success.

Except for another visit to Cornwall, 1914 was a fairly uneventful year—uneventful for Noël, that is. For the first time in a long while he did not work at Christmas, for puberty pursued him: he shot up, and his voice started breaking, putting paid to his part in *Peter Pan*. He was even more disappointed to find that Madge Titheradge, whom he greatly admired, was playing Peter (he made up for this later when she starred in his own plays).

But just after Christmas A. W. Baskcomb, who was playing Slightly, was suddenly taken ill, and Noël, notwithstanding the change in his voice, was summoned to the theatre to take over the role for his second year running at the Duke of York's. At the end of 1915 he again played in *Where the Rainbow Ends*, at the Garrick, and early in the following year he toured as Charles Wykeham in *Charley's Aunt*. The summer offered him a small part in *The Light Blues*, a new musical comedy with Albert Chevalier and Shaun Glenville. Jack Hulbert was in it too, in a smaller role, and supported by Cicely Courtneidge—whose father, Robert, a well-known theatre manager, was presenting the play. They toured Cardiff, Newcastle, and Glasgow before coming to London's Shaftesbury Theatre.

CICELY COURTNEIDGE: *Noël was very pompous in those days. Frightfully pompous. This young man, very tall, skinny, not good-looking*

31

Lessee and Manager
ROBERT COURTNEIDGE.

Proprietors : The Representatives of
the late Mr. JOHN LANCASTER.

Shaftesbury Theatre

ROBERT COURTNEIDGE'S Production of

"THE LIGHT BLUES"

by MARK AMBIENT and JACK HULBERT, with Lyrics by ADRIAN ROSS.
Music by HOWARD TALBOT and HERMAN FINCK.

Cast

Joe Brooke	...	ALBERT CHEVALIER
Sir Oliver Petrie, LL.D.	{Author of "Petrie's Aristotle"}	FRED LEWIS
Duke of Dorchester		STANLEY LOGAN
Clive Brooke	Undergraduates of St. Stephen's College Cambridge	AUBREY MILLWARD
Arthur Hobbs		JACK HULBERT
William McGee		K. BLAKE ADAMS
Hon. George Rawson		ALAN NICHOLS
Harry Hotblack		JOHN PERRY
Sydney Panting		NOEL DAINTON
Gundy	... (a College "Gyp")	SHAUN GLENVILLE
Mons. Gobelin	... (Caterer)	REX LONDON
Tom		WYATT ROTHWELL
Dick	his Assistants	L. BURMAN
Harry		HERBERT NORRIS
Basil Pyecroft	(Private Secretary to Sir Oliver)	NOEL COWARD
Inspector Walker	(of Scotland Yard) ...	FRED CREASEY
Topsy Devigne	(a Variety Artiste) ...	CICELY DEBENHAM
Cynthia Petrie	Daughters of Sir Oliver	CICELY COURTNEIDGE
Mildred Petrie		NANCIE LOVAT
Lady Peggy		PHYLLIS HUGHES
Lady Rose		JOAN BERYL
Lady Doris	Sisters to the Duke of Dorchester	STEPHANIE STEPHENS
Lady Gertrude		IVY LOUISE
Lady Kate		MONA FINUCANE
Lady Phyllis		MADGE COMPTON
Mary	the Lock-Keeper's Daughters	LESLIE GRAHAM
Phoebe		DUX DAVIS
Mrs. Budd	(a College Bedmaker) ...	ALICE MANSFIELD

Dances arranged by ESPINOSA.
Orchestra under the Direction of ARTHUR WOOD.

SYNOPSIS OF SCENERY.

Act I. Clive Brooke's Rooms at St. Stephen's (EVENING)

Act II. Outside Rose Cottage, Lytton Lock (a few miles down the Cam. (NEXT MORNING)

TIME—MAY-WEEK, CAMBRIDGE, 1914.
The Scenery of Act I. painted by R. C. McCLEERY. Act II. by CONRAD TRITSCHLER.

MATINEE EVERY WEDNESDAY and SATURDAY at 2
EVENINGS at 8.

Nearest Underground Stations : Leicester Square, Piccadilly, Tottenham Court Road.

Dresses by the Maison Chic, 38, Conduit Street, Bond Street, W.
Hats by Maison Lewis, Regent Street, W.
Gloves by H. C. Russell, Ltd., Leicester Sq. Boots and Shoes by H. and M. Rayne
Waterloo Road, S.E. Wigs by Clarkson.

Acting Manager	- - -	WILLIAM BLOORE
Stage Manager	- - -	DERICK KNOWLES

General Manager (for ROBERT COURTNEIDGE) DOUGLAS MILLAR

EXTRACT FROM THE RULES MADE BY THE LORD CHAMBERLAIN.—(1) The name of the actual and responsible Manager of the Theatre must be printed on every play bill. (2) The Public can leave the Theatre at the end of the performance by all exit and entrance doors, which must open outwards. (3) Where there is a fireproof screen to the proscenium opening it must be lowered at least once during every performance to ensure its being in proper working order. (4) Smoking is not permitted in the auditorium. (5) All gangways, passages and staircases must be kept free from chairs or any other obstructions, whether permanent or temporary.

The gentlemen of this company who are of military age have either served with the Colours, been rejected as medically unfit, or passed for home service.

Programme

and rather spotty, wasn't the sort of bloke you'd take to at all, but my goodness, was he clever!

He played a small part in The Light Blues, and behaved in a very—shall we say young way, and he wasn't popular with the rest of the company because he was too knowing.

We were of the school where you were not heard—you simply wouldn't dare to speak your mind at rehearsals. You did as you were told. The leading artists might say quietly, afterwards, 'Mr Courtneidge, do you think that perhaps ...' but never in front of everybody the way Noël did. He knew everything, and would speak his mind. He would say to my father, 'I think it would be much better if you did it this way,' or 'I don't think that's nearly so good.' He was dreadfully outspoken, and we were appalled at this, but my father took a good view of him, and would say, 'Yes, I think you're right,' which of course made us even more angry!

Anyhow, by the time we got to London and opened at the Shaftesbury Theatre we were more friendly, because of a particular incident. I remember it was on the show's first night in London, and the Zeppelins were over. The bombs started falling for the first time ever and we were all stunned and shocked because no one had ever experienced bombs before. Someone shouted, 'Quickly, bring down the curtain. Bring down the curtain!' but Noël and I rushed on the stage in an effort to calm the audience, singing, in the middle

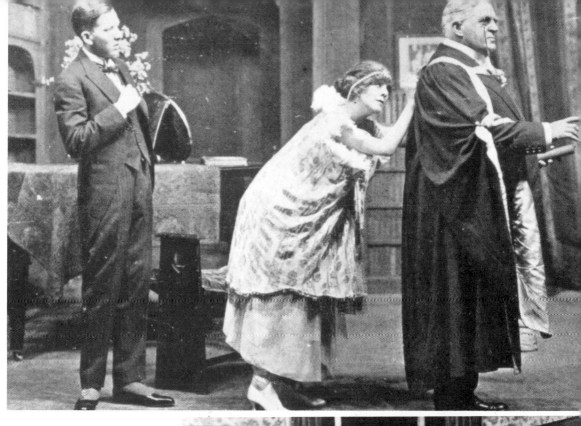

top, with Cicely Courtneidge and Fred Lewis in *The Light Blues*.
above right, with Charles Hawtrey in *The Saving Grace*.

of a love scene, at the tops of our voices, '*The May Week, The May Week, the jolly, jolly May Week!*'—*which was all about Cambridge, during which the bombs continued to fall, and finally the curtain came down. We ended up in shrieks of laughter, and became very good friends.*

My father admired him a lot—but only much later when he produced one of his first plays, The Young Idea. *Noël wanted to play in it, and my father didn't think he was suitable for the part, but Noël wouldn't agree to have it put on unless he played in it—and my father gave in.*

Until then Noël continued to find parts where he could. His professional dancing career began—and ended—with a season at the Elysée Restaurant (later the Café de Paris) with a dancer, Eileen Dennis.

At the end of 1916 he was in yet another Christmas play, *The Happy Family*. His next appearance was much briefer but it was on film. He was paid a pound a day to push a wheelbarrow in D. W. Griffith's *Hearts of the World*, starring Lilian Gish. The following summer in Manchester, he played Helen Hayes' son in *Wild Heather* by Dorothy Brandon, which led to a London engagement.

NOËL COWARD:

Charles Hawtrey offered me a leading part in The Saving Grace *at the Garrick Theatre, and that was the real start of my name being known.*

Also in *The Saving Grace* were Charles Hawtrey himself, Ellis Jeffreys, Emily Brooke and Mary Jerrold. It had a successful London run of several months, despite the bombing. It took Noël back to Manchester, where he met Ivor Novello for the first time and was asked to tea. Ivor was in Manchester for *Arlette*, a musical comedy then playing in Manchester and for which he had composed some of the music. The fashionable young matinée idol seemed to personify all that Noël had wished to be. He had enjoyed recent success with his patriotic composition 'Keep the Home Fires Burning'. He was romantically good-looking, elegant, sophisticated and rich, and Noël was greatly impressed by his personality, his assured position, his style and fame.

Noël began to look on all this as a model for his own career, and with scarcely a look back at his stable middle-class background, he proceeded with his talent, charm and determination and awaited the other element necessary for success; luck. But whilst both his craftmanship and his discipline were improving, he was still to learn to get on with people. During *The Saving Grace* he was to be severely reprimanded yet again for his outbursts of temper at what he considered an imposition—the stage manager's use of his dressing-room for auditions. He was threatened with dismissal from the company for his lack of discretion, but was saved by Hawtrey, a tolerant man who believed in his talent and dealt tactfully with his bad behaviour.

NOËL COWARD:

You see, he never, never discouraged me. He never lost his temper for one moment. He was never unkind. Now Basil Dean was a fiend, because he had no patience. Hawtrey had infinite patience. But Basil used to say, 'No, no, no, no!!' And you know, the gunpowder does *run out of the heels of your boots at moments like that. You can't act under those conditions. I'm surprised that he got so many wonderful performances. But he was a frightfully good director.*

But now Noël suffered another setback. His tuberculosis returned. Fortunately it was again a comparatively slight attack, but he was obliged to spend the following year resting. Some of that time was spent convalescing at the Pinewood Sanatorium at Wokingham, and there he continued to write.

He was considered sufficiently fit to be called up for Army service the following year, 1917, but that episode was not to prove an unmitigated success.

NOËL COWARD: *What happened about my Army career was one long series of sad little disasters. First of all I hated it. I hated making my bed out of boards, and having made my bed out of boards, I hated sleeping on them. And then, fortunately really for me, doubling back—one always doubles in the Army, you know —doubling back from a terrible parade I caught my toe in a slat and fell flat on my face and got concussion.*

The next thing I knew I was in the First London General Hospital with my mother weeping, a little bit overdoing it she was because she knew it wasn't really serious, but from then onwards it was really I think the end of my Army career, because I'd got something—I had this tubercular gland, and so I wasn't liable for foreign service.

And so a very very nice Captain sent for me and said, 'Do you think you are going to be of much use in the Army?'

And I said, 'Well, frankly—no.'

And he said, 'In that case don't you think it would be a good idea if you were discharged?'

And I said, 'I think it's one of the best *ideas I've ever heard.' And I was discharged from the Army!*

By now the Coward family had moved to the more select precincts of Ebury Street in Pimlico, with the author George Moore as their neighbour, but the address was something of a façade to their still slender means, for Mr Coward had been put out of work by the war, the demand for pianos having markedly declined.

Aunt Vida moved in with them, but Aunt Borby, who had seemed to be doomed ever since, during her youth, she had fallen out of a ship's port-hole in Madeira and landed on her head, had died the year before.

Their other neighbours were called Evans, and they too ran a lodging-house, and had a member of the theatrical profession in the family. Their daughter, Edith, was (and still is) an actress:

EDITH EVANS: *There was a time, all those years ago, when Noël's mother and father had a house next door, and we both had lodgers. Ours was called an apartment house. I don't know what theirs was called—it was probably much the same, but it*

111 Ebury Street.

was in Ebury Street, and they were right next door to us in number one hundred and eleven.

My mother decided with extreme valiance to try her hand at running a lodging-house, which she didn't care for. The lodgers seemed happy enough but it was a hell of a hard job for her.

But Noël was a Londoner now and he loved it. He was to write with affection and wit of the circles in which he moved, and in the lyrics of many of his songs recorded his affection for the town.

```
           'London Pride'
London Pride has been handed down to us,
London Pride is a flower that's free.
London Pride means our own dear town
   to us,
And our pride it for ever will be.
Woa, Liza,
See the coster barrows,
Vegetable marrows
And the fruit piled high.
Woa, Liza,
Little London sparrows,
Covent Garden Market where the costers
   cry.
Cockney feet
Mark the beat of history.
Every street
Pins a memory down.
Nothing ever can quite replace
the grace of London town.
```

Beatrice Lillie and Gertrude Lawrence.

NOËL COWARD

'NO TALENT WHATEVER!'

When he returned from his short-lived Army career he entered upon an increasingly active social life. Now that he was in London the acquaintances he had made while working in the theatre drew him into their circles, and he made new friends daily. Among them was Beatrice Lillie:

She introduced me to André Charlot. After I had sung several songs with incredible vivacity, Charlot took her aside and said, 'Bea, never do that to me again. That boy has no talent whatever!'

But at the next audition he was more successful. George Grossmith and Edward Laurillard were planning the production of an American musical comedy called *Oh Boy*, with music by Jerome Kern, and Noël joined the cast at the not inconsiderable salary of twelve pounds a week. Rehearsals were not due to begin for a few weeks, so he wrote to the novelist G. B. Stern, whose work he admired and with whom he had corresponded but never met, suggesting that he stay with her and her friends the Dawson-Scotts in Cornwall. Gladys Bronwen Stern was an English novelist and short-story writer who had at that time enjoyed some success with *Grand Chain* and *A Marrying Man*. In the years to come she was to help Noël choose the period songs for *Cavalcade*. Now he was duly invited—and asked to pay two pounds a week for his keep. The Dawson-Scotts took an instant dislike to him, and he responded in true style by driving 'Peter' Stern and her friends to near distraction by reading and re-reading them plays he had written.

André Charlot

George Grossmith.

NOËL COWARD:

He returned to London to find that not only had the musical comedy changed its title to *Oh! Joy* but that his part had been given to another actor. He stormed into Grossmith and Laurillard's office demanding an explanation. They had realised in fact that he had not sufficient musical comedy experience, but now they explained uneasily that they felt his talents as a straight actor would have been sadly wasted on a musical comedy. He was not mollified, and they hurriedly offered him a part in a play called *Scandal* by Cosmo Hamilton, which was to be produced at the Strand Theatre two months later with a first-rate cast headed by Arthur Bourchier, Kyrle Bellew and Nora Swinburne.

He spent those months writing a never-to-be-published novel called *Cherry Pan*, about the daughter of Peter Pan, and various short stories which he sold to magazines. His father was still out of work and helping to run the boarding-house, which now boasted three guests, but Noël, who had been writing songs steadily for the past four years, landed a contract with a music publisher that guaranteed him £50 a year, rising to £100 in the third year—a most welcome help in the support of his family.

But he didn't last long in *Scandal*. He was discontented with his paltry part and, fretful and angry, he banged about backstage during the other actors' performances. He succeeded in upstaging some of the cast and persistently upset an elderly actress by telling her that her dog smelt. His dismissal resulted in eight months' unemployment.

He enjoyed a mild success with his short stories, and the advance from the publishing company gave him confidence in his composing. He was now beginning to move in what he considered more interesting social circles. In his estimation he was going up in the world, and he moved down from his attic room at 111 Ebury Street to larger quarters in the house where he might entertain such friends as Esmé Wynne, the actress Betty Chester (later one of The Co-optimists), and a friend of Betty's, Lorn Macnaughton, who was to become his secretary and confidante, and remain so for forty-seven years.

That year he played Ralph in *The Knight of the Burning Pestle*, directed by Nigel Playfair. It opened at the Birmingham Repertory Theatre, with a cast headed by Betty Chester.

The play was by Messrs Beaumont and Fletcher, two of the dullest Elizabethan writers ever known. I had a very very long part. But I was very very bad at it.

At about this time he met Mrs Patrick Campbell. One of the greatest actresses of the period, she was almost as well known for her extraordinary and often cruel wit as for her considerable dramatic talent. An indefatigable talker

Mrs Patrick Campbell in *The Matriach*.

with an explosive manner, she was spiteful and generous, loathed and loved, admired and hated. She was dreaded by the actors with whom she played, but the audiences adored her, although her performances ranged from wonderful to perfectly dreadful, depending entirely on her mood. She liked to shock people, and often unwisely insulted those whose help she needed. Asked what she thought of a sister actress, she answered, 'Oh, admirable. If she only had a few more brains she'd be half-witted.'

Her bitterness at this time might easily have resulted from the fact that she hadn't worked for three years and her tremendous success in Shaw's original production of *Pygmalion*, in which she created the role of Eliza, was behind her. Her many subsequent performances included Mrs Alving in *Ghosts* and Anastasia in G. B. Stern's *The Matriarch*, adapted as a stage play from *Tents of Israel*, and *No Man's Land*, in the late twenties.

She telephoned me and asked for a box for one of the matinée performances of The Knight of the Burning Pestle. *That afternoon she came, and quite early in the play went into a deep sleep. She was awakened only by the applause at the end of the play—which was not very strident. I was so angry that I sent a message via a friend of hers to say that as I'd given her the seat, the least she could do was to* appear *to keep awake. She could have got behind the curtain or something.*

The next night I came on, there she was, with white gloves from here to here (gesturing from fingertip to armpit), *and she applauded every single line I said. So I think she really won. I got hysterical.*

JOYCE GRENFELL:

I was ten years old and Noël was about twenty-one the first time I met him. Actually it was my tenth birthday. He was brought to lunch with my mother by Mrs Patrick Campbell, and if I'm to be absolutely honest I don't remember a great deal about him because Mrs Patrick Campbell had on such a big black velvet hat, and I was kind of hypnotised by that. And she looked at me and boomed, 'Are you happy?' which did startle me a little.

But Noël did something marvellous, I think really more for my mother's sake than mine. When he left he sent me five books by E. Nesbit, and that's something I've never forgotten. He knew her, I think, quite well, and was a great fan of hers. And that was my introduction to E. Nesbit. And Noël.

The Last Trick, a play that Noël had written the year before, was a melodrama in four acts. He took it to

With Esme Wynne in *I'll Leave it to You*.

Gilbert Miller, who was leaving for New York a few weeks later, and nothing could have been further from his expectations than to have the option taken up for what seemed to him the enormous sum of £500. 'It was a very sophisticated play,' he said, 'but it didn't see the light of day.' However the money provided for his family some of the comforts that poverty had hitherto denied them, and with it came a change in his luck. His next play was taken for production as well, giving him the opportunity to act in the first of his plays to be produced.

Charles Hawtrey suggested my writing I'll Leave it to You. *It was a very light family comedy which Gilbert Miller put on in Manchester. It was a success there where it ran for a three-week season, redeemed by a marvellous performance by Kate Cutler. I just played a straight juvenile. It was fairly dull, on the whole. It opened on July 21st 1920 at the New Theatre in London. It ran four whole weeks.*

'I'll Leave it to You'
(Taken from Act One)
The action takes place in the hall of Mulberry Manor. It is late afternoon. Joyce (Moya Nugent), is wearing a fur coat and galoshes. Sylvia (Stella Jesse), twenty-one and pretty, is seated on the sofa.

JOYCE: (Rightly) My feet are simply soaking.

SYLVIA: (Sewing) Why on earth don't you go and change them? You'll catch cold.
            (Bobbie (Noël Coward) enters.
            He is slim, bright looking -
            twenty.)

JOYCE: I don't mind if I do. (Laughs) Colds are fun.

BOBBIE: She loves having a fuss made of her - beef tea, chicken, jelly with whipped cream and fires in her bedroom, little Sybarite.

JOYCE: So do you.

BOBBIE: No I don't; whenever my various ailments confine me to bed I chafe, positively chafe at the terrible inactivity. I want to be up and about, shooting, riding, cricket, football, ludo, the usual run of manly sports.

SYLVIA: Knowing you for what you are - lazy, luxurious -

BOBBIE: (Pained) Please, please, please, not in front of the child. It's demoralising for her to hear her idolised brother held up to ridicule.

SYLVIA: You're not my idolised brother at all – Oliver is.

BOBBIE: (Sweetly) If that were really so, dear, I know you have much too kind a heart to let me know it.

SYLVIA: What's the matter with you this afternoon, Bobbie? You're very up in the air about something.
(Joyce takes her coat off, puts it on back of chair.)

BOBBIE: (Rising and sitting on club fender) Merely another instance of the triumph of mind over matter; in this case a long and healthy walk was the matter. I went into the lobby to put on my snow boots and then – as is usually the case with me – my mind won. I thought of tea, crumpets and comfort. Oliver has gone without me, he simply bursts with health and extraordinary dullness. Personally I shall continue to be delicate and interesting.

SYLVIA: (Seriously) You may have to work, Bobbie.

BOBBIE: Really, Sylvia, you do say the most awful things, remember Joyce is only a schoolgirl, she'll be quite shocked.

JOYCE: We work jolly hard at school, anyhow.

BOBBIE: Oh no you don't. I've read the modern novelists, and I know all you do is walk about with arms entwined and write poems of tigerish adoration to your mistresses. It's a beautiful existence.

One of the great beauties of the London theatre, Gladys Cooper started out as one of George Edwardes's chorus girls. When she was once asked, 'If you had your life over again, what would you change?' she replied without hesitation, 'I'd be a man.'

I remember after Noël had written and played in that first play, I'll Leave it to You, *we were all together in Switzerland.*

We had a mutual friend [Lord Lathom, whom Noël wanted to finance a revue he had in mind], *who went there because he had lung trouble, and we all made up a party and went to see him. I remember it was at luncheon one day; Noël had had very good notices for the play saying it was very slight, not much plot, but the dialogue was very good, so I said to him, 'Why don't you collaborate, Noël? I mean, after all Edward Knoblock and Arnold Bennett collaborated,' and he turned on me, outraged and exasperated: 'Shaw never collaborated, Barrie never collaborated, Shakespeare never collaborated . . .!'*

And I exploded, 'Well, if you're setting yourself up to be a Shaw . . .!' and that's the kind of argument that went on all our lives! But he was great fun and a good friend. He's done some wonderful things for me which are very private, which I shall always love him for and be grateful to him for.

JOHN GIELGUD:

I played Noël's part in I'll Leave it to you *with Edward Chapman as the uncle* (played at the New in the original production by Holman Clark) *in an amateur production at the Tavistock Theatre in 1921, just before I became a professional actor. Of course in those days I had never met Noël himself, though I was introduced to him on one occasion at a tea party to which he came with Betty Chester, and I remember thinking him very conceited.*

Noël was now twenty-one. He was still poor and playing small parts in undistinguished plays, but he was working hard at his songs, sketches and plays, the latest of which was a comedy in three acts called *The Young Idea*, inspired by Shaw's *You Never Can Tell*. He sent the script to Shaw, who returned it with a long letter indicating that Noël might become a good playwright, provided he never read another of his plays.

'The Young Idea'

(Taken from Act Three)
Jennifer and George have been divorced for fourteen years. George has remarried, but his second wife has gone off with one of her lovers. Jennifer and her two precocious children have been living in Alassio, but the children, Sholto (Noël Coward), and Gerda (Ann Trevor), on a visit to their father in England, plot to reconcile their parents. But on their return to Italy they find that in the meantime their mother has decided to remarry someone else, thereby upsetting their carefully worked out ploy. They are about to meet their mother's Intended.
(Jennifer goes out. Sholto and Gerda look at one another in horror.)

THE HIGHLY
TRAINED
BABES IN
THE WOOD!

NOEL COWARD
ANN TREVOR

In The Young Idea.

SHOLTO:	What are we to do?
GERDA:	(Frantic) This is frightful - frightful! Let me think . . .
SHOLTO:	I suppose we couldn't make him drunk - like David Garrick - ?
GERDA:	We haven't time -
SHOLTO:	(Clutching his head; throws himself on to couch) This is appalling!
GERDA:	(Pacing up and down in anguish) Oh dear, oh dear - !
SHOLTO:	We must terrify him - lie to him - somehow -
GERDA:	I know! (Both down) Dreadful story about father - follow my lead, and try not to overdo it. 　　　　　(The door rattles)
SHOLTO:	All right - look out - 　　　(Enter Hiram, very sure of himself. He sees the children.)
HIRAM:	Good God!
SHOLTO:	Good afternoon.
GERDA:	How do you do.
HIRAM:	But, see here, I - you're not -!
SHOLTO:	I'm afraid we are.
HIRAM:	(Recovering himself) I guess you're much older than I expected.
GERDA:	(Politely) Are we?
HIRAM:	Your mother's a great little woman.
SHOLTO:	Isn't she?
HIRAM:	(Weakly) Yes - she sure is. (Pause) She told you that I - we - we're going to be married?
GERDA:	Yes. Ah! (Sigh) 　　(Hiram looks from one to the other.)
SHOLTO:	Oh! (Sighs)
HIRAM:	Well - what do you say to it?
GERDA:	(Firmly) Close the door, Sholto. 　　　　(Sholto obeys in silence. Hiram begins to fidget.)
HIRAM:	See here, you know I -
GERDA:	(Stops him) It's all right, Mr - mother never told us your name.
HIRAM:	Walkin. Hiram J. Walkin.
GERDA:	Thank you. I should like to tell you, Mr Walkin, how delighted we are that this has happened. (She smiles sweetly)

HIRAM:	Delighted! I thought you seemed a bit depressed about it.
GERDA:	(Seriously) We have almost prayed for this moment - haven't we, Sholto?
SHOLTO:	Yes - almost.
GERDA:	Our mother -
SHOLTO:	(Mechanically) God help her -
GERDA:	Our mother - we've got to tell you this, Mr Walkin.
HIRAM:	See here, are you two trying to put something over on me?
SHOLTO:	(Reprovingly) We should never do that, even if we knew what it meant.
GERDA:	You must listen attentively to what we have to say. It's very upsetting, but somehow I feel that you have strength of mind, and that I can trust you.
SHOLTO:	We can both trust you.
GERDA:	Sholto and I have felt it our duty always to tell the truth to all the people who have wanted to marry our mother; but, thank heaven, something tells me that you won't be like the others, and - run away!
HIRAM:	What are you getting at?
GERDA:	Mother told you that she divorced father?
HIRAM:	She did.
GERDA:	(Impressively) Well, it's not true!
HIRAM:	Not true? But - why - what do you mean?
GERDA:	Our father - (Her voice breaks) - our father was put into a lunatic asylum eight years ago.
HIRAM:	(Astounded) What! (Drops on to sofa)
SHOLTO:	Mother pretends she divorced him - she carried her head high in spite of all the shame and horror she has had to endure - gallant, gallant little woman -
HIRAM:	(Incredulously) Lunatic asylum! But I -
GERDA:	(Sits beside him. Gently) Now, Mr Walkin, why should we try to tell lies to you? (Sholto sits) You will be able to take care of mother; you will be able to comfort her when she has these uncontrollable fits of depression, which we have endured, willingly, but for so long -

HIRAM:	(Still distrustful) But it's incredible! I mean to say –
GERDA:	Lots of frightful things that happen are incredible.
SHOLTO:	Father used to be so gay, so merry – and now – (He turns away)
GERDA:	Now –! (She turns away)
SHOLTO:	(Brokenly) Now he eats the buttons off padded chairs!

Polly with a Past (Noël, *second from left*, Edna Best *extreme right*).

In 1921 Noël appeared in another Gilbert Miller offering, *Polly with a Past*. This American comedy had been a big success in New York, where it starred Ina Claire, a great American beauty, but the English production ran for only three months. *Polly* was written by George Middleton and Guy Bolton, the title role was played by Edna Best, and the cast included C. Aubrey Smith, Helen Hayes, Claude Rains, Henry Kendall and Donald Calthrop.

NOËL COWARD: *There was trouble with* Polly with a Past *because there were three main parts, and I was the feed. Now in all my career in the theatre I've never cared very much for being a feed, so by the time we got half-way through the run the amount of 'business' that had been put in by me . . . .! I had to be ticked off and had it all cut out. But I put it back, so I wasn't terribly popular with the rest of the cast.*

EDITH EVANS:

I don't remember much about Noël's acting, nor indeed about mine, but we walked home together, and I used to like that, because he talked to me, and he once told me he'd had something published. I thought that was terrific; being published, I mean. So grown-up and grand. And he had, too, and he started at about seventeen.

Noël's social life continued to develop in the way he had hoped. He sought out stars and celebrities and enjoyed their company. He liked the aristocracy and became a friend of Jeffrey Holmesdale, son of the Earl of Amherst, who became a close, life-long friend. Today Jeffrey sits in the House of Lords, but in the early twenties, when Noël first met him, he was a captain in the Coldstream Guards.

Noël also became a friend of Ivor Novello, whose profile by now had become almost as famous as Valentino's. When, years later, Noël was asked about the comparison between him and Novello, he quipped, 'The two most beautiful things in the world are Ivor's profile and my mind'.

At dinner with Novello one evening in London he met the American star Jeanne Eagles, famous for her brilliant performance in the name-part of Sadie Thompson in Somerset Maughams *Rain* in New York. Noël was fascinated by Miss Eagles talk of Broadway and the American theatre, and soon afterwards he borrowed the money for a steamer ticket to America, hoping that New York might offer him the rewards which London had hitherto been foolish enough to deny him.

He had only a one-way ticket, but was perfectly confident of earning the return fare from the fruits of what he knew would be his great success in America. Jeffrey Holmesdale was sailing for New York on his father's business at the same time, and this became the first of their many journeys together. Noël got himself released from *Polly with a Past*, and, this accomplished, he and Jeffrey set out for the Promised Land in the Spring of 1921.

'EXTRAORDINARILY UNSPOILED'

NOËL COWARD:

I landed in America with ten pounds in my pocket and no return ticket. It was the month of May, when all the theatres close, and I was under the impression that everybody would rush out and snap up my plays, but they'd all gone away for their holidays.

So there I stayed. Fortunately I was lent a flat in Washington Square, and I lived for six months on practically nothing. That was the only time in my life that I've ever virtually starved. But there was a very nice Italian grocer who used to give me things on credit. And there I stayed until the autumn when the new plays began to open, and I'd made enough to live on by writing articles (for Vanity Fair).

However he made a number of new friends, mostly in the theatre; Tallulah Bankhead and Ronald Colman, whom he had first met in London, the George Kaufmans, and Lynn Fontanne and Alfred Lunt (not yet married, but soon to become the most famous husband and wife acting partnership in America). He also met Laurette Taylor, the great American star with whom Lynn Fontanne had often acted before she married Alfred Lunt. Miss Taylor came to London at the beginning of the First World War to make an enormous success in *Peg o' my Heart*, written by her husband, J. Hartley Manners. She was a magnificent actress—Irish, wayward, and full of charm. After many reverses of fortune she made history in her last years by performances as an old charwoman in a revival of *Outward Bound* and as the mother in Tennessee Williams' *The Glass Menagerie*—a part which she created shortly before her death.

NOËL COWARD: *Laurette used to give these Sunday evening parties at Riverside Drive to which a few pros were invited. Good ones.*

And then Dwight and Marguerite [Laurette Taylor's children by her first husband, playwright Charles A. Taylor] *used to invite their friends who of course didn't understand any of the theatre jargon and were really not very happy. And then to everybody's horror Laurette invariably said, 'Now we'll play a word game.' Well, the guests shrank with horror and some poor beast had to pick up a box and put it somewhere, and Laurette would say, 'No, no, no! That's not the way to do it at all.' So then she would do it. Beautifully. And her family and we would all applaud, and then we'd go on to the next word. And those evenings got such a reputation for* dread *in America that hardly anyone ever went at all. And I see their point.*

Those evenings did, however, provide Noël with the plot for *Hay Fever*, which he wrote in 1924, substituting Judith Bliss for Laurette Taylor:

above, Laurette Taylor.
right, Marie Tempest (Judith Bliss) Robert Andrews (Simon) Helen Spencer (Sorel) in *Hay Fever*, Ambassador's Theatre, June 1925.

'Hay Fever'
(Taken from Act Two)
Judith Bliss has decided to play a
word game after dinner. Her husband
David is reluctant to play - he
knows only too well how it will end
but her precocious son and
daughter, Simon and Sorel, are
eager as ever - at the expense of
their guests - in this particular
case, Richard, Sandy, Jackie and
Myra.
(Sorel leaves the room. The others
decide on the word for her to guess)

SOREL:	Don't be too long. (She goes out)
SIMON:	(Rises, faces the company) Now then.
JUDITH:	'Bitterly.'
SIMON:	No, we did that last time; she'll know.
DAVID:	'Intensely.'
JUDITH:	Too difficult.
RICHARD:	There was an amusing game I played once at the Harringtons' house. Everyone was blindfolded except –
SIMON:	This room's not big enough for that. What about 'winsomely?'
JACKIE:	I wish I knew what we had to do.
JUDITH:	You'll see when we start playing. (Rises, takes a cigarette and lights it) If we start playing.
SIMON:	Mother's brilliant at this. Do you remember when we played it at the Mackenzies?
JUDITH:	Yes, and Blanche was so cross when I kissed Freddie's ear in the manner of the word.
RICHARD:	What was the word?
JUDITH:	I can't remember.
MYRA:	(Having lit her cigarette, returns to her seat) Perhaps it's as well.
DAVID:	What about 'drearily?'
JUDITH:	Not definite enough.
SIMON:	'Winsomely' is the best.

49

JUDITH:	She's sure to guess it straight off.
SANDY:	(Confidentially to Jackie) These games are much too brainy for me.
DAVID:	Young Norman Robertson used to be marvellous - do you remember?
SIMON:	Yes, wonderful sense of humour.
MYRA:	He's lost it all since his marriage.
JUDITH:	I didn't know you knew him.
MYRA:	Well, considering he married my cousin - (Pause)
RICHARD:	We don't seem to be getting on with the game.
JUDITH:	We haven't thought of a word yet.
MYRA:	'Brightly.'
SIMON:	Too obvious.
MYRA:	Very well - don't snap at me!
JUDITH:	'Saucily.' I've got a lovely idea for 'saucily'.
MYRA:	(To Simon) I should think 'rudely' would be the easiest.
SIMON:	Don't be sour, Myra.
JUDITH:	The great thing is to get an obscure word.
SIMON:	What a pity Irene isn't here - she knows masses of obscure words.
MYRA:	She's probably picked them up from her obscure friends.
SIMON:	It's no use being catty about Irene; she's a perfect darling.
MYRA:	I wasn't being catty at all.
SIMON:	Yes you were.
SOREL:	(Off) Hurry up!
JUDITH:	Quickly, now! We must think - (Rises)
JACKIE:	(Helpfully) 'Appendicitis.'
JUDITH:	(Witheringly) That's not an adverb. You're thinking of Charades. (Jackie sinks back into her seat.)
SANDY:	Charades are damned good fun.
SIMON:	Yes, but we don't happen to be doing

	them at the moment.
SANDY:	Sorry.
JUDITH:	'Saucily.'
SIMON:	No, 'winsomely' is better.
JUDITH:	All right. Call her in.
SIMON:	(Calling) Sorel - come on; we're ready.
SANDY:	(Hoarsely to Simon) Which is it - 'saucily' or 'winsomely'?
SIMON:	(Whispering) 'Winsomely.'

(Sorel re-enters.)

| SOREL: | (To Judith) Go and take a flower out of that vase and give it to Richard. |
| JUDITH: | Very well. |

(She trips lightly over to the vase on the piano, gurgling with coy laughter, selects a flower, then goes over to Richard, pursing her lips into a mock smile, she gives him the flower with a little girlish gasp at her own daring and wags her finger archly at him, and returns to her seat. Richard puts flower on sofa table and sits again.)

SIMON:	Marvellous, Mother!
SOREL:	(Laughing) Oh, lovely! (Looking round the company) Now, Myra, get up and say goodbye to everyone in the manner of the word.
MYRA:	(Rises and starts with David) Goodbye. It really has been most delightful -
JUDITH:	No, no, no!
MYRA:	Why - what do you mean?
JUDITH:	You haven't got the right intonation a bit.
SIMON:	Oh, Mother darling, do shut up!
MYRA:	(Acidly) Remember what an advantage you have over we poor amateurs, Judith, having been a professional for so long. (Returns to her seat)
JUDITH:	I don't like 'so long' very much.
SOREL:	Do you think we might go on now?

MYRA:	Go to the next one; I'm not going to do any more.
SIMON:	Oh, please do. You were simply splendid.
SOREL:	It doesn't matter. (To Richard) Light a cigarette in the manner of the word. (Richard rises.)
RICHARD:	(Takes cigarette from box on sofa table) I've forgotten what it is.
JUDITH:	(Grimacing at him violently) You remember . . .
RICHARD:	Oh yes.
	(He goes to Sorel and proceeds to light a cigarette with great abandon, winking and chucking Sorel under the chin, then looks round panic stricken.)
JUDITH:	Oh, no, no, no!
MYRA:	I can't think what that's meant to be.
RICHARD:	(Offended) I was doing my best.
JUDITH:	It's so frightfully easy, and nobody can do it right.
SIMON:	I believe you've muddled it up.
RICHARD:	(Returns to his seat.) You'd better go on to the next one.
JUDITH:	Which word were you doing? Whisper –
RICHARD:	(Leans over to her, whispering) 'Saucily.'
JUDITH:	I knew it! – He was doing the wrong word. (She whispers to him)
RICHARD:	Oh, I see. I'm sorry.
JUDITH:	Give him another chance.
SIMON:	No, it's Jackie's turn now; it will come round to him again, I'm afraid.
SOREL:	(Moves to Jackie) Do a dance in the manner of the word.
JACKIE:	(Giggling) I can't.
JUDITH:	Nonsense! Of course you can.
JACKIE:	I can't – honestly – I . . .
SIMON:	(Crosses and pulls her to her feet) Go on; have a shot at it.
JACKIE:	No, I'd much rather not. Count me out.

JUDITH:	Really, the ridiculous fuss everyone makes –
JACKIE:	I'm awfully stupid, at anything like this.
SOREL:	It's only a game, after all.
DAVID:	Come along – try.
JACKIE:	(Dragging back) I couldn't – please don't ask me. I simply couldn't. (Sits again)
SIMON:	Leave her alone if she doesn't want to.
SOREL:	(Irritably) What's the use of playing at all, if people won't do it properly!
JUDITH:	It's so simple.
SANDY:	It's awfully difficult if you haven't done it before.
SIMON:	Go on to the next one.
SOREL:	(Firmly) Unless everyone's in it we won't play at all.
SIMON:	Now don't lose your temper.
SOREL:	Lose my temper! I like that! No one's given me the slightest indication of what the word is – you all argue and squabble –
DAVID:	Talk, talk, talk! Everybody talks too much.
JUDITH:	It's so surprising to me when people won't play up. After all –
JACKIE:	(With spirit) It's a hateful game, anyhow, and I don't want to play it again ever.
SOREL:	You haven't played it at all yet.
SIMON:	Don't be rude, Sorel.
SOREL:	Really, Simon, the way you go on is infuriating!
SIMON:	It's always the same; whenever Sorel goes out she gets quarrelsome.
SOREL:	Quarrelsome!
SIMON:	(Patting her hand in a fatherly fashion) Don't worry, Jackie; you needn't do anything you don't want to.
JUDITH:	I think for the future, we'd better confine our efforts to social

53

	conversation and not attempt anything in the least intelligent.
SIMON:	How can you be so unkind, Mother!
JUDITH:	(Sharply) Don't speak to me like that!
JACKIE:	(Speaking winsomely) It's all my fault – I know I'm awfully silly, but it embarrasses me so terribly doing anything in front of people.
SOREL:	(With acidity) I should think the word was 'winsomely'.
SIMON:	You must have been listening outside the door, then.
SOREL:	Not at all – Miss Coryton gave it away.
SIMON:	Why 'Miss Coryton' all of a sudden? You've been calling her Jackie all the evening. You're far too grand, Sorel.
SOREL:	(Stamping her foot) And you're absolutely maddening – I'll never play another game with you as long as I live!
SIMON:	That won't break my heart.
JUDITH:	Stop, stop, stop!
SIMON:	(Grabbing Jackie's hand – he pulls her up to window) Come out in the garden. I'm sick of this.
SOREL:	(Following them up and shouting after them) Don't let him take you on the river; he isn't very good at it.

With the arrival of autumn in New York came the return of the theatre managers to whom Noël hoped to sell his plays. They, however, had other ideas. He was so broke that he had to borrow twenty dollars from Lynn Fontanne. However, he was asked by the Editor of *Metropolitan Magazine* to turn his play *I'll Leave it to You* into a short story for $500. 'I reflected gleefully that for five hundred dollars I would gladly have considered turning *War and Peace* into a music-hall sketch.' And so *I'll Leave it to You* provided his return ticket home.

He came back to London with few financial prospects. His father was still out of work, and his mother needed a rest from the arduous chores of running their boarding-house. The family was deeply in debt, for Noël's six-month absence had deprived them of his much-needed subsidy, and there seemed no prospect of getting back into the black. No one appeared to be interested in his plays, nor in offering him acting parts. But there were five mouths to feed, and the responsibility for keeping the wolf from the door fell squarely on his shoulders. He managed to borrow from friends, and mortgaged the piano.

NOËL COWARD: *I was so sick of watching mother slaving herself to death that I rented a cottage from Athene Seyler in Dymchurch in Kent and popped mother into that. Father coped with the lodging-house very very well, and was very very popular. A convivial character, he was very jolly and made jolly jokes.*

SYBIL THORNDIKE: *My mother was devoted to Noël. Of course he was wonderful with old ladies—she wasn't that old then, I mean not as old as I am now* (nearly ninety). *But they were*

Noël.

Noël.

tremendous pals, and my mother always said, 'That boy's going places.'

He was always so wonderful with old people, he'd got a knack with them. He was devoted to his old mother. He was wonderful. We always spent our summers in Dymchurch, me and my four small children. And Noël was wonderful with them. He was awfully funny. He would never go in swimming with us. I don't know why. Perhaps he didn't like swimming . . .

He was such an entertaining talker—and then one day he brought us down a play to read—it was his first play that was produced, called I'll Leave it to You. *I thought it was an excellent play, and we all knew that he was going to do things because he was so funny. We knew he was on the way!*

He was indeed. Robert Courtneidge now took *The Young Idea*, with Herbert Marshall and Kate Cutler playing the leading parts.

The play opened to fairly good reviews in Bristol, and ran for six weeks in the provinces, but as there was no theatre available in London during the pantomime season, it was taken off in the hope of the Savoy becoming free in February. Noël took the opportunity of spending the three winter months out of England, and left for Davos in Switzerland to stay with his benefactor and friend Ned Lathom, still recovering from tuberculosis.

Lathom had poured money into theatrical enterprises, including the impresario André Charlot's most recent revue, *A to Z*, and Noël now proposed that he write a revue himself, and that Ned Lathom put up the money. An author himself, Lathom had founded The Ventures, a society for plays which were refused public performance by the Lord Chamberlain. His own play *Wet Paint* was considered outstanding by some critics, and two others, *Tuppence Coloured* and *Twenty Houses in a Row*, were also produced by The Ventures.

Lord Lathom liked Noël's idea and cabled Charlot to join them in Switzerland to discuss the project. Charlot read the sketches Noël had prepared and listened to the music and lyrics he had composed, but felt the material not strong enough to carry an entire revue, especially one in which it was hoped that Gertrude Lawrence and Maisie Gay would star. It was agreed, therefore, that Noël should share the writing of the book of *London Calling!* with Ronald Jeans, and the composing with Philip Braham. At that

56

above, Maisie Gay in *London Calling!*

time Noël could not himself write music down on paper, but he was fortunate enough to meet Elsie April, a rehearsal pianist who transcribed each note he sang at her. This was to be a lasting and valuable partnership and for almost fifteen years he used no one else to arrange his music and act as accompanist at his rehearsals.

With the opening of *London Calling!* Noël's name went up in lights for the first time. Edward Molyneux designed the dresses, even those of the chorus, and Fred Astaire, who was appearing in *Stop Flirting* at the time, arranged some of the musical numbers.

Charlot opened with a matinée, which was then considered a great innovation, and it became a great hit. Particularly successful were Gertrude Lawrence and Noël singing 'You Were Meant for Me', and Gertrude Lawrence's performance of Noël's composition 'Parisian Pierrot'.

'Parisian Pierrot'
from 'London Calling!'

Parisian Pierrot,
Society's hero,
The lord of a day,
The Rue de la Paix
Is under your sway.
The world may flatter,
But what does that matter,
They'll never shatter
Your gloom profound.
Parisian Pierrot,
Your spirit's at zero,
Divinely forlorn,
With exquisite scorn
From sunset to dawn,
The limbo is calling,
Your star will be falling,
As soon as the clock goes round.

During the run of *London Calling!*, Noël wrote two more plays: *Fallen Angels* and *The Vortex*. But Charlot now decided to mount a new revue in New York, including all the hit numbers from his recent successes together with those from *London Calling!*, as a vehicle for three stars, Jack Buchanan, Beatrice Lillie and Gertrude Lawrence. This meant that Gertrude Lawrence would leave the London production of *London Calling!*, and even though Joyce Barbour took over the role the show closed after three months.

However, it ran long enough for Noël to have received the anticipated financial reward from music royalties from the show, and he was thrilled to hear his own music played as he dined and danced in restaurants and night-clubs.

He too left the cast of *London Calling!* after his six-month contract had expired, in order to make a trip to New York, but his visit this time differed from the last. Now he could afford the luxury of an uptown hotel. André Charlot's *London Revue of 1924* opened at the Times Square Theatre and Noël saw three of his numbers performed on Broadway for the first time. Also in New York, at a party at Laurette Taylor's, he met Douglas Fairbanks and Mary Pickford, the then royalty of the screen. When Noël learned that they were sailing for England on the *Olympic* he booked a passage on the same vessel and got to know the celebrated couple better through mutual friends. He placed himself beside them at the deck-rail when the ship set sail to the screams and shouts of adoration from the thousands who had gathered on the dock to bid the couple farewell, and shared in their greeting when the ship docked at

below, Noël and Gertrude Lawrence in *London Calling!* *opposite*, Gertrude Lawrence singing 'Parisian Pierrot' from *London Calling!*

Joyce Barbour.

Noël with Gladys Calthrop.

Southampton to the excited cheers of the crowd on the docks.

On his return to London, he had planned to do *Fallen Angels*, with Madge Titheradge and Gladys Cooper, to be presented by Gladys Cooper's own management at the Playhouse Theatre, but he found that the leading ladies had other contracts to fulfil and would not be free at the same time. And so both *Fallen Angels* and *The Vortex* went the rounds of theatre managements. He had since completed *Oranges and Lemons*, the play based on the Laurette Taylor/Hartley Manners family, changed the title to *Hay Fever* and sent it round with the other two plays; but none of the managements took any notice.

Three years previously, on holiday in Alassio, Noël had met a young English artist, Gladys Calthrop who was about his own age. She was separated from her husband,

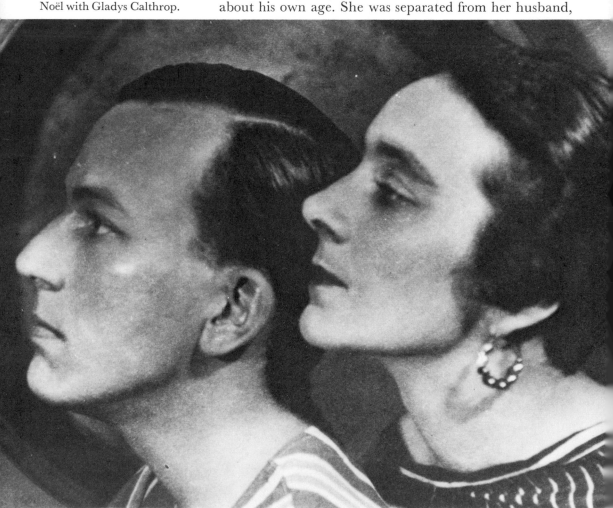

and had a young son, Hugo. She and Noël became close friends, frequently holidaying together.

GLADYS CALTHROP:

As a matter of fact, the reason no management would touch the script of The Vortex *was because of Noël. They were all mad about the play, and said it was one of the best they had ever read, but would have nothing to do with it if Noël played the lead. You see, they didn't consider him good enough. But as he'd written it for himself, he wasn't having any of that, and wouldn't give way.*

However Norman Macdermott, who ran a converted drill hall called the Everyman Theatre in Hampstead (now a cinema) read *Hay Fever* and *The Vortex*, and liked them both. He called Noël to discuss which he considered the more economical to produce, for the Everyman had a very small auditorium, with no balconies.

Noël's own preference was for *The Vortex*, and Macdermott agreed to put it on. Since the maximum salary he paid to any artist, stars included, was £5 a week, the choice of cast was limited. However Noël's friend Kate Cutler agreed to play the leading role of Florence, a society mother who has a young lover, with Noël as her drug-taking son Nicky. The Lord Chamberlain had refused at first to grant it a licence because of the unpleasantness of the theme, but Noël managed to persuade him of its moral importance.

He asked Gladys Calthrop to design the sets and costumes.

GLADYS CALTHROP:

It was certainly an easy play to design because there are just three rooms, but it was the first designing I'd ever done; and certainly the first designing I'd done out of doors, because I had to paint the scenery out in the streets in the rain, as there was no room anywhere inside, but it was a good beginning, very good training. It was learning the hard way.

At the eleventh hour, however, Macdermott called Noël in to tell him that he hadn't the money to put it on.

GLADYS CALTHROP:

By chance Noël happened to be lunching with Michael Arlen, the Armenian novelist whose new book The Green Hat *was a best-selling success in London that year. They were discussing their work, and Noël told him that* The Vortex *was in a ghastly mess because of the financial problem.*

'How much do you need to put it on?' Michael asked.

'Oh, about £200,' Noël replied, *and with that, Michael took out his cheque-book at the luncheon table, wrote out a cheque for £250, and handed it to him without so much as asking to read the play.*

Money, however, was not to be the answer to all their problems. Soon after *The Vortex* went into rehearsal Helen Spencer, who had one of the minor parts, developed diphtheria and was replaced by Mollie Kerr. Worse was to come. Only a few days before the opening Kate Cutler resigned from the cast, having apparently decided at that late date that her part was less good than Noël's, and

unsympathetic into the bargain. Noël was both angry at her abrupt departure and disappointed in her since she had appeared in his first two plays, *I'll Leave it to You* and *The Young Idea*. In despair he appealed to Lilian Braithwaite, though with opposition from Norman Macdermott, who considered her wrong for the part. Noël, however, drew Macdermott's attention to the source of the play's backing, and the objections to Miss Braithwaite faded away. She learned the part in two days.

All the same, one could see Macdermott's point. Lilian Braithwaite had excelled in sympathetic parts. She was known for her wit, but it was of a wry kind, where the knife slipped in gently and the tiny flick of the wrist provided the laugh.

One of her victims was her close friend Ivor Novello,

who was known to be as careful with his money as she was generous with hers. He had gone so far as to install a coin-operated telephone in the hall of his country home, Red Roofs, for the benefit of his many visiting friends. Drink did not flow, and many a half-bottle was to be packed in the luggage of week-ending chums. When Noël was playing in *The Constant Nymph*, Lilian Braithwaite went back stage to see him. Pointing to a brooch clipped to her dress, she said, '*Ivor* gave me this tiny diamond. Can *you* see it?'

For years she had been type-cast on the West End stage as a respectable and conventional hostess, but now she surprised her critics in her performance as the man-hunting society mother in *The Vortex*.

left, with Gladys Calthrop at rehearsals.
right, Lilian Braithwaite.

Her daughter, actress Joyce Carey, is a friend of Noël's and has been in many of his plays. (She also wrote, under the pseudonym of Jay Mallory, the highly successful play *Sweet Aloes*.)

JOYCE CAREY:

I was playing in something and couldn't get to the first night of The Vortex, *so they let me go to a dress rehearsal. It was one of the most thrilling theatrical experiences I've ever had in my life.*

George Bishop of the Telegraph *and I were the only two people in the theatre, so there was no question of audience reaction, and it was so exciting. It's the only time I've ever known for sure that something was going to be a success.*

Joyce Carey.

GINETTE SPANIER:

I flew round to the back and found them all sitting round a stove. The Everyman was rather a primitive little theatre. I wasn't encouraged as a rule to give my ideas on things, but I flew down and, very articulate, I did the opposite of Cassandra and said, 'It's all wonderful, and you'll have a huge success. You'll move at once to the West End and run for ever,' which indeed it did.

I don't think any of you realise what Noël Coward meant to us, the audience, the young people, when he burst upon the world in 1924 with The Vortex. *We'd seen him before, in* London Calling!, *and suddenly in Hampstead* The Vortex *was born.*

It horrified our parents, but for us young people it was revelation. Noël Coward was the Beatles of our day. Do you realise that up till then nobody had ever called somebody 'darling' unless they were having a love affair with them? And the fact of everybody being so sophisticated and calling each other 'darling' was a habit started by Noël which has gone on till today.

Our parents forbade us to go, but we went to the Everyman and there on stage was a young man taking dope; his mother having an affair with a young man—with one of his friends! I mean this was absolutely horrifying. But to us it was revelation.

I wanted to meet him so badly. I used to look round the corner in case he came down the street. And then after the war, it must have been 1945 or 1946, quite by chance we met in the South of France, and in three minutes we became intimate, close and wonderful friends.

He would come and stay with my husband and me, here, in Paris, in what he called acute discomfort, because I'm a very bad housekeeper, and when he left, instead of sending me a bread-and-butter letter he sent me a list of complaints— which was very useful. I've done quite a lot of things on that list!

The Vortex opened on Noël's twenty-fifth birthday, December 16th 1924, and took London by storm. It transferred from the Everyman after two weeks, first to the Royalty Theatre, then to the Comedy and finally to the Little Theatre in the Adelphi (which vanished after the Second World War), and it played for more than a year. From that night when the curtain rose in Hampstead,

Noël was never poor again. He was to know everyone, and everyone knew him, or wanted to know him.

But the critics were mixed in their reviews. The *Express* accused it of being 'a dustbin of a play'. James Agate criticised the length of the last act, and Hannen Swaffer, the most dreaded critic of the day, was sufficiently enraged to devote a full page of the *People* to a virulent attack, accusing Noël of writing 'the most decadent play of our time'. Even Sir Gerald du Maurier wrote a deprecating article, to which Noël replied in the *Express*, politely putting him in his place. It is probably fair to say that this play changed the face of the British theatre in the twenties in the way that John Osborne changed it in the fifties with *Look Back in Anger*.

NOËL COWARD:

My original motive in The Vortex *was to write a good play with a whacking great part in it for myself. We opened in November, which was rather tricky as it was generally a pea-soup fog, and it was also very difficult to get to the theatre. The first night was wonderful, that went all right, but after that it was extremely uncomfortable and very cold. There was no heating. And our relief when we finally moved into the West End to the Royalty Theatre was something. We could hardly believe we weren't shuddering. I used to watch poor Lilian's hands shaking with cold. Horrible.*

SYBIL THORNDIKE:

It was an astonishing play. Noël was before his time, but it didn't matter because he was so funny—because he carried it off with his humour. And I think that if you're before your time and you're solemn you're no good at all. Oh my goodness, what an actor! As an actor he was absolutely in the front. He could play these nervous strange people, hysterical people, which is very rare. I think that if he hadn't been such a wonderful playwright he could have been right in the forefront as a really hysterical actor. And it's only people who are hysterical who can play hysterical parts. He was absolutely wonderful. You see, he could scream!

I remember one awful *scream, driving up Sloane Street one day. He was in front of us in an open taxi and we were coming along in our old car making a terrific noise, trying to attract his attention, and he screamed at us: 'Stop it, stop it!' He didn't recognise us. We rocked with laughter. But he was nervous, you know. He had awful nerves. But he couldn't have been the hysterical actor he was if he hadn't.*

The Vortex brought him the kind of success he had always longed for—material things—money, new clothes, a fine car, friends . . . and some of the responsibilities and penalties of fame.

NOËL COWARD:

I've never really minded publicity. In fact sometimes I've been known to encourage it. But the thing about sitting up in bed with a cigarette-holder was unfortunate, because I had Chinese pyjamas and a cigarette, and they insisted. They took it, and as the flash went my eyes shut so the result was I looked like an advanced Chinese decadent in the last phases of dope.
That photograph was published all over the world.

It was an unfortunate incident, for drug-taking was one of the themes of *The Vortex*, and when the photograph appeared in the Press, suggesting that Noël was a little high when it was taken, it resulted in scurrilous attacks on his 'decadence'. Noël, however, was not noticeably upset, for the publicity boosted the play overwhelmingly, guaranteeing box-office sell-outs, and, moreover, attracted attention to Noël himself—of which it cannot be said he entirely disapproved.

He was to be seen dancing at the Embassy Club in Bond Street with Gertrude Lawrence, and was invited to all the smart parties, where he would sing his own songs

NOËL COWARD AND GERTIE LAWRENCE.

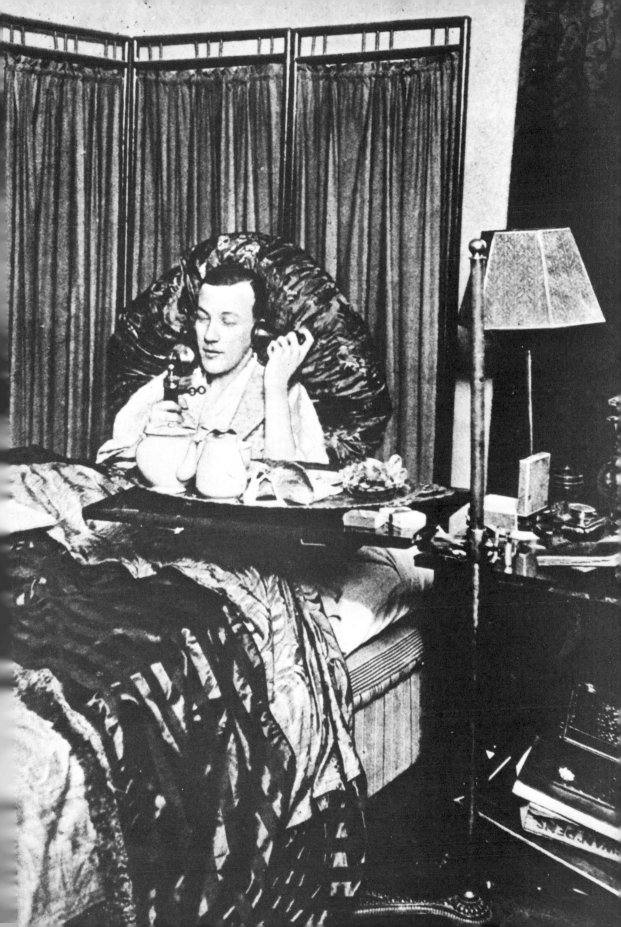

and talk wittily with untiring charm and zest. Gladys Calthrop redecorated his bedroom in pillar-box scarlet, and painted sinuous pink nudes over the chimney-piece.

NOËL COWARD: *I became extraordinarily unspoiled by my great success after* The Vortex. *As a matter of fact I still am.*

The Vortex, 1924, Everyman Theatre, Hampstead.

'The Vortex'
(Taken from Act Three)

The scene takes place in Florence's (Lilian Braithwaite) bedroom. Her son Nicky (Noël Coward) has discovered her affair with a friend of his, who is half her age, and has attacked her for it.

FLORENCE: Don't talk like that. Don't - don't - it can't be such a crime being loved - it can't be such a crime being happy -

NICKY: You're not happy - you're never happy - you're fighting - fighting all the time to keep your youth and your looks - because you can't bear the thought of living without them - as though they mattered in the end.

FLORENCE: (Hysterically) What does anything matter - ever?

NICKY: That's what I'm trying to find out.

FLORENCE: I'm still young inside - I'm still beautiful - why shouldn't I live my life as I choose?

NICKY: You're not young or beautiful; I'm

68

	seeing for the first time how old you are - it's horrible - your silly fair hair - and your face all plastered and painted -
FLORENCE:	Nicky - Nicky - stop - stop - stop! (She flings herself face downwards on the bed. Nicky goes over to her).
NICKY:	Mother!
FLORENCE:	Go away - go away - I hate you - go away -
NICKY:	Mother - sit up -
FLORENCE:	(Pulling herself together) Go out of my room -
NICKY	Mother -
FLORENCE:	I don't ever want to see you again - you're insane - you've said wicked, wicked things to me - you've talked to me as though I were a woman off the streets. I can't bear any more - I can't bear any more!
NICKY:	I have a slight confession to make -
FLORENCE:	Confession?
NICKY:	Yes.
FLORENCE:	Go away - go away -
NICKY:	(Taking a small gold box from his pocket) Look -
FLORENCE:	What do you mean - what is it -?
NICKY:	Don't you know? (Florence takes the box with trembling fingers and opens it. She stares at it for a moment. She speaks again, her voice is quite dead.)
FLORENCE:	Nicky, it isn't - you haven't -?
NICKY:	Why do you look so shocked?
FLORENCE:	(Dully) Oh, my God!
NICKY:	What does it matter? (Florence suddenly rises and hurls the box out of the window.) That doesn't make it any better.
FLORENCE:	(Flinging herself on her knees beside him) Nicky, promise me, oh, promise you'll never do it again - never in your life - it's frightful - horrible -
NICKY:	It's only just the beginning.
FLORENCE:	What can I say to you - what can I say to you?

NICKY:	Nothing - under the circumstances.
FLORENCE:	What do you mean?
NICKY:	It can't possibly matter - now.
FLORENCE:	Matter - but it's the finish of everything - you're young, you're just starting on your life - you must stop - you must swear never to touch it again - swear to me on your oath, Nicky - I'll help you - I'll help you -
NICKY:	You!

(He turns away)

FLORENCE:	(Burying her face in her hands and moaning) Oh - oh - oh!
NICKY:	How could you possibly help me?
FLORENCE:	(Clutching him) Nicky!
NICKY:	(Almost losing control) Shut up - shut up - don't touch me -
FLORENCE:	(Trying to take him in her arms) Nicky - Nicky -
NICKY:	I'm trying to control myself, but you won't let me - you're an awfully rotten woman, really.
FLORENCE:	Nicky - stop - stop - stop - (She beats him with her fists)
NICKY:	Leave go of me! (He breaks away from her and going up to the dressing table he sweeps everything off on to the floor with his arm)
FLORENCE:	(Screaming) Oh - oh - Nicky -!
NICKY:	Now then! Now then! You're not to have any more lovers; you're not going to be beautiful and successful ever again - you're going to be my mother for once - it's about time I had one to help me, before I go over the edge altogether -
FLORENCE:	Nicky - Nicky -
NICKY:	Promise me to be different - you've got to promise me!
FLORENCE:	(Sinking on to the end of the couch, facing audience) Yes - yes - I promise - (The tears are running down her face)

NICKY: I love you, really – that's why it's so
           awful.
               (He falls on his knees by her side
               and buries his face in her lap)
FLORENCE: No. No, not awful – don't say that – I
           love you, too.
NICKY: (Sobbing hopelessly) Oh, mother –!
FLORENCE: (Staring in front of her) I wish I were
           dead!
NICKY: It doesn't matter about death, but it
           matters terribly about life.
FLORENCE: I know –
NICKY: (Desperately) Promise me you'll be
           different –
FLORENCE: Yes, yes – I'll try –
NICKY: We'll both try.
FLORENCE: Yes, dear. Oh, my dear –!
               (She sits quite still, staring in
               front of her – the tears are
               rolling down her cheeks, and she is
               stroking Nicky's hair mechanically
               in an effort to calm him.)
                         Curtain

NOËL COWARD: *The most hilarious thing that happened to me in* The
               Vortex *was in America after we played the London run.
               We opened in Washington and Lilian, at one great moment
               in the last act, used to take the box of drugs from my
               hand and throw it with tremendous vehemence. She threw
               it out of the window, and a stage-hand who happened to
               be passing threw it back, and she caught it. She had her
               hands in that position still—and she gave it one look and
               threw it back with such* venom *that it broke the edge of the
               window. And then the audience broke up and the curtain
               had to come down and we had to start the act again.*

               *There are certain actors who are haunted throughout
               their theatrical careers by inanimate objects. The inanimate
               objects that have haunted my career have always been
               fireplaces. Once a fireplace on stage fell down, knocking
               Alan Webb on to his face, leaving a perfectly plain blank
               wall behind it, so that there could obviously have been no
               fireplace there. Ever.*

               And then there was another great moment when Constance

Collier, who was playing in Serena Blandish, *had to make a splendid entrance with two enormous greyhounds. They were rather straining at the leash and she was holding them back and the doors were flung open and she was announced. They lost their heads at the sight of the audience and came on at a* gallop, *followed hotly by Constance, who hadn't let go, and they went straight off through the fireplace and Constance had the* wit *to bend her head so that she didn't hit her head on the fireplace, and the curtain had to come down. The audience laughed so dreadfully that the whole play had to start from the beginning again.*

When Constance was playing with Wilson Barrett in The Sign of the Cross, *she had to hand him a little lamb. Now it was rather a mean management, Wilson Barrett didn't pay much, and so gradually the lamb started to grow and by the end of the run she handed him a full-sized sheep at every performance which weighed her down so much that finally she fell on to her knees, sheep and all. And the audience applauded and cheered and roared. It didn't help* The Sign of the Cross *a bit.*

Noël had met the great English impresario Charles B. Cochran several times since their first luncheon together during the run of *The Young Idea*, and their discussions about his writing a new revue had progressed apace. Now, during the run of *The Vortex*, he completed work on sketches and the music for the revue, to be called *On with the Dance*.

Noël left *The Vortex* for a few performances for the Manchester opening of *On with the Dance*, and his role was taken over by John Gielgud:

JOHN GIELGUD: *I had been acting in a repertory company in Oxford and was released to understudy him. I took over the role in London while he was away and subsequently succeeded him in the part when he left the company; but stepping into someone else's shoes in a success can be a nerve-racking experience, and I found myself copying his mannerisms and style of speaking. This made it rather difficult for me to find my own way of playing later on, though it certainly gave me my first big chance in the West End.*

But on his arrival in Manchester for the try-out, not only did Noël find to his horror that his name was nowhere to

Alice Delysia.

be seen on the bills, which instead announced 'Charles B. Cochran's Revue', but at rehearsal the next day he discovered that Cochran had considered 'Poor Little Rich Girl' too dreary and cut it out of the show. Noël rushed over to the Midland Hotel, burst in on Cochran, who was in his bath at the time, and shrieked at him:

'*Not* only have I done three-quarters of the score, *all* the lyrics and the *entire* book, but I directed the dialogue scenes and most of the musical numbers!'

Cochran received the outburst with calm dignity, and offered him a glass of sherry in return for the bathtowel Noël was brandishing. Drying himself, he agreed to Noël's demands to be billed as he saw fit and restored 'Poor Little Rich Girl' to the show; it turned out to be the big song hit of the revue and one of Noël's biggest royalty-earners.

This established a satisfactory working partnership with Cochran, and they formed an alliance that was to present to the British public a decade of successful musicals.

The cast of *On with the Dance* included Douglas Byng, Nigel Bruce, Hermione Baddeley and Ernest Thesiger, and the star of the show was Alice Delysia, an enchanting entertainer who had made her début at the Moulin Rouge in Paris as a chorus girl in *The Belle of New York*, and became an overnight star in London in 1914 at the

Ambassador's Theatre in *Odds and Ends*. She it was who sang 'Poor Little Rich Girl.'

'Poor Little Rich Girl'
from 'On with the Dance'

Poor little rich girl,
You're a bewitched girl,
Better beware!
Laughing at danger,
Virtue a stranger,
Better take care!
The life you lead sets all your nerves
  a jangle,
Your love affairs are in a hopeless
  tangle,
Though you're a child, dear,
Your life's a wild typhoon,
In lives of leisure
The craze for pleasure
Steadily grows.
Cocktails and laughter,
But what comes after?
Nobody knows.
You're weaving love into a mad jazz
  pattern,
Ruled by Pantaloon.
Poor little rich girl, don't drop a
  stitch too soon.

The opening of *On with the Dance* at the London Pavilion meant that Noël had two hits playing simultaneously in London, and *Fallen Angels*, with Edna Best and Tallulah Bankhead, made it a hat-trick. He was not yet twenty-six years old, and when *Easy Virtue* opened in New York that same year, he had achieved more than any author, composer and actor of the age. He was labelled the second Somerset Maugham and the second Sacha Guitry by everybody except Maugham and Guitry.

But even though he pleased the public and his backers, he found the critics harder to please.

THE DARLING OF THE LONDON THEATRE

If there had been panic over the re-casting of *The Vortex* there was positive pandemonium over *Fallen Angels*. In 1925 Anthony Prinsep, who was in joint management of the Globe Theatre with his wife Marie Löhr, bought *Fallen Angels* as a vehicle for Margaret Bannerman, a Canadian actress who had been appearing in West End plays ever since her arrival in England ten years before (Prinsep was to marry her after the dissolution of his marriage to Miss Löhr in 1928). Margaret Bannerman had scored a striking success as Lady George Grayston in *Our Betters* at the Globe two years before, in 1923, but now she was physically and mentally exhausted as the result of a run of not-so-successful plays. She therefore announced four days before the production's opening that she was unable to go on. All hell broke loose. The part demanded a star of equal ability and rating to that of Edna Best, and the range of out-of-work stars of that calibre was limited.

One star who was apparently not out of work was Tallulah Bankhead. Jeanne Eagles had electrified the New York critics with her performance as Sadie Thompson in *Rain*, and Basil Dean had promised Tallulah the coveted part for the London opening. It would not be her first British appearance. She had invaded the West End eighteen months before with Gerald du Maurier in *The Dancers* (written by du Maurier and Viola Tree under the pseudonym Hubert Parsons), and the effects were, to say the least, sensational. Alabama-born, the daughter of a Congressman (and grand-daughter of a Senator) Tallulah was aristocratically arrogant and wildly beautiful with golden hair. She was exciting, witty and outrageous. When told that Bette Davis was portraying her in the movie *All*

With Tallulah Bankhead
during *Fallen Angels*.

About Eve, she cracked, 'Tell her when I get back to Hollywood I'll pull every hair out of her moustache.' She liked
to shock, which was fortunate, considering her talent for it.

Basil Dean offered Tallulah £40 a week for the star part
in *Rain*, subject to Somerset Maugham's agreeing the
casting. She learned the part, and offered to visit New
York to see Jeanne Eagles' performance, but Maugham
didn't want her, and she was sacked on the second day of
rehearsal. Since her contract hadn't been signed, that was
that. The newspapers were full of speculation as to who was
to play Sadie, and the winner was Olga Lindo, a good
actress but said to be lacking in the necessary sex appeal
for the role. Dean, when he explained the situation to
Tallulah, added insult to injury by offering her Olga
Lindo's current role in *Tarnish*, to which Tallulah hollered
a polite 'NO THANKS!'

Her professional pride punctured, she was contemplating
the various forms of suicide the following morning when
Noël telephoned asking whether she could learn the role
of Julia Sterroll in *Fallen Angels* in four days.

'In four days? I'll do it in four *hours*!'

'What's your salary?' Noël asked.

'One hundred pounds a week.'

'But you were only getting forty pounds for *Rain*.'

'That's because I wanted to play Sadie Thompson. I
don't give a goddam if I play *Fallen Angels* or not.'

'Agreed. If you can open Tuesday.'

'I'll open Tuesday.'

And true to her word she did, word perfect, *and* the play
was a hit. The Press, however, went to town, accusing it

of being (among other things) vulgar, disgusting, shocking, nauseating, vile and obscene. This did not prevent Winston Churchill from seeing Tallulah Bankhead's performance five times. But there was no doubt about the play's effect upon one horrified section of the public.

One scene, which produced an onslaught of obscene anonymous letters, involves two young women getting drunk.

'Fallen Angels'

(Taken from Act Two)

The scene is evening, in Julia Sterroll's apartment. Julia (Tallulah Bankhead), and Jane (Edna Best), both bored with their respective marriages, are expecting the arrival of Maurice — the Frenchman with whom both had affairs before their marriages, seven years before. They are now to see him for the first time in seven years — in the hope of rekindling the flames. They are in the middle of dinner, served by the maid, Saunders, whose real name is Jasmin.

(There is a ring at the door. Saunders answers it, and re-enters.)

SAUNDERS: It's a foreign gentleman, ma'am.

JANE: There now!

JULIA: Why didn't you show him in?

SAUNDERS: He says he won't come in. He only wants to know if there's a Madame Gambelitti living here.

JANE: What's he like?

SAUNDERS: Quite respectable, ma'am, but with a long moustache.

JULIA: Come on, Jane, we'll peep.
(They go to the door and peep round it into the hall — then return to the table crestfallen.)

JULIA: Why didn't you tell him there was no Madame What's her name here, and get rid of him?

SAUNDERS: You said you were expecting a foreign gentleman, ma'am, and I thought I'd better keep him in case.

JULIA: Well, get rid of him now.

SAUNDERS:	Very good, ma'am.
	<u>(Exit)</u>
JANE:	<u>(Almost in tears)</u> It's downright cruel, that's what it is.
JULIA:	It's the first time that anybody not aggressively English has rung that bell since we've been here.
JANE:	And he would come after his beastly Madame Gambelitti tonight of all nights. It's indecent!
JULIA:	More champagne?
JANE:	<u>(Loudly)</u> Yes.
JULIA:	Well, don't shout.
JANE:	I shall if I want to, Julia; you mustn't be dictatorial.
	<u>(Julia fills both glasses again.)</u>
JULIA:	Let's have a toast!
JANE:	<u>(Rising and holding up her glass)</u> Maurice Duclos.
JULIA:	<u>(Also rising)</u> Maurice Duclos! No heeltaps.
	<u>(They both drain their glasses)</u>
JANE:	<u>(Sitting down quickly)</u> That was silly of us, Julia.
JULIA:	<u>(Also sitting)</u> Eat some steak quickly. <u>(There is silence for a moment while they devote themselves to their food.)</u>
JANE:	Wouldn't it be awful if a tree blew down and killed Fred and Willy on the golf links?
JULIA:	<u>(Shocked)</u> Jane, how can you!
JANE:	It would serve us right.
JULIA:	It would be too awful - I should never forgive myself.
JANE:	Neither should I.
JULIA:	There's a dreadful gale blowing.
JANE:	Things like that do happen.
JULIA:	No, they don't - not if you don't think about them. Mind over matter.
JANE:	I do admire you, Julia, you're so strong - and sensible.
JULIA:	Nonsense, dear, I'm just not <u>afraid</u> of life.
JANE:	You're brave.
JULIA:	No braver than you.

JANE:	(Verging on tears) We must both be brave always, Julia.
JULIA:	(Slightly maudlin) Whatever happens.
JANE:	Even if Fred and Willy were killed we should have to bear it.
JULIA:	Yes, Jane - we wouldn't break down - we'd face the world with a smile.
JANE:	Not quite a smile, dear, it would be misunderstood.
JULIA:	Poor darling Fred, I can see him now being carried in on a stretcher -
JANE:	With Willy on another stretcher. Oh, dear - (She breaks down)
JULIA:	Jane dear - don't - (Re-enter Saunders with sweet - Profiteroles au chocolat.)
JANE:	I've eaten much too much already.
JULIA:	So have I, but we must go on, it will keep up our strength.
JANE:	They look lovely - tinker, tailor, soldier, sailor -
JULIA:	(Giggling) No, you do that with cherry stones.
JANE:	(Also giggling) I like doing it with these.
JULIA:	Have some more champagne?
JANE:	No, thank you.
JULIA:	Here you are. (She pours it out)
JANE:	Thanks, darling.
JULIA:	What's so silly is that I'm beginning to feel sleepy.
JANE:	I'm not - exactly - just cosy.
JULIA:	Bring the coffee straight away, Saunders.
SAUNDERS:	Yes, ma'am.
	(Exit)
JANE:	What a pretty girl Saunders is!
JULIA:	Yes, isn't she?
JANE:	She ought to be a great success in life, she's so calm.
JULIA:	(Suddenly bursting out laughing) Oh, dear -!
JANE:	What are you laughing at?
JULIA:	You look frightfully funny.
JANE:	What's the matter with me? (She gets up

	just a little unsteadily and looks at herself in the glass)
JULIA:	(Giggling hopelessly) I don't know – you just do!
JANE:	So do you.
JULIA:	(Also getting up and looking in the glass) It's our heads, I think – they're too big!

MICHEÁL MACLIAMMÓIR: *The only naïve thing I've ever known Noël do—one cannot associate naïvety with Noël Coward really, he might appear naïve in about a hundred years time, but who won't? —was in* Fallen Angels. *It was the elaborate menus described in the stage directions, not in the dialogue, all those elaborate things that were brought on by the maid for those two disgraceful ladies dining together. It was very funny—'She brings on so-and-so, and so-and-so, and uncovers the foie gras and puts out the caviar and so on, and the sole bonne femme à la crême-de-something', and so on, and it goes on and on. And it struck me as being, ah yes, he's doing that because he was in his early twenties when he wrote it, and was showing off that he knows all about French food. That was typical of Noël.*

Noël was in an enviable position. He had a comedy, a revue and a play on, and everywhere he went he heard orchestras playing 'Poor Little Rich Girl'. He was a success and he knew it, and what's more he thoroughly enjoyed it. Others knew it too, and didn't enjoy it, least of all his critics.

His closest friends and inseparable companions were Gladys Calthrop, Jeffrey Amherst and Lorn Loraine (née Macnaughton), but soon the quartet was to become a quintet.

A friend told Noël that a young American was anxious to meet him, and might he bring him round after the performance one evening? 'Of course', said Noël, and was delighted to be introduced to a handsome young man whom he'd noticed enthusiastically applauding *The Vortex* from the front row of the stalls.

Jack Wilson was a young New York stockbroker. He was courteous, tactful and charming. Noël took an instant liking to him, as did Gladys. Later he was to become one of the most important people in Noël's professional life.

In June 1925 Alban B. Limpus and Charles Kenyon, the theatre managers who had brought *The Vortex* to the West End, approached Noël and asked if Marie Tempest could do *Hay Fever*. Noël was both flattered and amazed, for the play had already been turned down by what

Jack Wilson.

GLADYS CALTHROP:

seemed to be every management in London, and Miss Tempest was one of the most attractive and delightful actresses on the English stage. She was short, with golden hair, exquisite in her appearance and always beautifully dressed. She was a disciplinarian in the theatre, but had charm and wit, and Noël had in fact written the part of Judith Bliss with her in mind.

'But', he was quick to point out, 'she refused *Hay Fever* herself last year.'

Oh, they explained, she'd been doing a world tour, but since her return she'd been unable to find any suitable parts until now. Needless to say, Noël had little hesitation in accepting their offer, especially as he was invited to direct the play himself.

Even the most confident twenty-year-old could have been forgiven for feeling a little nervous at having to direct an actress of Marie Tempest's professional stature and personal attributes, but she proved surprisingly co-operative. *Hay Fever* opened on June 8th 1925 at the Ambassador's Theatre, with the supporting roles played by Helen Spencer, Ann Trevor, W. Graham Browne and, in the part of Simon Bliss, Robert Andrews, once a leading juvenile actor and later a lifelong friend of Ivor Novello. The critics greeted it with the bad or indifferent reviews with which they had welcomed most of Noël's previous work, except that this time they accused him of being flippant and trivial as well, but this did not prevent it from being as successful as *The Vortex*, *On with the Dance* and *Fallen Angels*. The last thing that mattered to Noël was what the critics wrote, as he thumbed through the weekly box-office returns and counted his share of the royalties.

Various American managements had asked to present *The Vortex* on Broadway, and Noël finally agreed to allow Basil Dean, who had a string of successes behind him, to re-produce it for New York in association with Charles Dillingham and Abe Erlanger, and also to direct it. All the principals from the English production were to play their original roles, and the rest of the cast would be found in New York. John Gielgud again took over from Noël in London. Together with his mother, Gladys Calthrop, Basil Dean and Alan Hollis, Noël sailed for New York on the *Majestic*.

When we took The Vortex *to America I had a splendid idea which sounds very old-fashioned now but it was new then. The first act is really nothing but social conversation and establishing personalities, so I thought it would be fun to do it with newspapers pasted on the wall, like wallpaper. Basil Dean, who was on the ship with us, had thought it a very good idea, so off I went. I'd already had to join the Painters Union in America, which was very alarming and far worse than any examination anyone's ever done.*

Jane Cowl in *Easy Virtue*.

There was a little man who presided over the whole affair with such ceremony that when I came out I believed he'd married me.

However, I was now told to join the Paperhangers Union, which I promptly did, and, as a Union member myself was able to employ other Union members to hang the paper up, and that's how the first act was presented to the great American public.

Noël was by now considered in America as the white hope of the English theatre, and he was received in New York with unprecedented and unexpected applause. The Press notices were good, and the advance sales terrific. Seats were bought and sold on the black market for twenty-five dollars a pair, and Noël was photographed, caricatured, interviewed, publicised and launched by the Press like a new soap powder. He was guest of honour at luncheons, invited to smart weekends on Long Island, wined and dined by American society—in short, he had arrived.

While he was in New York he renewed his contact with Jack Wilson. They became friends, and their association developed from then onwards until Wilson gave up his stockbroking to become Noël's manager. In the years to come they were to form their own theatre management, presenting Noël's own works under the John C. Wilson banner.

Once *The Vortex* was established as a success Noël was asked to do *Hay Fever* in New York as well. Unfortunately the play ran into trouble over the casting. All the parts are of course utterly and typically English, and Noël was delighted with Laura Hope-Crews as Judith Bliss, but was horrified on the first day of rehearsal at the Broadhurst Theatre to be introduced to the actress playing Myra—a brassy blonde with a *décolleté* black lace dress, a broad Bronx accent and a watertight contract.

It opened in Brooklyn for a week's trial run, and moved to the Maxine Elliot Theatre in New York, where it played to a specially invited Sunday night audience. In their attempts to be in at the birth of another Noël Coward success, every star, writer and critic was present. The curtain fell to gentle applause, the notices next day were bad and the advance sales non-existent. The play closed after six weeks.

Easy Virtue, Noël's new play, was bought by Basil Dean for a considerable advance, and it seemed marked out for success, in view of the triumphs his last four plays had enjoyed in London. Because of his considerable financial outlay, however, Dean decided to try for an American production first. Dean was an astute man, unpopular with actors, whom he directed with a rod of iron, but powerful in the theatre, influential and clever, and with a string of past successes to vindicate his judgement.

The play called for a real star to play the role of Larita, the lady with a past. Jane Cowl seemed the ideal choice, but this beautiful American actress was also notably capricious. She and Basil Dean did not see eye to eye from the start and she exasperated Noël by playing a key scene for sympathy rather than for theatrical effect. Still, she got the laugh at the curtain, and scored a considerable success in the play

During the New York run of *Easy Virtue* Basil Dean returned to London and induced Violet Melnotte, the proprietress of the Duke of York's theatre, to present the play with the original Broadway cast. After running successfully for five months in London, however, the play came to an abrupt close when Miss Cowl, never one to overstay her welcome, saw the writing on the wall and decided to leave, ostensibly to fulfil a New York engagement. Had she stayed, the play would have stood a considerable chance of recouping the management's London costs, but Miss Cowl was motivated more by concern for her own good than for that of the management.

The film version of *Easy Virtue* was directed by Alfred Hitchcock, and starred Isabel Jeans, who had always been ragged for the famous line she had in the Jacobean pastoral *The Faithful Shepherdess* by John Fletcher, 'It's *impossible* to ravish me—I'm too *willing*!'

ISABEL JEANS:

I was very happy to do the film because it was one of Noël's big early successes, and of course with Hitchcock directing I knew I couldn't go wrong.

The next thing I did with Noël wasn't one of his own plays, it was Mademoiselle *by Jacques Duval. There were Madge Titheradge and Greer Garson, Cecil Parker and Nigel Patrick, and Noël produced it brilliantly. He wanted pace, pace, the whole time, he wouldn't let anybody slow up at all. At least I'm talking about the comedy scenes. The comedy scenes had to go right through and when he gave a direction one knew at once that he was right. It was really inspired. It was bang on.*

While Jane Cowl was packing them in with *Easy Virtue* at the Empire Theatre, New York, Noël was seeing the New Year in with *The Vortex*. It entered 1926 with the enthusiasm that it had left 1925. He spent New Year's Eve alone with his mother in their apartment overlooking Central Park, sipping champagne and wondering how the family were faring at home in Ebury Street. That evening he confirmed his vow never to return to his early days of want. Then he downed another glass of champagne and retired early to bed.

The Vortex closed on Broadway after five successful

months, and Noël bade farewell to the circle of friends he had acquired during its run. He had renewed the acquaintance of Elsa Maxwell, the famous party giver, on whose 'come as you are' parties he was to write 'I've been to a marvelous party'. (When asked what he considered exceptional about her, he replied in one word: 'Bounce'.) It had been decided to take *The Vortex* on a short road tour which would include Newark, Brooklyn, Cincinnati and Chicago.

In the latter city a six-week season was advertised. Noël had bought a Rolls-Royce in New York, and arranged for it to meet him at the station to escort his party to the de luxe Lake Shore Drive Hotel. The play opened at the packed Selwyn Theatre on the night of George Washington's birthday celebrations, but Chicago, supposedly the high spot of the tour, turned sour on him. Mistaking the play for a farce, the audience proceeded to laugh at every straight line. Exasperated to say the least, Noël was tempted to go before the curtain to explain the play's purpose to the misguided audience, but was fortunately prevented from doing so by Lilian Braithwaite trumpeting, 'You're English! Remember, you're English!'

After the tour Noël, his mother, Jack Wilson and the Rolls-Royce left for London, and from there the men sped off to a holiday in the South of France and Italy.

In Palermo Noël had written a comedy called *This was a Man* which was refused a licence by the Lord Chamberlain because of its flippant approach to the theme—a faithless wife whose husband is having an affair with another woman. It was presented in New York, Berlin and Paris, but never in Britain.

When *Easy Virtue* closed at the Duke of York's, Noël's new play *The Queen was in the Parlour*, with Francis Lister, Madge Titheradge and Herbert Marshall playing the leads, transferred there from the St Martin's Theatre, and played to even bigger audiences. He had another success on his hands.

Noël had had seven full-length plays and two revues on in the West End in two years, and the royalties were flooding in. He set to work to find a place where he, Gladys and Jack could work, and large enough to accommodate the rest of the family; mother, father, Aunt Vida and brother Eric. He found a farmhouse called Goldenhurst, at Aldington in Kent, and rented it for fifty pounds a year. It was a late seventeenth century house, with six acres of land, a new wing, thatched barns, two small ponds, —all in need of repair—and a view of Dymchurch and the sea-wall across the marshes.

Since the Lord Chamberlain would not licence *This was a Man* for production in England, Noël decided to open it in America, but now Basil Dean came up with the idea that Noël should play Lewis Dodd in Dean's adaptation with Margaret Kennedy of her best-selling novel, *The Constant Nymph*.

Meanwhile *The Rat Trap*, which he had written eight years before, was at last being tried out by a new management at the Everyman Theatre, with a cast headed by Joyce Kennedy, Robert Harris, Raymond Massey and Massey's future wife Adrianne Allen. Gilbert Miller had failed to sell it to America. Of it, Noël remarked, '*The Rat Trap*, my first serious play, fizzled out at the end of its regulation two-week run. It was neither good enough nor bad enough to merit a West End run.'

Madge Titheradge as Nadja in *The Queen was in the Parlour*.

above, Noël's parents at
Goldenhurst.
centre, Raymond Massey in
The Rat Trap (1926) Everyman
Theatre.
right, Goldenhurst.

A WORLD RECORD

Shortly after he had agreed to play the part of Lewis Dodd, Noël met John Gielgud at the Ivy restaurant.

'Have you heard?' he said, 'I'm to play the part of Lewis Dodd in *The Constant Nymph*. Isn't it exciting?'

'Yes, it is,' Gielgud replied, 'I'm so glad. You'll be very good in it.'

What Noël did not himself know was that the part was officially under offer to John, who in his turn had not been told by the management that Noël had been asked, and had accepted, to play the role for the first month of its run.

JOHN GIELGUD: *When he was offered the part of Lewis Dodd in* The Constant Nymph, *Noël realised he must try to suppress his characteristic mannerism of clipped speech for the first time. With the help of Basil Dean he succeeded in giving a character performance of greater variety and depth than he had attempted since* The Vortex.

SYBIL THORNDIKE: *Oh, what an actor! Noël's Lewis Dodd was beautiful. It was perfection. It was the part she* [Margaret Kennedy] *had written. John gave a lovely performance of it, but there was the streak of cruelty that was in Noël. It was so awfully valuable, in that in spite of his sympathy and his lovingness and his adorableness you felt that slight* jab *that Noël always had, and which was so exciting always.*

Mrs Patrick Campbell did not share Dame Sybil's enthusiasm, however. Having insisted on being invited to a dress rehearsal, pleading that she was too poor to afford a seat when the play opened, she telephoned Noël after the performance, groaning, 'You're the wrong *type*. You have no *glamour*. You should wear a *beard*!'

NOËL COWARD:

Edna [Edna Best, his co-star] *looked quite frail, but she weighed a ton. I used to stagger across the stage with her and put her on the bed to die, and then go to the window very sadly and throw it up and say the last line of the play, 'Tessa's got away. She's safe. She's dead.'*

Well, one night the cord of the window broke and the window came down on my fingers, and I said, 'Tessa's got away. She's safe. She's OW!' Whereupon Tessa, who was dead, jumped three feet into the air and the curtain fell amid roars of laughter.

In October 1926 Noël and Jack Wilson sailed for New York to attend the opening of *This was a Man* on Broadway. The difficult role of leading lady was played by Francine Larrimore, and her leading man was A. E. Matthews. On the first night his infidelity (in the play) to Miss Larrimore was paralleled by his disloyalty to the script. Noël remarked: 'A. E. Matthews ambled through *This was a Man* like a charming retriever who has buried a bone and can't quite remember where.'

But most of the fashionable New York audience who had applauded *The Vortex* and come expecting another Noël Coward winner failed to return to their seats after the second act. The play closed after a fortnight.

The result of five years almost unbroken hard work now caught up with Noël. A perfectionist who drove himself to the limit, he paid for his efforts with a nervous breakdown. He went to White Sulphur Springs in Virginia to convalesce, and there he wrote *The Marquise*, the play he had promised Marie Tempest a long while before (it was put on in London shortly after, with only modest success).

above, as Lewis Dodd in *The Constant Nymph*.
right, 'A Room with a View'. Jessie Matthews and Sonnie Hale in *This Year of Grace*; London Pavilion, March 1928.

Still unwell, he decided that to recover completely he must get far away from all that was familiar to him, and he set sail for Hong Kong. The sea-trip aggravated his condition, however, and his temperature shot up to a hundred and three. The boat stopped in Honolulu, and while lunching with some friends, Charles and Louise Dillingham, he realised that the trip to Hong Kong would do him less good than a few weeks in the serenity of Honolulu, and he returned to the boat to collect his belongings. But his health, far from improving, worsened, and his symptoms revealed that he was suffering from a recurrence of his early tuberculosis. The Dillinghams insisted on his staying on their ranch on the other side of the island, and there, while cooped up in his room overlooking the beach, he composed one of his most successful songs 'A Room with a View'.

NOËL COWARD:

. . . and it comes in very handy if I'm doing any cabaret performances, because you know, it's now so well known that as I start the first bars, people applaud—and that gets me through to the end if—I'm quick.

'A Room with a View'
from 'This Year of Grace!'

A room with a view, and you,
With no one to worry us,
No one to hurry us through
This dream we've found,
We'll gaze at the sky, and try
To guess what it's all about,
Then we will figure out why
The world is round.

We'll be as happy and contented
As birds upon a tree,
High above the mountains and the sea.

We'll bill and we'll coo-oo-oo
And sorrow will never come,
Oh, will it ever come true,
Our room with a view.

He returned to England in the spring, much restored, and now he decided to buy Goldenhurst, which he was only renting at the moment. Remodelled and redecorated it provided accommodation for his family and closest friends.

That summer Lynn Fontanne and Alfred Lunt came down to Goldenhurst. They had been playing in S. N. Behrman's comedy *The Second Man* for the Theatre Guild in New York, and persuaded Noël to play it in London.

NOËL COWARD:

There have only been three plays since the twenties that I acted in that weren't my own. The Constant Nymph,

| Nancy Barnett | Madeline Gibson | Marjorie Browne | Peter May | Jessie Matthews | | Florita Fey | Marjorie Robertson | Peggy Wynne | Gr... Tay... |

In " Teach me to dance like Grandma," JESSIE MATTHEWS idealises the poetry of motion.

Noel Coward's New Play.

Comedy of a Wagon-lit, a Modern Husband, and a Still More Modern Wife.

Arthur Margetson; Madge Titheradge, Henrietta Watson, Helen Spencer, Marda Vanne, George Curzon, Nina Boucicault, George Relph.

top, This Year of Grace.

The Apple Cart *and* The Second Man. *And two performances of* Journey's End *in Singapore.*

I think that, like all actors, I look at the part, so naturally if I've written it for myself it's liable to be a fairly good part. But The Second Man *was right up my street.*

He managed to arrange a January opening, and in the meantime wrote *Home Chat*.

The play concerns a respectable young married woman, Janet Ebony, who returns from Egypt with a good-looking

PLAYS AND PICTURES.

"HOME CHAT."

MR. NOEL COWARD'S NEW PLAY BOOED.

The first night of a new play by Mr. Noel Coward is always an event and usually a sensation. The sensation, caused by his newest piece, *Home Chat*, at the Duke of York's Theatre, was provided, not by the play, but by the audience. For at the end it was 'booed". The booing too came not from the rough seas of the gallery, whence it might have been expected, but from the usually quiet back waters of the upper circle. Mr. Coward seemed quite unperturbed. "We expected better", said the collective voice of the upper circle. "So did I", answered Mr. Coward, and for the moment the

FANTASTIC FARCE.

What *was* clear was that the whole of this act was purely fantastic farce and quite out of the mood of the remainder of the play. Mr. Coward is clever but even he found it impossible to do this difficult piece of juggling with success for, after the shock of the second act, the audience is suddenly brought back to the mood of the first. Janet really does fall in love now and goes to Paris with her lover but there is no railway accident this time and when she comes back, burning with righteous guilt, they again refuse to

young man whom she has known for years and with whom she is caught in a railway accident. Accounts appear in newspapers of how she and the young man were in the same sleeping car in their pyjamas at three in the morning. Naturally enough, Janet's husband, a well-known and respected novelist (played by George Relph), expects an explanation, as does the young man's fiancée, and the play sets out to resolve the situation. On the opening night, however, it failed to do so to the satisfaction of either the audience or the critics.

The opening performance of Home Chat *was rendered agonising by one of the elderly actresses in the company continuously forgetting her lines.* [He carefully avoids naming the culprit, Nina Boucicault, an actress of great charm who, twenty-three years before had created Peter Pan on that same stage, when Gerald du Maurier doubled as Mr Darling and Captain Hook]. *The pauses she made, coupled with the intentional pauses Basil Dean had carefully rehearsed, frequently brought the play to a standstill.*

Noël stood on the stage at the end of the play to be greeted with boos and cries of 'Rubbish!' from the upper circle.
    'We expected better!' called out one voice.
    'So did I!' replied the author.
    The *Daily Mail* put paid to the proceedings by

describing it as 'Acting of the best, and Noël Coward at his worst'. The *Daily Mirror*, which had discovered he had written it in a week, commented: 'Personally I wish Mr Coward had taken a fortnight in which to write *Home Chat*, for then we might have had two good laughs during the evening instead of only one.'

NOËL COWARD: *Home Chat is my least favourite play. It was a silly little play, really. It could have been so much better. I was awfully cock-a-hoop in those days and wrote it without taking enough trouble.*

When you have a failure, it's always your own fault. Nobody else's. But when you're writing something, you know at the time that it's good beyond belief, otherwise you wouldn't go on with it. And then rehearsals begin and doubts start creeping in. Even so, a success doesn't mean that it's a very good play. It may mean that the leading lady's got a very good part, and is very good in it. It may mean a lot of things.

The fascination about playwriting is that it has got to be written to play for two and a half hours, so you've got to start practising economy from the first page. The secret of play-writing is economy.

But the reaction to *Home Chat* was a mere curtain-raiser to what lay in store for *Sirocco*'s first night. It opened at Daly's a month later, and more than thirty years since a straight play had been presented at the famous theatre where *The Merry Widow* and *The Geisha* had each run for two years.

The rather novelettish story of *Sirocco* involved a bored young English wife who, left alone by her husband in an hotel in Italy, is carried off her feet by a handsome young Italian. She goes away with him, but after a week, decides that they are unsuited, refuses to return to her pompous husband, and sets off to live her own life.

The leading parts were played by Ivor Novello, the great matinée idol of the day, and Frances Doble. Both were possessed of tremendous physical beauty, but neither had sufficient acting ability to sustain the parts Noël had created.

Each time Novello came on in his blue-striped pyjamas, the audience sniggered. Each time he kissed Frances Doble in the first act, the gallery giggled. When he made love to her in the second act, they laughed.

'Give the old cow a chance!' cried out a sympathetic fan from the gods.

'Thank you sir. You're the only gentleman here', called back the leading lady. With that, they grew hysterical. By the time the curtain fell, booing and hissing was followed by pandemonium. All hell broke loose. The loud cries of 'Rubbish! Rubbish!' from the gallery were swamped by

Daily Express

NOEL COWARD PLAY SCENE.

PANDEMONIUM AT THE END.

IVOR NOVELLO BOOED.

The Play: "Sirocco."
Author: Noel Coward.
Theatre: Daly's.

The most extraordinary scene which has taken place in a London theatre since "The Rainbow" provided the finish of "Sirocco" at Daly's last night.

During the last act the gallery roared with laughter every time Ivor Novello came on wearing light blue pyjamas. When he carried a spaniel puppy and went out to buy some milk the laughter grew even more cynical. It was supposed to be drama. Really, it was roared at like a farce.

The first two acts had been dull, but when, at the end, there came scenes of weak drama, crudely written, and utterly uninspired, and with Ivor Novello, the darling of the films, in light blue pyjamas, it was too much even for his fans.

When the curtain fell the play was booed, Ivor Novello was booed, Noel Coward, the author, was booed, and there were derisive noises made at Basil Dean, the producer. For nearly ten minutes wild scenes went on.

EXCITEMENT.

Whenever Frances Doble was pushed forward by the author, however, there was wild excitement from upstairs. "Bravo, Bunny!" they shouted. "You're wonderful, Bunny! Bunny! Bunny!" Then, although they had asked for a speech from Miss Doble, they would not listen to it, but shouted "Rubbish!"

Finally, Mr. Dean shouted for silence, and then Miss Doble said it was the happiest night of her life! This was greeted with laughter, because of the pitiful tragedy of the rest of it—a hall of actors and actresses, mostly in fancy dress, who all stood by in rows, knew that it meant a short run and then a search for new work.

The dull first act, which was about how an English husband left his kinglish wife alone on the Riviera, was unillumined by any sparkle of wit. The second act, which took place in a bar, was chiefly a lot of noise in Italian,

Mr. Ivor Novello.   Miss Frances Doble.

at the end of which a young artist persuaded the wife to go away with him.

Every time Ivor Novello as the artist, kissed Miss Doble, the gallery shrieked out with merriment.

Then, in the last scene, a week later, they were both tired of it.

The husband came back, and in stilted words reproved his wife. She said she was sorry! Then, when he had gone, she upbraided her lover, who lost his temper.

Ivor Novello started chasing Miss Doble round the table.

"Free love is hateful and sordid and cheap," she sobbed. "I can never get back!"

"I go to my mother," said the lover. That made the whole house scream again.

This amateurish play is full of sneers at the English and jokes like calling a dog "Mrs. Robinson." It is baby talk.

Ivor Novello acted the last scene almost like an amateur, but Miss Doble nearly held it up with her unexpected cleverness. She could not save it, though; it was too silly.

Surely, in future, when there is a failure, managers will ring down the curtain and let the company go home. Last night's scene was disgraceful. In fact, it was cruelty.

Daily Herald

SERIOUS MR. NOEL COWARD

"Sirocco" Smacks of the Novelette

Mr. Noel Coward's hand appears to have lost its cunning. "Sirocco," which opened last night at Daly's, was, we were told, a *serious* play. Last night its most passionate kisses convulsed the gallery with laughter.

The story is a simple one. A bored young English wife, left alone by her husband in an hotel in Italy, is carried off her feet by a handsome young Italian; she goes away with him, but after a week decides that they are unsuited, refuses to return to her pompous husband, and sets off to live her own life in the good old Ibsen way.

The dialogue derives mainly from the novelette. It was permissible for the flashy young Italian to talk theatrically, but the trouble was that it did not stop at the Italian. The simple English heroine assured him that she would go down to the dregs with him, and her dreary English husband uttered every known cliché, beginning with, "You have dishonoured my name" up to "Have you no shame!"

The action was eked out by much singing and dancing, and in the last act the "big scene" detailed pursuing the lady round and round the breakfast table in the best Lyceum tradition. Miss Frances Doble achieved a personal success in this struggle.

M. E.

Daily Mail

NEW PLAY HISSED.

MR. NOEL COWARD'S "SIROCCO."

ACTRESS SOBS.

At the end of "Sirocco," Mr. Noel Coward's new play, which was produced at Daly's last night (and of which the Dramatic Critic writes in Page 12), there were witnessed some of the most remarkable scenes that have occurred in any theatre for several years.

Some people applauded, others booed and hissed with equal loudness. For the most part the reception was hostile.

It soon became obvious that the applause was for the acting, the "boos" for the play. Yet time after time the curtain was raised, and Mr. Coward, with something of courage, came on to the stage. But although he shook hands with his leading actors he made no attempt to make a speech.

"RUBBISH!"

"It's rubbish!" someone shouted, and the author made no verbal reply, but merely smiled and bowed.

Yet, in spite of a reception decidedly hostile, the curtain was raised once more, and at last Miss Frances Doble was brought—or dragged perhaps would be a better term—to the front of the stage.

"This is the happiest moment of my life," she sobbed between trembling lips. Actually she was almost crying. She may have been proud of her own reception; but she must have realised that the play was a failure.

It seemed an act of cruelty to bring her forward. It seemed a mistaken policy to allow so many curtain calls to be taken when the play for the most part was unpopular.

Those who had come to see something "nasty" had been disappointed. And there was not sufficient wit in the piece to compensate them for the absence of the ugly.

Daily News

"SIROCCO."

MR. NOEL COWARD'S NEW PLAY.

SNEERS AT ENGLISH CONVENTIONS.

By THE DRAMATIC CRITIC.

A new Noel Coward play is still regarded as a big event, in spite of a recent failure.

Last night, when his very latest, "Sirocco," was produced at Daly's Theatre, there was present the usual Coward audience, willing to laugh at everything they considered a "Noelism."

They even laughed when one of the characters remarked, "One of my greatest friends died of consumption."

Now, really, is there anything funny about that?

The scene is laid in Italy, and a story which supports Mr. Coward's light, bright, often cynical lines concerns a woman whose husband decides to go abroad on a business "deal," and who refuses to take his wife with him. The result is of the kind so familiar in many and many a film. There is another.

In this case he is a handsome "foreigner"—one might say a pretty foreigner, since the character is played by Mr. Ivor Novello. Naturally that clearcut, cinema profile of his infatuated the wife, even as it seemed to infatuate so many of an audience so largely composed of women.

AN ARTIFICIAL STORY.

The story matters little. It is entirely artificial. The characters are puppets moved by the author's strings—not by human motives. There is no sign of any attempt at characterisation. No one has a soul. Several have a sneer—especially at the alleged niceness of English life and at English conventions.

Mr. Novello, disguised in a foreign accent, makes love and says "smart" things with the ease of one who is sure of his reception. He does, in fact, his best to get some colour out of a colourless part; Mr. Aubrey Mather is entirely a figure from farce, and Miss Ada King, Miss Margaret Watson, and Miss Helen Ferrers show that they can give a little life-blood to figures almost composed of sawdust.

There remains the dialogue, which has many a laugh in it, but which suggests that Mr. Coward is working more than a little too fast.

At his present pace his future threatens to "be behind him," to use an ancient Irishism.

... With ...
author ...
Dor ...

Daly's Uproar.

NOT SINCE "Ashes" was produced at the Prince of Wales Theatre early last year has there been such a noisy and tumultuous scene at a first night as at Daly's, when Noel Coward's play, "Sirocco," was booed and hissed.

This is the second time within five weeks that Noel Coward has had a play booed. If again took it coolly enough, but it was a cruel ordeal for Frances Doble, who was made to speak.

There was a very fashionable audience for this—the first "straight" play at Daly's since Ada Reban played in Shakespeare there. In the stalls I saw Lady Gory of Faldodon, Lady Plunkett, Cornelia Countess of Craven, Lady Pollock, the Marchioness of Headfort, Sir Percy Simmonds, Mr. Gordon Selfridge, Sir Patrick Hastings, K.C., Mr. E. G. Hemmerde, K.C., Mr. Somerset Maugham, and Mr. Alfred Sutro.

---

below, Ivor Novello and Frances Doble in *Sirocco.*

calls for 'Bunny! Bunny!' the nickname given by fans in the stalls to the engaging Miss Doble.

The stage manager, confusing the mixture of applause and shouting as calls for the author, gestured to Noël to make the curtain speech his audiences had come to expect, but Noël, who had seen the audience's reaction from his box, was only too aware of what lay in store for him, and stood in the wings, shaking his head vigorously and refusing to budge. Finally he rushed on stage, grabbed Frances Doble's and Ivor Novello's hands, shook them feverishly in thanks for their performances and dashed off the stage with the speed of an antelope, pursued by more boos and hisses. And then Basil Dean led Frances Doble forward. A momentary hush fell. The audience were aghast. Surely she wouldn't attempt a speech? But Miss Doble, bewildered by the mixed reception and the calls for 'Bunny! Bunny!' took the initiative, clasped her hands tightly and said, 'Ladies and gentlemen, this is the happiest night of my life!' With that, shrieks of hysterical and incredulous laughter came flooding across the footlights. Basil Dean, in a fury, rushed to her defence: 'Ladies and gentlemen, if there *are* any gentlemen in the house . . .' and after that, there was no stopping them. Frances Doble grew pale and seemed about to faint, Ivor Novello looked dazed, backstage Noël was seething with indignation, and the orchestra struck up 'God Save the King' in an effort to drown the chaos.

Infuriated fans rushed round to the stage-door and railed at Noël as he left the theatre, and newspapers the next day reported the evening's events in appalling detail. It was a field day for Hannen Swaffer, who dived in: 'At last the public seem to appreciate the truth of what I have said now for over three years, in season and out of season, that Noël Coward has nothing whatever to say, that he has no wit, and that his sneers at ordinary, respectable people are irritating to the point of painfulness.

'Noël Coward has been booed off the London stage now twice in four weeks. That is a world record.'

NOËL COWARD: *After the first night of* Sirocco *they spat at me in the streets. Literally spat all over my tailcoat, and I felt I must be a good playwright because nobody's going to take all that trouble unless they feel badly disappointed. But they needn't have made all that fuss. The play wasn't all that bad. There were a lot worse running triumphantly at the time. But I'd set a standard for myself, and the audience had felt let down.*

My first instinct was to leave England immediately, but this seemed too craven a move and also too gratifying to my enemies, whose numbers by then had swollen in our minds to practically the entire population of the British Isles.

FAMILY CARE

Unwilling to have his name up in the West End again until he had cooled his heels, Noël was nevertheless obliged to honour his agreement to appear in *The Second Man*. Also in the cast were Raymond Massey, Ursula Jeans and Zena Dare, one of the most celebrated figures of English musical comedy. Zena is now eighty-five, and looks all of sixty:

ZENA DARE:

I first met Noël about fifty years ago, just casually and socially because I wasn't on the stage at the time [she had given up acting when she married Maurice Brett, second son of Lord Esher].

Well, a little time went by, and with a growing family, I thought I must make some money. So I was offered The Last of Mrs Cheyney, *which I played, touring on and off for a year.*

When I got back home to the country, the telephone rang from London. Would I play in S. N. Behrman's comedy The Second Man *with Noël Coward? Of course I was very excited and pleased about it, and they sent me the script. It was a very sophisticated,* chic *play—rather* avant-garde *for 1927, and with such a cast I accepted.*

I rang up a friend in the country and said, 'Isn't it exciting, I've been asked to play with Noël Coward in London.'

'Oh, but you can't possibly do that,' came the reply.

'Why not?'

'Well haven't you heard?'

'Heard what? No. I've heard nothing, I've been away. What is there to hear?'

'Well, he wrote a play called Sirocco. *It was booed off*

With Zena Dare in
The Second Man.

*the stage, there were catcalls and hisses and pandemonium—
and Ivor Novello was playing the lead too—Zena, now
really, think about it. It's a great mistake to play with
Noël Coward.'*

*Well, I took no notice of this advice. 'Don't know what
they're talking about,' I told myself.*

*I go up to London and we have the first rehearsal. Noël
has got a part as long as* Hamlet. *He arrives at the first
rehearsal* word perfect. *This is shattering to everybody,
especially to me, who had been off for such a long time.
Well, I struggled for two or three days, and then I began to
cry. I never stopped crying at all. There I was, supposed to
be a very wealthy, sophisticated woman, Noël's mistress,
and here was just a teared-stained drab every time he looked
at me, which was really rather trying for him. However,
he called me over and said, 'Now look, Zena. Zena, you
can't go on like this. After all, if you were working for the*
Post Office *you couldn't behave like this, could you!'*

*'However,' he said, 'come up to my flat now and we'll
work together.' His patience and forbearance were terrific
and of course I did get better. The American author came
over from New York, and was very pleased with the
company and the production, so I thought, 'Well, that's all
right.'*

*Now comes the first night. I was wearing the most
beautiful, gorgeous and glamorous dress, and as I came out
of my dressing-room Noël came out of his dressing-room
and we met in the corridor.*

*'Well, if you look like that it doesn't matter how you
play the part,' he said.*

*I wasn't quite sure how to take this, and I didn't ask him.
And I'm certainly not going to ask him now!*

The Second Man opened to good notices; for once the critics and the audiences were in accord.

Noël, who had never been content to do only one thing at a time, was at the same time auditioning artists for his new Cochran revue, *This Year of Grace!* which opened with a cast headed by Sonnie Hale, then married to Evelyn Laye. The hit of the show was the number 'Dance Little Lady'.

'Dance Little Lady'

from 'This Year of Grace'

```
Though you're only seventeen
Far too much of life you've seen.
Syncopated child.
Maybe if you only knew
Where your path was leading to,
You'd become less wild,
But I know it's vain
Trying to explain
While there's this insane
Music in your brain.

Dance, dance, dance little lady,
Youth is fleeting to the rhythm beating
In your mind.
Dance, dance, dance little lady,
So obsessed with second best,
No rest you'll ever find,
Time and tide and trouble
Never, never wait.
Let the cauldron bubble
Justify your fate.
Dance, dance, dance, little lady,
Leave tomorrow behind.
```

One of the chorus girls in the show was Marjorie Robertson, one of the first British actresses to win international film stardom in films such as *The Lady with the Lamp*, *Nell Gwynn*, *Odette* and *Spring in Park Lane*—after she changed her name:

ANNA NEAGLE: *Noël was always so kind to all the girls—the Cochran Young Ladies. He was always encouraging and helpful.*

There was a marvellous day when we were in this great bare rehearsal room in Poland Street, when the numbers were first being tried out, and Sonnie Hale was to sing 'Dance, Little Lady'. Now 'Dance, Little Lady' at that time was such a new rhythm altogether, and we didn't really know what to make of it. We were the girls and the boys dancing as robots in the background, wearing rather sinister masks, with Sonnie singing this number.

DANCE LITTLE LADY

"THIS YEAR OF GRACE"

CHARLES B. COCHRAN'S 1928 REVUE

Book, Lyrics and Music by

NOËL COWARD

COMPLETE VOCAL SCORE - Price 8s. od. net
BOOK OF LYRICS - Price 12. od. net
SEPARATE NUMBERS
Price - 2s. net each

A ROOM WITH A VIEW	CABALLERO
DANCE, LITTLE LADY	LORELEI
I'M MAD ABOUT YOU	TRY TO LEARN TO LOVE
MARY MAKE-BELIEVE	

TEACH ME TO DANCE LIKE GRANDMA
" " " " (Novelty Dance)
A ROOM WITH A VIEW (Pianoforte Transcription)
PIANOFORTE SELECTION - Price 2s. 6d. net
VALSE - - " - 2s. net

CHAPPELL & Co. Ltd. 50, New Bond St. London, W1. New York & Sydney

Sonnie was in despair at rehearsal, not knowing how to do the routine, and the rather young Noël Coward was sitting there watching him. One could see him getting agitated because it wasn't going the way he wanted it, and Sonnie said to him, 'I don't know what to do with the number.'

'Well let me show you, dear boy, let me show you', Noël replied, and got up and did it. Well, the vitality, the magnetism when he went into it—it was astonishing! To us, it was a very very new rhythm. It was gorgeous. Just gorgeous.

This Year of Grace! was a triumph. Maisie Gay, Jessie Matthews and Tilly Losch scored their own successes, and the show netted Noël a thousand pounds a week in royalties. What with this and his weekly salary for his appearance in *The Second Man*, the wolf was very far from the door.

Cochran and his American associate Archie Selwyn were keen to open a second company of *This Year of Grace!* in New York with a cast led by Noël and Beatrice Lillie, so when *The Second Man* closed, Noël and Cochran set sail for America. Two weeks later they were back in London, having failed to find a suitable cast. The trip had one good result, nevertheless, which was that Noël conceived the idea for *Bitter-Sweet* in New York, and began composing it there and on the return boat journey. He outlined to Cochran the idea of an operetta in the popular Viennese style of Strauss's *Die Fledermaus* and Léhar's *The Merry Widow*. It concerns the daughter of a society hostess, who falls in love with her Viennese singing teacher in London, and elopes with him to Vienna where she marries him. They live in blissful poverty while he completes his new operetta, but he is killed in a duel, fighting for her virtue. Cochran was enthusiastic, and agreed to present it in the spring of the following year if Noël could complete the score by that time. That gave him precisely five months in which to write the book, compose the music and write the lyrics. Despite this limitation *Bitter-Sweet* turned out splendidly. Even an operation for a malady of an intimate nature during rehearsals for the American production of *This Year of Grace!* did not prevent him from composing, in acute discomfort, the delightful 'Dear Little Café'.

```
            'Dear Little Café'

            from 'Bitter-Sweet'
We'll have a sweet little café
In a neat little square,
We'll find our fortune
And our happiness there.
We shall thrive on the vain and
   resplendent
And contrive to remain independent.
We'll have a meek reputation
   and a chic clientèle,
Kings will fall under our spell.
We'll be so zealous
That the world will be jealous
Of our sweet little café in a square.
```

On his return to London, Noël sold the lease of 111 Ebury Street, only retaining his own rooms, and moved his family down to Goldenhurst.

His brother Eric, who seemed to have no clear vocation or talent apart from the ability to strum a tune on the piano, and who was always in the shadow of a famous brother so much better at it than he, was by now twenty-three and old enough to go out and find work. He was promptly sent to Ceylon to plant tea.

The American production of *This Year of Grace!* was finally cast and rehearsed in London, with Beatrice Lillie playing Maisie Gay's roles and Noël the Sonnie Hale parts. It opened in New York at the Selwyn Theatre on November 7th 1928, and played to packed houses.

Beatrice Lillie took *This Year of Grace!* on to Philadelphia, with Billy Milton playing Noël's roles, and Noël rushed off to Vienna and Berlin with Cochran, looking for a tenor for the male lead. They eventually hired George Metaxa—in London. The heartbreaking role of Manon la Crevette was no problem, though, for Noël had written it for the temperamental and tiny Ivy St Helier.

'Have you heard?' an actor rushed up to Noël one day, 'Ivy's broken her leg in two places.'

'I didn't know there *were* two places,' came the reply.

The production was designed by Gladys Calthrop and the brilliant German designer, Ernst Stern.

GLADYS CALTHROP:

On Bitter-Sweet *Noël worked upstairs in his bedroom at Goldenhurst, while I worked downstairs in the sitting-room, so that one was close at hand, and never got into trouble over things because one could always get together to discuss it before it was too late. We worked on* Cavalcade *in the same way. So there have never been any really bad moments, except very very short rows, explosive and very quickly over.*

He's wonderful to work with because he concentrates absolutely on what he's doing as if he were blinkered from the rest of the world, and working with him, you become the same. You catch this thing of work being life—work being the whole importance of living and the only reason for 'being'. He's always had this. And tremendous energy, which is another thing that is terribly useful, and my goodness, it's seen him through a lot of trials!

below, with Gladys Calthrop at Goldenhurst.

By now, 1928, Noël was on the way to completing the score of *Bitter-Sweet*.

NOËL COWARD:

That *was my favourite of all. It combines my talents in almost perfect balance. The dialogue is very good, the music is the best I ever wrote, with the possible exception of the score of* Conversation Piece, *which I love more than anything I've ever done. The book part of* Bitter-Sweet *took ten days to write. I had some of the tunes in my head, but on the whole I'd say the complete show was ready to go into rehearsal in about five months.*

His first choice for *Bitter-Sweet*'s leading lady had been Gertrude Lawrence, but she hadn't the voice for the semi-operatic score. Noël cabled Cochran to offer the part to Evelyn Laye, but she seemed to feel that Cochran had condoned, if not actually encouraged the friendship between her husband, Sonnie Hale, and his leading lady Jessie Matthews, whom he subsequently married, and turned down the role. It was a decision she was to regret.

Then Noël ran into Peggy Wood in the lobby of New York's Algonquin Hotel, and that solved that casting problem.

Ernst Stern's costume designs for the Ladies of the Town for *Bitter Sweet*.

ROBERT HELPMANN: *The first thing of Noël's I did was* This Year of Grace! *in Australia with Maisie Gay in 1927, four years before I came to England. I understudied Pat and Terry Kendall— Terry was Kay Kendall's father—they were the principal dancers, and I played several of Douglas Byng's parts in the sketches.*

Although I was terribly young I'd been in a lot of other revues, but this was the first sophisticated revue in Australia. It had considerable critical acclaim and anyone however slightly theatrical absolutely adored it, but in spite of its enormous success the general public couldn't understand some of the typically English jargon and situations. A 'depressing English beach', for instance. They didn't know what a depressing beach was. Or a bus queue. They weren't used to them. There was a big number called 'Waiting in a Queue', with Maisie Gay doing a very funny thing about a woman waiting in a queue, frightfully grandly dressed, with balloons and parcels and hair very smart, and of course by the time she got on the bus she had no balloons left and her hair was all over the place. Bea Lillie did it in America, but I don't think they understood that sketch there either.

Herr Schlick (Clifford Heatherley), the café proprietor, being "sauced" by Gussi (Norah Howard), a cheery cocotte

Bitter-Sweet was a success from the start. Cochran came to rehearsals and felt assured of a long run. The two-week try-out in Manchester was already sold out. Word was getting around about the perfectly captivating score, and excitement grew both backstage and front of house.

The first-night audience in London included Prince George, Lady Mountbatten, Ivor Novello and a string of friends, celebrities and Noël Coward fans. The performance was given a rapturous reception, but not from the Press, who gave it less than six weeks. It ran for over eighteen months.

HERBERT WILCOX:

Manon (Ivy St. Helier), known as La Creoste, the star of Herr Schlick's Viennese Café indulges in a song and dance

I have a unique memory of Noël because I was with him on the first night of Bitter-Sweet. *I've never known anybody so apprehensive. It was obviously a classic, and I think as years go on the music becomes more important. All the same, he was very apprehensive.*

'Herbert, I want you to tell me one thing,' he said. 'This is the best thing I've done ever, isn't it?'

'Yes of course it is, Noël,' I replied. 'It's very very good.'

'I wanted you to tell me that,' he said, 'because this is going to take care of my family for as long as they live.'

In the last act, Sari, the runaway society daughter, manages to get her late husband's new operetta performed, sings the delightful 'Zigeuner', and the final curtain falls on the last chords of 'I'll See You Again'.

(George Metaxa), a violinist with himself as a beau

EVELYN LAYE:

'I'll See You Again'
from 'Bitter-Sweet'

```
I'll see you again,
I live each moment through again.
Time has lain heavy between,
But what has been
Can leave me never;
Your dear memory
Throughout my life has guided me.
Though my world has gone awry,
Though the years my tears may dry,
I shall love you till I die,
Goodbye!
```

Sarah Millick (Peggy Wood) elopes with Carl Linde

Cochran now decided to repeat the great London success of *Bitter-Sweet* on the American stage.

I think Noël was absolutely stunned at my turning down the London production, and so was I when a few weeks later I saw it at His Majesty's Theatre, and realised what an idiot I'd been. When I came out of the theatre, I thought,

Evelyn Laye.

'I've got to get that part for New York somehow, I've simply got to.' I thought, 'I wonder if he'd look at me after turning it down', so I rang up a great friend of his who worked with him consistently, Elsie April. I told her my plight, and asked her to talk to Noël—which she did. Noël was generous. He rang me up and asked me to play the part in New York. Oh, I was thrilled! I got a script right away and started working on it.

Noël was wonderful at the beginning of rehearsals. I found him very exciting and inspiring, very curt and to the point. He often used to make funny remarks with a smile on his face, but behind them you knew that he meant what he said, that he was going to have exactly what he wanted.

I remember having a rather bad habit of whirling my arms about in the air for no apparent reason while I was singing, and Noël cracking: 'Is it necessary, dear, for you to perform like a windmill?' I was very frightened of him.

The TATLER

Vol. CXVIII. No. 1531. London, November 1, 1930. Price One Shilling

BITTER . . . to lose PEGGY
SWEET . . . . to regain EVELYN

Noël, Jack, Gladys and Evelyn Laye sailed for New York, followed later by the rest of the company and the production opened in Boston. George Metaxa was unable to go with the show to America, and Alexandro Rosati the Italian tenor now playing Carl, was swiftly replaced because of his inability to make the English language, or at any rate that percentage of it contained in his dialogue, comprehensible. He failed, too, to demonstrate an acceptable ability to act, and his part was taken over at the last minute by Gerald Nodin, who had sung Tokay and understudied Carl in the London production.

The play was due to open at the Ziegfeld Theatre in New York. It seemed to Florenz Ziegfeld to lack the abundance of leggy showgirls and spruce male chorus that were in his view essential to any musical show, and when Noël resisted his daily demands to add leggy showgirls to the production, he not only promised to discourage any advantageous publicity for the New York opening, but refused to raise the prices for the first night seats. Noël, however, persisted with the production as it stood—after all, it had succeeded in London with its present staging— and he stood his ground even though Cochran wasn't present to support his decision.

On the first night in New York special police were called up to hold back the surging crowds outside the theatre, and seats changed hands for as much as two hundred and fifty dollars a pair. Floodlights illuminated the celebrities as they entered the theatre, and Florenz Ziegfeld, despite his earlier misgivings, put his private box at Noël's disposal, equipped with bouquets of flowers, lashings of caviar and magnums of champagne. But the evening was clearly Evelyn Laye's.

NOËL COWARD: *She played as though she were enchanted. Early on in the ballroom scene she conquered the audience completely by singing the quick waltz song, 'Tell me, what is Love?' so brilliantly, and with such a quality of excitement, that the next few minutes of the play were entirely lost in one of the most prolonged outbursts of cheering I have ever heard in the theatre.*

EVELYN LAYE: *Noël came into my dressing-room that night before the curtain. He had a gift for me. It was a small Fabergé box, and it had a little knob on it. As you pressed it, up came a little bird. A little feathered bird which sang its head off.*
'Do let me be the first to give it to you, dear,' he said.

'What is Love?'
from 'Bitter-Sweet'

Play something gay for me,
Play for me, play for me,
Set me free.
I'm in a trance tonight,
Can't you see
How I want to dance tonight?
Madly my heart is beating,
Some insane melody possessing me,
Is my brain thrilling and obsessing me?
How can I leave it to call in vain?
Is it joy or pain?
Live your life, for time is fleeting,
Some insistent voice repeating,
Hear me – hear me,
How can I leave it to call in vain?
Is it joy or pain?

Tell me – tell me – tell me, what is
    love?
Is it some consuming flame;
Part of the moon, part of the sun,
Part of a dream barely begun?
When is the moment of breaking –
    waking?
Skies change, nothing is the same,
Some strange magic is to blame;
Voices that seem to echo round me and
    above,
Tell me, what is love, love, love?

When asked why he never wrote another *Bitter-Sweet*, Noël replied, 'That's what I want to know, too.'

'After Metro-Goldwyn-Mayer's dreadful film [made in 1940 with Jeanette MacDonald and Nelson Eddy] I can never revive *Bitter-Sweet*,' he told John Barber of the *Daily Telegraph*.

'A pity,' he added, 'I was saving it up as an investment for my old age.'

NOËL COWARD:

A star is somebody whose name over the title drags the audience into the theatre, and the only quality they've got to have is 'star' quality. I think that my darling Anna Neagle, who started her career with me as one of my chorus girls is a star [she later starred in the first film version of *Bitter-Sweet*, produced by Herbert Wilcox].

Now I know many actors and actresses and singers and dancers who can do it as well as Anna, but when Anna comes on, the lights go up a little bit. Rather like Gertrude Lawrence, except that Gertie was a much more experienced

Anna Neagle and Fernand Gravey in the original film version of *Bitter-Sweet*.

and accomplished actress than Anna. Gertie could play anything. *She could have played Hedda Gabler or whatever you like, provided she had a good director.*

And it was as a vehicle for Gertrude Lawrence and himself that Noël wrote *Private Lives*.

After the Broadway triumph of *Bitter-Sweet*, he slipped away to San Francisco and spent ten days in Hollywood, where he made a great many new friends—Charles Chaplin, who became a lifelong friend and a neighbour in Switzerland, Gloria Swanson, Clifton Webb, Leslie Howard and many others.

Then followed a six month trip to Japan, Korea and Shanghai with Jeffrey Amherst, during the course of which Jeffrey was stricken with amoebic dysentery. While awaiting his recovery Noël himself contracted flu, and wrote what was to be his most famous comedy, in bed, in Singapore.

NOËL COWARD: *Gertie Lawrence had given me a most beautiful Cartier picture frame with a photograph of* her *on one side, and another of* me *on the other side, so as to remind me that I'd promised to write a play for us. And when I was getting over my flu in Shanghai, there was nothing much to do so I wrote* Private Lives—*in four days—and not one word was changed.*

When I started writing it, Gertie cabled me to say that she would be perfectly delighted to do it, but she had a contract with Charlot and would I join her in a revue beforehand. And so I cabled back, 'Certainly not. Private Lives *comes first.' And it did.*

That trip was also to result in his writing one of his most original and well-known songs, 'Mad Dogs and Englishmen'.

NOËL COWARD:

below, with Marlene Dietrich.
right, with Charles Chaplin.
bottom right, with Jeffrey Amhurst travelling.

That was written, very appropriately, driving from Hanoi, in Tonkin, to Singapore. I sang it triumphantly and unaccompanied to Jeffrey on the verandah of a small jungle guest house. Not only Jeffrey but the lizards and the tree frogs gave every vocal indication of enthusiasm. But I didn't use it until years later in my revue Words and Music. *and Romney Brent sang it.*

'Mad Dogs and Englishmen'
from 'Words and Music'

In tropical climes there are certain
   times of day
When all the citizens retire
To tear their clothes off and perspire.
It's one of the rules that the greatest
   fools obey,
Because the sun is much too sultry
And one must avoid its ultry-violet ray.

The natives grieve when the white men
   leave their huts,
Because they're obviously, definitely
   nuts!

Mad dogs and Englishmen
Go out in the midday sun,
The Japanese don't care to,
The Chinese wouldn't dare to,
Hindus and Argentines sleep firmly from
   twelve to one
But Englishmen detest a siesta.
In the Philippines
There are lovely screens
To protect you from the glare.
In the Malay States
There are hats like plates
Which the Britishers won't wear.
At twelve noon
The natives swoon
and no further work is done,
But mad dogs and Englishmen
Go out in the midday sun.

It's such a surprise for the Eastern
   eyes to see,
That though the English are effcte,
They're quite impervious to heat,
When the white man rides every native
   hides in glee,
Because the simple creatures hope he
Will impale his solar topee on a tree.

It seems such a shame
When the English claim
The earth,
They give rise to such hilarity and
   mirth.

1. Mad dogs and Eng-lish-men Go out in the mid-day sun. The
2. Mad dogs and Eng-lish-men Go out in the mid-day sun. The
3. Mad dogs and Eng-lish-men Go out in the mid-day sun. The

Mad dogs and Englishmen
Go out in the midday sun.
The toughest Burmese bandit
Can never understand it.
In Rangoon the heat of noon
Is just what the natives shun,
They put their Scotch or Rye down,
And lie down.
In a jungle town
Where the sun beats down
To the rage of man and beast
The English garb
Of the English sahib
Merely gets a bit more creased.
In Bangkok
At twelve o'clock
They foam at the mouth and run,
But mad dogs and Englishmen
Go out in the midday sun.

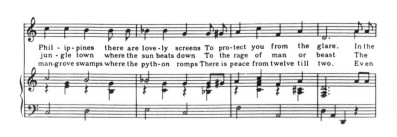

Phil-ip-pines there are love-ly screens To pro-tect you from the glare. In the
jun-gle town where the sun beats down To the rage of man or beast The
man-grove swamps where the pyth-on romps There is peace from twelve till two. Even

Jap - an -ese don't care to, The Chin - ese would - n't dare to,
tough -est Bur- mese ban - dit Can nev - er un - der - stand it. In
small -est Ma - lay rab - bit De - plores this stu - pid ha - bit. In

Mad dogs and Englishmen
Go out in the midday sun.
The smallest Malay rabbit
Deplores this stupid habit.
In Hong Kong
They strike a gong
And fire off a noonday gun,
To reprimand each inmate
Who's in late.
In the mangrove swamps
Where the python romps
There is peace from twelve till two.
Even caribous
Lie around and snooze,
For there's nothing else to do.
In Bengal
To move at all
Is seldom if ever done,
But mad dogs and Englishmen
Go out in the midday sun.

Hin - doos and Ar - gen - tines sleep firm - ly from twelve to one. But
Ran - goon the heat of noon Is just what the na - tives shun. They
Hong Kong they strike a gong And fire off a noon - day . gun. To

John Mills.

Jeffrey spent another month recovering, and Noël explored the island. Among other novelties he discovered an English theatrical touring company that was appearing in repertory at the Victoria Theatre. John Mills was a member of that company.

It was my first visit to Singapore. I'd been travelling round the world doing a play with a company that went under the extraordinary name of 'The Quaints' and we did Shakespeare, and some rather beautiful comedy.

The night Noël arrived in Singapore, we happened to be playing Journey's End. *He told me that it was his favourite play and that he'd always longed to play Stanhope, so he asked our manager if he could play the part of Stanhope with the company. Well of course the manager had a fit, and we all fainted. We were thrilled to death. And so to cut a long story short, he learned the part, which is about as long as Hamlet, in about three days, and went on with us one Thursday night. Even with so little time for rehearsal he was able to think up new bits of business.*

When Raleigh (which I played) died in the dug-out in the last scene in the play, Stanhope used to walk to the dug-out steps, wait for a second, and then walk away. 'No,' said Noël, 'I think after you've died, I'll just walk back once more, and look at you on the bed, and then walk out.' And I said, 'Marvellous! Marvellous idea.' Terribly thrilled about the whole thing.

The great night arrived and I tried not to overact my head off in the death scene, and died.

I heard his footsteps go toward the dug-out steps, and then pause, and his return to the bed. Suddenly I heard the most terrific crash, and a very heavy object fell on a very tender part of my anatomy. Noël's tin hat had fallen plonk on the crutch of the corpse. With that, I sat up, let out a terrifying screech and collapsed again. And that was the end of Journey's End *in Singapore.*

In due course Jeffrey Amherst left hospital, and the tour of the Far East continued. After a brief stay in Colombo with Noël's brother Eric, still planting tea, they returned to their hotel where a cable from Gertrude Lawrence awaited Noël: 'YOUR PLAY IS DELIGHTFUL', (she had clearly received the manuscript of *Private Lives*) 'AND THERE'S NOTHING THAT CAN'T BE FIXED.'

'THE ONLY THING TO BE FIXED', cabled back the incensed author, 'WILL BE YOUR PERFORMANCE.'

left, Gertrude Lawrence.
above, John Mills with Steffi
Duna and Doris Hare in
'Children's Hour' from *Words
and Music*, 1932.

Gertrude Lawrence was an instinctive actress. She was incredibly quick, often inspired and invariably unreliable. She would never give the same performance, for her inventiveness would spark off impromptu business, throwing into disarray not only those with whom she acted, but the author as well. When the actor and the author were the same person, and when that person was Noël, there was a certain tendency for the situation to get just the tiniest bit out of hand.

She danced exquisitely, dressed expensively and effectively, and was outrageously extravagant, her excesses leading her at length to the bankruptcy courts. She could play comedy and drama with equal brilliance and sing enchantingly. Her grace and poise, her talent, fun, madness and sheer brilliance never failed to entrance her audiences.

Adrianne Allen.

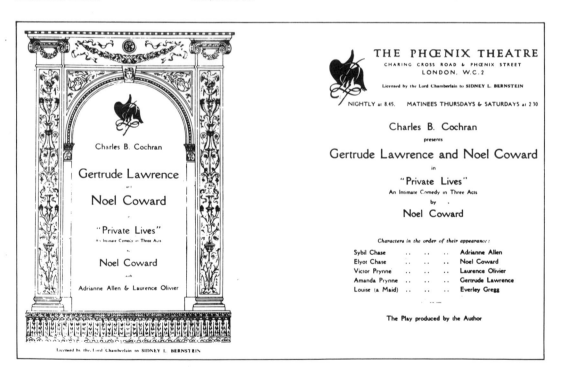

Charles B. Cochran

Gertrude Lawrence
and
Noel Coward

"Private Lives"
An Intimate Comedy in Three Acts

Noel Coward

with
Adrianne Allen & Laurence Olivier

Licensed by the Lord Chamberlain to SIDNEY L. BERNSTEIN

THE PHŒNIX THEATRE
CHARING CROSS ROAD & PHŒNIX STREET
LONDON, W.C.2
Licensed by the Lord Chamberlain to SIDNEY L. BERNSTEIN

NIGHTLY at 8.45.   MATINEES THURSDAYS & SATURDAYS at 2.30

Charles B. Cochran
presents

Gertrude Lawrence and Noel Coward
in

"Private Lives"
An Intimate Comedy in Three Acts
by
Noel Coward

Characters in the order of their appearance:

Sybil Chase	..	..	..	Adrianne Allen
Elyot Chase	..	..	..	Noel Coward
Victor Prynne	..	..	..	Laurence Olivier
Amanda Prynne	..	..	..	Gertrude Lawrence
Louise (a Maid)	..	..	..	Everley Gregg

The Play produced by the Author

Private Lives was the first play to be presented at the Phoenix Theatre in London, where it opened in 1930. The two supporting parts were played by Laurence Olivier as Victor Prynne, and Adrianne Allen (at that time Mrs Raymond Massey), as Sybil. Victor, although a rather priggish character, required the talents of a handsome and fine actor.

NOËL COWARD:

I had to have somebody physically attractive otherwise Amanda would never have married him.

Larry was a terrible giggler on stage and I had to stop him. It's one thing to have an actor's joke, but it's not very fair on the audience. If I did anything in the part that was at all funny, Larry would be in fits of laughter instead of being cross, so I said, 'From now on I'm going to try and make you laugh, and every time you do so, I'll kill you.' He got so angry with himself for falling for it, and I ruined several of his performances, but it was worth it.

One incident occurred in the breakfast scene towards the end of the play.

NOËL COWARD:

When Amanda spluttered over the coffee, Victor had to slap her hard on the back. One day she choked and turned round to him and said, 'You great clob!' 'Clob?' I said, and she replied, 'Yes, clob'. To which I added, 'The man with the clob foot!' And of course Larry had to restrain himself from giggling. I finally cured him.

ADRIANNE ALLEN:

Daniel Massey.

Being in the first production of Private Lives *was one of the most lovely experiences that any actress could have. Noël made Larry and me, who were playing the small parts, as important as him and Gertie, which of course enabled us to give much better performances. He would call us on to the stage two or three times a week and give notes, always keeping us up to scratch. Amongst other things, while we were playing in* Private Lives, *he taught me to play backgammon, and I must say I paid for that production!*

Adrianne Allen was pregnant and couldn't go with the production to New York. The resultant baby was Daniel Massey; Noël was his godfather, and he played Noël in the film about Gertrude Lawrence, *Star*.

Private Lives is perhaps Noel's best comedy—a simple, light and witty piece about two attractive lovers unable to live together and unable to live apart.

'Unique theatrical magic,' a critic wrote. 'Mr Coward's a first rate conjuror; the seeming spontaneity of the character has been attained by the most industrious stagecraft and remarkable sense of timing.'

115

'Private Lives'
(Taken from Act One)

The scene takes place on the terrace of a hotel in the South of France. Amanda (Gertrude Lawrence) and Elyot (Noël Coward) once married, have divorced and both remarried. They meet by chance, staying at the same hotel.

ELYOT:	We were so ridiculously over in love.
AMANDA:	Funny, wasn't it?
ELYOT:	(sadly) Horribly funny.
AMANDA:	Selfishness, cruelty, hatred, possessiveness, petty jealousy. All those qualities came out in us just because we loved each other.
ELYOT:	Perhaps they were there anyhow.
AMANDA:	No, it's love that does it. To hell with love.
ELYOT:	To hell with love.
AMANDA:	And yet here we are starting afresh with two quite different people. In love all over again, aren't we? (Elyot doesn't answer) Aren't we?
ELYOT:	No.
AMANDA:	Elyot!
ELYOT:	We're not in love all over again, and you know it. Good night, Amanda. (He turns abruptly, and goes towards the French windows.)
AMANDA:	Elyot - don't be silly - come back.
ELYOT:	I must go and find Sibyl.
AMANDA:	I must go and find Victor.
ELYOT:	(Savagely) Well, why don't you?
AMANDA:	I don't want to.
ELYOT:	It's shameful, shameful of us.
AMANDA:	Don't: I feel terrible. Don't leave me for a minute, I shall go mad if you do. We won't talk about ourselves any more, we'll talk about outside things, anything you like, only just don't leave me until I've pulled myself together.

ELYOT:	Very well. (<u>There is a dead silence</u>)
AMANDA:	What have you been doing lately? During these last years?
ELYOT:	Travelling about. I went round the world, you know, after –
AMANDA:	(<u>Hurriedly</u>) Yes, yes, I know. How was it?
ELYOT:	The world?
AMANDA:	Yes.
ELYOT:	Oh, highly enjoyable.
AMANDA:	China must be very interesting.
ELYOT:	Very big, China.
AMANDA:	And Japan –
ELYOT:	Very small.
AMANDA:	Did you eat sharks' fins, and take your shoes off, and use chopsticks and everything?
ELYOT:	Practically everything.
AMANDA:	And India, the burning Ghars, or Ghats, or whatever they are, and the Taj Mahal. How was the Taj Mahal?
ELYOT:	(<u>Looking at her</u>) Unbelievable, a sort of dream.

Noël and Gertie in *Private Lives*.

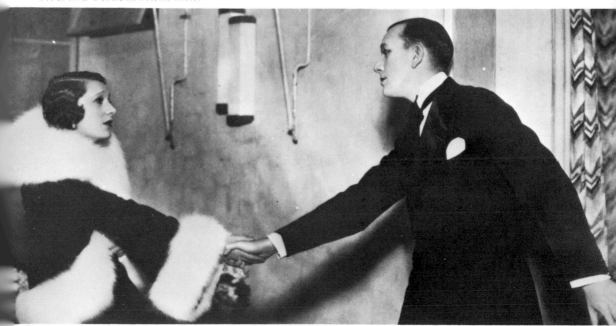

AMANDA:	That was the moonlight, I expect, you must have seen it in the moonlight.
ELYOT:	(Never taking his eyes off her face) Yes, moonlight is cruelly deceptive.
AMANDA:	And it didn't look like a biscuit box, did it? I always felt that it might.
ELYOT:	(Quietly) Darling, darling, I love you so.
AMANDA:	And I hope you met a sacred Elephant. They're lint-white I believe, and very, very sweet.
ELYOT:	I've never loved anyone else for an instant.
AMANDA:	(Raising her hand feebly in protest) No, no, you mustn't - Elyot - stop.
ELYOT:	You love me too, don't you. There's no doubt about it anywhere, is there?
AMANDA:	No, no doubt anywhere.
ELYOT:	You're looking very lovely you know, in this damned moonlight. Your skin is clear and cool, and your eyes are shining, and you're growing lovelier and lovelier every second as I look at you. You don't hold any mystery for me, darling, do you mind? There isn't a particle of you that I don't know, remember and want.

AMANDA:	(Softly) I'm glad, my sweet.
ELYOT:	More than any desire anywhere, deep down in my deepest heart I want you back again - please -
AMANDA:	(Putting her hand over his mouth) Don't say any more, you're making me cry so dreadfully.

> (He pulls her gently into his arms and they stand silently, completely oblivious of anything but the moment, and each other. When finally, they separate, they sit down, rather breathlessly, on the balustrade.)

The music: 'Someday I'll find You' that has been playing on the gramophone in the background, stops.

'Someday I'll find You'
from 'Private Lives'

Someday I'll find you,
Moonlight behind you,
True to the dream I am dreaming.
As I draw near you
You'll smile a little smile,
For a little while
We shall stand
Hand in hand.
I'll leave you never,
Love you for ever,
All our past sorrow redeeming;
Try to make it true,
Say you love me too,
Someday I'll find you again.

GOOGIE WITHERS:

I took over from Kay Hammond in Private Lives *in 1946 —the first revival. Noël directed us, which was wonderfully exciting for me, because I was young and it was a great chance for me in that marvellous part—a God-given part for a girl.*

I felt that I was doing quite well, my second act was good and the third act was all right, but the first act—there was something wrong somewhere and I said to Noël, 'What's wrong, darling—you know there is *something wrong.'*

'Yes my dear, yes my dear—too piss-elegant. Too piss-elegant,' he said. It was perfect for me, just what I needed.

SOMEDAY I'LL FIND YOU

Photo by SASHA (By Permission)

Sung by
GERTRUDE LAWRENCE & NOËL COWARD
in
"PRIVATE LIVES"
AN INTIMATE COMEDY IN THREE ACTS
By NOËL COWARD

Presented by CHARLES B. COCHRAN.

Words & Music
by
NOËL COWARD

PRICE 2/- NET.

CHAPPELL & Cọ LTD
50, NEW BOND ST, LONDON, W.I.
NEW YORK & SYDNEY

PRINTED IN ENGLAND

Photo by DOROTHY WILDING (By Permission)

TIIE MASTER

It was Noël's policy never to play in any one production for more than six months—half in London and half in New York—and although *Private Lives* could well have run a further six months in the West End he closed it after three, in order to open on Broadway. A film was made of the entire play in New York as a guide for M.G.M., who were preparing the film of it (with Norma Shearer and Robert Montgomery).

While on Broadway Noël started to write a musical, the mammoth *Cavalcade*. This spectacular Cochran presentation tested all the technical facilities the Drury Lane stage had to offer—one scene included a complete laden troopship leaving for the Boer War. The musical's time–span stretched over thirty years, and featured the brilliant 'Twentieth Century Blues'.

JOHN MILLS: *Noël never forgets that he was once a bit player and a crowd artist; the one thing I remember about the rehearsals for* Cavalcade *was that he had about eighty-five or a hundred artists in small parts, and he gave every old actor and actress a job in the show. He went to great lengths to try and find them, and to give them a job.*

He did something I've never seen done before or since. He had all the small parts and crowd wearing numbers, like football teams, and I couldn't see what this was all about, but I soon realised that as he was directing the play from the front row of the dress circle, he couldn't really identify every one of the crowd from that distance. He would whisper to somebody on his left, 'Who's number thirty-two?'

'Sybil,' came the reply.

'Sybil,' he'd say, 'Sybil, would you mind moving . . .'

and gave her a direction, and of course Sybil fainted because she was now the leading lady of the play, and he did this with all of them. The rehearsals were a joy—it was a marvellous experience to be with him.

But the first night almost ended in disaster.

NOËL COWARD:

There was a scene when the troopship had to go away. We did this by moving platforms, and another platform slid on for the other scene. But on the first night, owing to the enthusiasm of the company, and the nervousness, the crowd waiting got on to the under *platform too soon, which made the other one stick. And so we sat. Me tee'ed up in the Royal Box, and with the theatre dark, everybody starting to whisper. Finally Jack Wilson came back into the Box and said, 'Danny says it might take a few minutes or two hours.'*

JOHN MILLS:

At that moment, I was on the stage with the rest of the abandoned company. I peeped through the curtain, and saw the author sitting in the Box, with a long white cigarette holder, and a very relaxed smile on his face. I looked very closely and there were small beads of perspiration just dripping off his chin.

NOËL COWARD:

Gladys [who had designed the production] *and I sat smiling bravely, and just as I was about to go on the stage and say, 'Dear audience, there's been a terrible hitch, and I'm afraid you must all go home,' the little red light went on in the conductor's desk, and we went on again. But it*

Troop Ship departure 1900.
One of twenty-two scenes
from *Cavalcade* at the
Theatre Royal, Drury Lane,
October, 1931.

JOHN MILLS:

ruined the first performance. It made everybody nervous, and the opening night of Cavalcade *was not a good performance.*

The show finished in a blaze of glory, and I think it was—well, I know it was the most exciting night in the theatre, the most exciting first night that I have ever had anything to do with.

Terence Rattigan was just nineteen when he was sent to see *Cavalcade*.

TERENCE RATTIGAN:

When I went up to Oxford in 1930, Noël had just written Cavalcade, *and he was a sort of God to all of us. I was dramatic critic on the undergraduate paper,* Cherwell, *and our rival newspaper,* Isis, *had come out with a great article saying, 'Noël Coward—Genius and Prophet', and as our editorial policy was always to contradict our rivals, I was sent up to London with a fairly heavy hint from the editor that I wasn't expected to be too effusive about* Cavalcade, *and somehow or other I managed to get myself into the dress circle, and thoroughly enjoyed it. But of course I had to obey my editor, and my little piece when it came out was headed,* 'NO, NO, NO!!!'

I can only say that if he'd read it, which of course I'm sure he never did, I would have had no chance of friendship with him. [Noël was much later to compose the music and write the lyrics for the Broadway musical version of Rattigan's *The Sleeping Prince*, re-entitled *The Girl who Came to Supper*.]

Cavalcade got rave notices, some of the best Noël had ever had, and congratulations poured in. The King and Queen and the entire Royal Family went to see it, and so, it seemed, did the major proportion of the inhabitants of the British Isles.

Not included in that number was George Bernard Shaw. When Noël heard that Shaw was reluctant to see it, he wrote to him, 'As you've lived through this period, I'm sure that you will enjoy it.' But Shaw declined the invitation. Not one to be easily dismissed, Noël this time sent him a ticket for a box with the note, 'The box contains four seats—so you'll be able to bring *all* your friends.'

But the next time Noël was dismissed by someone, he had no quick retort to suit the occasion.

An actress in London went to every one of his auditions for every show he ever did—musical, straight and revue. And each time she came, she was well dressed, sang a few songs—rather badly—and didn't fit into anything.

Finally, Noël got upset and said, 'We've got to find something for that woman. She's so lovely, and she's so nice.' So after many years when he auditioned for another show, she came again, sang one of her songs—and at last he had something for her. He went down the aisle to the edge of the stage, and looked up at her. 'I'm very happy to tell you that at last we have a part for you.'

'Oh no, Mr Coward,' she replied, 'I don't take parts. I just audition,' and grandly swept out.

Noël sold the *Cavalcade* film rights for a hundred thousand dollars; the film, made in Hollywood with a cast headed by Clive Brook and Diana Wynyard, was both a critical and box-office success, but it could not be said really to have captured the patriotic English atmosphere of the early part of the century.

Noël now left for a nine-month trip to South America,

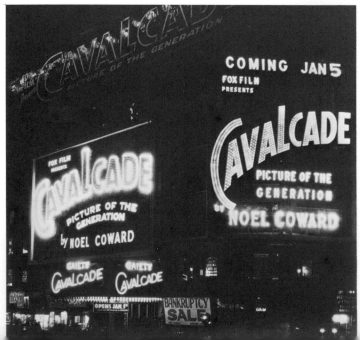

again accompanied by Jeffrey Amherst, to recover from the exhaustion of getting *Cavalcade* into production. No sooner had he reached Argentina, however, when he received a cable from Alfred Lunt and Lynn Fontanne, saying that they were free to accept his offer of a play he had promised to write as a star vehicle for the three of them.

NOËL COWARD: *I was having a lovely holiday in Bora-Bora or somewhere around the Pacific when I suddenly had a cable saying,* 'OUR CONTRACT WITH THE GUILD IS UP NEXT APRIL. WHAT ABOUT IT? LOVE.'

But on returning to London, he had a new revue to get off the ground. This was *Words and Music*, which he had offered Cochran with the suggestion that they co-produce. Whereas up till then revues normally contained contributions from various writers, lyricists and composers, Noël now wanted there to be no other contributor. After the successes of *Bitter-Sweet* and *Cavalcade*, he was in a strong enough position to persuade Cochran.

NOËL COWARD: Words and Music *was almost a very very good revue, but it wasn't quite. I've never quite made up my mind why. It could possibly have been my fault. But it wasn't entirely. It had no great big star in it, though there was a wonderful cast—Ivy St Helier, Romney Brent. It ran for about eight months. Notices were terrible. They always were.*

Words and Music (1932), Joy Spring and Norah Howard in original performance 'Mad about the Boy'.

Apart from 'Mad Dogs and Englishmen' it featured two other Noël Coward evergreens, 'The Party's over Now', and 'Mad About the Boy'.

'Mad About the Boy'
from 'Words and Music'

I met him at a party just a couple of
   years ago,
He was rather over-hearty and ridiculous
But as I'd seen him on the Screen
He cast a certain spell.
I basked in his attraction for a couple
   of hours or so,
His manners were a fraction too
   meticulous,
If he was real or not I couldn't tell,
But like a silly fool, I fell.

Mad about the boy,
I know it's stupid to be mad about the
   boy,
I'm so ashamed of it,
But must admit
The sleepless nights I've had about the
   boy.
On the Silver Screen
He melts my foolish heart in every
   single scene.
Although I'm quite aware
That here and there
Are traces of the cad about the boy
Lord knows I'm not a fool girl,
I really shouldn't care,
Lord knows I'm not a schoolgirl
In the flurry of her first affair.
Will it ever cloy?
This odd diversity of misery and joy,
I'm feeling quite insane
And young again
And all because I'm mad about the boy.

Home work, home work,
Every night there's home work,
While Elsie practises the gas goes pop,
I wish, I wish she'd stop,
Oh dear, oh dear,
Here it's always, 'No, dear,
You can't go out again, you must stay
   home,
You waste your money on that common
   Picturedrome,

Don't shirk - stay here and do your
   work.'
Yearning, yearning,
How my heart is burning.
I'll see him Saturday in 'Strong Man's
   Pain',

And then on Monday and on Friday week
   again.
To me he is the sole man
Who can kiss as well as Colman,
I could faint whenever there's a close
   up of his lips,
Though John Barrymore is larger
When my hero's on his charger
Even Douglas Fairbanks Junior hasn't
   smaller hips.
If only he could know
That I adore him so.

Mad about the boy,
It's simply scrumptious to be mad about
   the boy,
I know that quite sincerely
Housman really
Wrote 'The Shropshire Lad' about the boy.
In my English prose
I've done a tracing of his forehead and
   his nose
And there is, honour bright,
A certain slight
Effect of Galahad about the boy.
I've talked to Rosie Hooper,
She feels the same as me,
She says that Gary Cooper
Doesn't thrill her to the same degree.
In 'Can Love Destroy?'
When he meets Garbo in a suit of
   corduroy,
He gives a little frown
And knocks her down.
Oh dear, oh dear, I'm mad about the boy.

JOHN MILLS:

Words and Music *was a wonderful show to be in. I think
it contains some of the most brilliant words and music that
Noël ever wrote.*

   At that time I was a song-and-dance man, and I did a

127

number in it called 'Something to do with Spring' with
Joyce Barbour, and just to show how censorship has altered,
there was one line in it, the last line in the lyric, which I
remember went 'I'd love to know what that stallion thinks,
maybe it's something to do with Spring', and it was so
utterly disgusting that we had to cut it out on the second
night!'

By the age of thirty-two, Noël had enough successful plays
on the books for a repertory group called The Noël
Coward Company to be formed to tour the English provinces. Its repertoire included *Private Lives, Hay Fever,
Home Chat, Fallen Angels* and *The Vortex*, and it was headed
by Kate Cutler, who had once walked out on *The Vortex*.
James Mason was in the company too, playing small parts.

JAMES MASON:

*Noël showed up at rehearsal one morning in London,
presumably to satisfy himself that the leading members of
the company were likely to perform adequately. The
company was actually a sort of spin-off from the 'Brandon-
Thomas Seasons', a repertory company which was run by
Jevon Brandon-Thomas, the son of the author of* Charley's
Aunt. *The leading man was always Wilson Barratt. For
some reason Jevon wanted to lay off, and his stage manager,
a man called Gatenby Bell, decided to keep the company
together, and specialise in Noël Coward plays. Wilson
Barratt played both the Noël Coward parts, and other
leads. I played the rather dull young men in the plays.*
    *The tour was a disaster. At one point Bell thought that
it might be a good idea to throw on two plays for the price of
one. The theatre was going badly all over, and the notion of
a curtain-raiser was in its infancy. I can't remember
whether we were obliged to make minor cuts in order to
present the two plays of an evening—the curtain-raiser, and
the main play—but in any event the public didn't go for it.
They continued to stay determinedly away in Exeter,
Eastbourne, Brighton and Bournemouth. Poor Bell was
badly hit financially.*
    *The Master may have nodded politely in my direction
when he came to the rehearsal but he wasn't heard to say
anything witty on that occasion.*

Noël spent all his spare time down at Goldenhurst, where

he entertained innumerable weekend guests. To be asked to Goldenhurst was like being asked to a Royal Garden Party.

While at Goldenhurst, towards the end of 1932, he finished *Design for Living*, the play he had promised the Lunts, and he left for New York before the end of the year to work on it with them. It was tried out in Cleveland, Ohio, early in the New Year, and opened at the Ethel Barrymore Theater, New York, on January 24th 1933.

NOËL COWARD:

We'd been playing Design for Living *for some time, and one night Alfred said my line instead of his own in the drunk scene. It couldn't have been done if it hadn't been in the drunk scene because everything was haywire, but he did, and I answered him with his line.*

Now there was lots of business that he'd invented that I envied and lots of stuff I did that he liked. And so we changed parts. It didn't make any difference to the psychology of the play, and we had a lovely time and never missed a laugh. When we came off stage, Lynn was waiting in the wings in a fury.

'Nothing that either of you did in that scene was even remotely amusing!' she said angrily, and walked into her dressing-room. So Alfred and I went to a movie, a matinée, to forget our grief.

Rex Harrison.

'Doesn't the eye of heaven mean anything to you?' asks Leo in the play.
'Only', replies Gilda, 'when it winks.'

When Paramount made the film of *Design for Living* with Frederic March, Gary Cooper and Miriam Hopkins, Noël commented: 'I'm told that there are three of my original lines left in the film—such original ones as "Pass the mustard".'

But it scored as great a success as it had in New York when it opened six years later on the London stage with Diana Wynyard, Anton Walbrook and Rex Harrison.

'You're an impossible person,' Noël said to Rex Harrison, who much later accepted the role of Henry Higgins in *My Fair Lady* which Noël had turned down. 'If, next to me, you weren't the finest light comedy actor in the world, you'd be good for only one thing—selling cars in Great Portland Street.'

'The ending of *Design for Living* is equivocal,' Noël wrote. 'After various partings and reunions and partings again, after torturing and loving and hating one another, the three star characters are left together as the curtain falls, laughing. Some saw in it a lascivious anticipation of a sort of triangular carnal frolic. Others, with less ribald imaginations, regarded it as a meaningless and slightly inept excuse to bring the curtain down. As the author, however, I prefer to think that Gilda, Otto and Leo were laughing at themselves.'

Noël Coward as Leo, Alfred Lunt as Otto, and Lynn Fontanne as Gilda, in the last act of *Design for Living* Ethel Barrymore Theater, New York.

'Design for Living'
(Taken from Act Three)

After a triangular romp with Leo (Noël) and Otto (Alfred Lunt), Gilda (Lynn Fontanne) has gone away, married their mutual friend Ernest and settled down in New York. But Leo and Otto have traced Gilda, and have come to reclaim her. The bond is too strong for Ernest to break, and in exasperation, he breaks out, decrying their amoral behaviour.

GILDA: Ernest, Ernest, be friendly. It can't hurt you much.

ERNEST: Not any more. I've wasted too much friendship on all of you, you're not worth it.

OTTO: There's a lot of vanity in your anger, Ernest, which isn't really worthy of your intelligence.

ERNEST:	(Turning on him) Don't speak to me, please!
LEO:	Otto's perfectly right. This behaviour isn't worthy of your intelligence. If you were twisted up inside and really unhappy it would be different; but you're not, you're no more than offended and resentful that your smooth habits should be tampered with -
ERNEST:	(Losing control) Hold your tongue! - I've had too much of your effrontery already!
GILDA:	(Peaceably) Once and for all, Ernest, don't be bitter and so dreadfully outraged. Please, please calm down and you'll find it much easier to understand.
ERNEST:	You overrate my capacity for understanding! I don't understand; the whole situation is revolting to me. I shall never understand; I never could understand; I never could understand this disgusting three sided erotic hotch-potch!
GILDA:	Ernest!
LEO:	Why, good heavens! King Solomon had a hundred wives and was thought very highly of. I can't see why Gilda shouldn't be allowed a couple of gentlemen friends.
ERNEST:	(Furiously) Your ill-timed flippancy is only in keeping with the rest of your execrable taste!
OTTO:	Certain emotions transcend even taste, Ernest. Take anger, for example. Look what anger's doing to you. You're blowing yourself out like a frog!
ERNEST:	(Beside himself) Be quiet! Be quiet!
LEO:	(Violently) Why should we be quiet? You're making enough row to blast the roof off! Why should you have the monopoly of noise? Why should your pompous moral pretensions be allowed to hurtle across the city without any competition? We've all got lungs; let's

	use them! Let's shriek like mad! Let's enjoy ourselves!
GILDA:	(<u>Beginning to laugh</u>) Stop it, Leo! I implore you! - This is ludicrous! Stop it - stop it -
ERNEST:	(<u>In a frenzy</u>) It is ludicrous! It's ludicrous to think that I was ever taken in by any of you - that I ever mistook you for anything but the unscrupulous, worthless degenerates that you are! There isn't a decent instinct among the lot of you. You're shifty and irresponsible and abominable, and I don't wish to set eyes on you again - as long as I live! Never! Do you hear me? Never - never - never!

> He stamps out of the room, quite beside himself with fury; on his way into the hall he falls over the package of canvases. This is too much for Gilda and Otto and Leo; they break down utterly and roar with laughter. They groan and weep with laughter; their laughter is still echoing from the walls as the curtain falls.

Gladys Calthrop's design for Yvonne Printemps costume for the Ballroom scene in *Conversation Piece*.

When Noël returned to England in the spring of 1933, he found Goldenhurst was in mourning for his brother Eric, who had died of a tropical disease at the age of twenty-eight, in Ceylon. The painful illness and subsequent death of a second of three sons, taken from her so young in life, came as a bitter blow to Mrs Coward.

Conversation Piece, a sentimental extravaganza set in the Regency period, was written and composed by Noël for the French singer Yvonne Printemps. In it she played Melanie, the little girl who falls in love with her elderly guardian, Paul. The latter was to be played by American actor Romney Brent until Noël himself took over the role.

Romney Brent's French was perfect, but he was entirely unromantic, and Conversation Piece *was a romantic musical. Four days before rehearsals began, I went round to him and said, 'Listen, I'm not going to let you open.'*

I've never seen anyone so happy in my life. He said, 'Okay. I won't make a scene. I'll go on condition that I can come to every rehearsal and watch you struggle with that awful part.'

132

CHARLES B. COCHRAN
presents

YVONNE PRINTEMPS

in

CONVERSATION PIECE

A Play with Music

BY

NOEL COWARD

THE PLAY DIRECTED BY THE AUTHOR

CHAPPELL & CO., LTD
50, NEW BOND ST.
LONDON, W.1
NEW YORK & SYDNEY
CHAPPELL S.A.
PARIS

PRINTED IN ENGLAND

ILL FOLLOW MY SECRET HEART	2/- NET
NEVERMORE	2/- "
REGENCY RAKES	2/- "
THERE'S ALWAYS SOMETHING FISHY ABOUT THE FRENCH	2/- "
VALSE (PIANO SOLO)	2/- "
PIANO SELECTION	2/6 "

The cast included Louis Hayward, George Sanders playing a Regency Rake, and Valerie Hobson was in the chorus. The successful run only ended when Yvonne Printemps returned to Paris to fulfil a film commitment. Despite such enchanting music as 'I'll Follow my Secret Heart', sung by Printemps, it closed after six months, still playing to packed houses, as no substitute for Printemps could be found. The entire production transferred to New York later that year with Pierre Fresnay (who subsequently married Yvonne Printemps after her marriage to Sacha Guitry had been dissolved), co-starring in the role of the guardian, with Printemps in her original role. It closed after only two months.

'I'll Follow my Secret Heart'
from 'Conversation Piece'

PAUL:	Now then, what did Lord Sheere say to you last night?
MELANIE:	Not very much, but he was very ardent.
PAUL:	Good. He is coming here this morning.
MELANIE:	This morning?
PAUL:	Yes. I wrote him a little note from you. I will receive him and when I have talked to him for a little he will propose marriage.
MELANIE:	He seemed last night to wish for something a little less binding.
PAUL:	Never mind. When he proposes, you will accept him.
MELANIE:	When may I love somebody, please?
PAUL:	Not until you are safely married, and then only with the greatest discretion.
MELANIE:	I see.
PAUL:	(After a pause) What's the matter?
MELANIE:	It doesn't feel like my birthday any more. (Sings) A cloud has passed across the sun, The morning seems no longer gay.
PAUL:	I want to get on with these bills. You'd better go and dress.
MELANIE:	(Listlessly) Very well – With so much business to be done, Even the sea looks grey.
PAUL:	Don't be silly.

MELANIE:	C'est vrai, C'est vrai.
	  It seems that all the joy has faded
	    from the day
	  As though the foolish world no longer
	    wants to play.

PAUL:	Go and dress.
MELANIE:	What shall I wear? A black crêpe with a little bonnet?
PAUL:	What on earth is the matter with you this morning?
MELANIE:	White, white for a bride. But the sun ought to shine on a bride.
PAUL:	You're not a bride yet.

MELANIE:	But I shall be soon, shall I not? A
	very quiet, aristocratic bride with a
	discreet heart!
	  You ask me to have a discreet heart
	  Until marriage is out of the way,
	  But what if I meet
	  With a sweetheart so sweet
	  That my wayward heart cannot obey
	  A single word that you may say?

PAUL:	Then we shall have to go away.

MELANIE:	No.
	  For there is nowhere we could go
	  Where we could hide from what we know
	  Is true.

PAUL:	Do stop talking nonsense.
MELANIE:	It is not nonsense. You are so sure that everything in life can be arranged just so, like arithmetic.
PAUL:	Why not? Emotion is so very untidy.
MELANIE:	The sun has come out again. I feel a little better.
PAUL:	Good.

MELANIE:	I'm sorry.
	  Don't be afraid I'll betray you
	  And destroy all the plans you have made,
	  But even your schemes
	  Must leave room for my dreams.
	  So when all I owe to you is paid
	  I'll still have something of my own,
	  A little prize that's mine alone.

```
I'll follow my secret heart
My whole life through,
I'll keep all my dreams apart
Till one comes true.
No matter what price is paid,
What stars may fade
Above,
I'll follow my secret heart
Till I find love.
```

Opera star Joan Sutherland recently recorded 'I'll Follow my Secret Heart', together with other Noël Coward tunes.

JOAN SUTHERLAND: *For me it's a great joy to sing his music, because I find it so operatic in quality. I think he's a great opera buff, and his music has a strong influence of Massenet and Puccini, who are, I think, his favourite operatic composers. I find that to sing his music in an operatic fashion isn't easy at all, because it's not easy music. People are led astray into believing them to be marvellously simple tunes, but they're not simple to sing at all, and I find them rather wonderful.*

RICHARD BURTON: *As you probably know, Noël Coward is always known in the theatre, and indeed in the professional world that I belong to, as The Master, and when I was very young in this business, I couldn't understand why he was called The Master. I knew, of course, that Noël Coward was a brilliant playwright, and a brilliant actor, and a brilliant writer of songs etcetera, and all the many things that he could do, but I still didn't see why he should be called The Master, and perhaps some of the other more towering figures in the business should not also be called either Second Master or Third Master and so on.*

Anyway, I was very young, and I'd just had my first success, when one tends to become a little big-headed, and whilst in New York I suddenly received a telephone call from Sir Noël asking whether I'd do one day's work on a recording he was doing of his musical comedy Conversation Piece.

I said of course I'd be thrilled and delighted, and then an agent called me up and offered me two hundred dollars to do this particular recording, and I said, 'I don't work for two hundred dollars, I mean I get that a minute. I mean two hundred dollars, even if it is Noël Coward. It's quite absurd. No. No, I can't do it for two hundred.'

I put the telephone down and felt self-righteous, and about ten minutes later the telephone rang again, and a voice said, 'You will do Conversation Piece *for two hundred dollars, and you will like it.' It was him. And I did it for two hundred dollars.*

QUICK AND EXCITABLE

Conversation Piece was Noël's last production under the Cochran banner, as he decided to go into management himself, backing his own plays, with Jack Wilson as his partner. Since it was thought that his own name on the posters might confuse the critics and the public, it was decided that they should use Wilson's name. Their first enterprise in London was S. N. Behrman's *Biography*, which unfortunately flopped, followed shortly after by George S. Kaufman's and Edna Ferber's comedy *Theatre Royal*, with Laurence Olivier, Marie Tempest and Madge Titheradge, which didn't.

Theatre Royal paid for *Biography*, but when the management's next presentation, *Point Valaine*, the new play that Noël had written for the Lunts, appeared on Broadway, it proved to be one of the Lunts' greatest failures. It closed after seven weeks, costing Noël a great deal of his own money. His bank accounts were overdrawn for the first time in ten years.

Still in New York, he agreed to play in his first film since his walk-on role in D. W. Griffith's *Hearts of the World* seventeen years before. *The Scoundrel* was a low-budget picture for which he was paid five thousand dollars to play a cynical publisher, with Julie Haydon as his co-star. It was written and directed by Ben Hecht and Charles MacArthur (who later married Helen Hayes), and filmed on Long Island. It was an enormous critical success.

Noël then returned to England via New York and the Far East. He was invited to become Chairman of the Actors' Orphanage, a particular interest of his, and he held the Chairmanship for twenty years (until he left England to live in Bermuda), organising and helping to raise funds for orphans, presiding over fashionable theatrical charity garden parties, and enlisting the support of celebrities.

top right, with Julie Haydon
in *The Scoundrel* (1934).
above, Theatrical garden party.
right, with Marlene Dietrich
and children from Actors'
Orphanage.
below right, Lord Mountbatten.

He never stopped writing, and by now had ready a
handful of short plays assembled as a vehicle for Gertrude
Lawrence and himself. *Tonight at Eight-Thirty* consisted
of nine one-act plays: *Fumed Oak, We Were Dancing, Still
Life, Red Peppers, The Astonished Heart, Shadow Play, Ways
and Means, Family Album* and *Hands Across the Sea*. A tenth,
Star Chamber, was added in place of *Hands Across the Sea*,
but subsequently taken out of the repertoire.

LORD MOUNTBATTEN: *I remember in 1936 Noël sent me six free tickets for the Phoenix Theatre, so my wife Edwina and I went with a party.*

It wasn't until we got to the second play, Hands Across the Sea, *that we knew why we'd been sent the tickets. It was a bare-faced parody of our lives, with Gertie Lawrence playing Lady Maureen Gilpin and Noël Coward playing me. Absolutely outrageous, and certainly not worth six free tickets!*

NOËL COWARD: *Lord Louis and Lady Louis Mountbatten used to give cocktail parties and people used to arrive that nobody had ever heard of and sit about and go away again; somebody Dickie had met somewhere, or somebody Edwina had met— and nobody knew who they were. We all talked among ourselves, and it was really a very very good basis for a light comedy.*

It was beautifully played by Alison Leggat and Joyce Carey and Alan Webb. Great fun to do and no trouble at all. I had nothing to do—just wander on and off occasionally and say, 'Hello', and go away.

I loved playing Fumed Oak, *I loved playing* Red Peppers, *I hated playing* The Astonished Heart. *It depressed me. I loved playing* Brief Encounter, *or* Still Life *as it was called.*

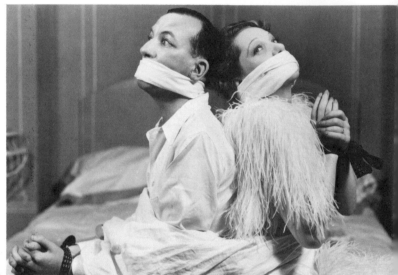

Shortly after the London opening Noël received word from the Palace that King Edward VII would like seats for one of the performances.

NOËL COWARD:

Of course I was delighted that he wanted to come, but word didn't reach me till late in the afternoon, and he wanted seats for himself and his party for that evening's performance. The theatre was booked solidly for weeks ahead, and I had no alternative but to ask friends of mine who I knew would be at that evening's performance to give up their seats—which they very kindly did. The King came, and afterwards went back-stage to Gertie's dressing-room and spent half an hour with her. To my astonishment, he left the theatre without so much as thanking me for the seats.

Now as I happened to have been the author, the star, and the producer of the show, I thought it rather ill-mannered of him, and got word through letting him know.

'Tell him', I said, 'that he may be the King of England, but I'm the King of the Theatre and I expect him to respect me as such.'

The reply he sent back was, 'Tell Noël Coward to go and . . . himself.'

I took my hat off to him for that—he managed to knock me down a peg or two!

When Noël appeared in the film version of *The Astonished Heart* with Celia Johnson and Margaret Leighton, he said of his two leading ladies, 'The only thing that prevents Celia Johnson from becoming the greatest actress of her time is her monotonous habit of having babies.'

And defining the difference between the two actresses, 'Margaret is so *chic!* Celia is so *understanding!*'

MARGARET LEIGHTON:

top left, *Red Peppers.*
top right, *Family Album.*
centre left, *Hands Across the Sea,* Gertrude Lawrence (Lady Maureen Gilpin) and Everley Gregg as the Hon. Clare Wedderburn.
centre, *Ways and Means.*
centre right, *Shadow Play.*
bottom left, *We Were Dancing.*
bottom right, *Fumed Oak.*

Before The Astonished Heart, *Noël sent me to Molyneux to get my clothes, and I had everything made there. I don't mean he paid for them, but he supervised the whole operation, demanded the right dresser and so forth, and they very kindly took me on and I became terribly well dressed. Noël always makes one feel so good—unless one isn't good . . . When I was with him, he'd make me feel I was a million dollars, and I'd think, 'Well, I'm not that bad after all. I'm wearing a Molyneux frock, and he makes me feel a treat.' That's a great thing about him, and it's a gift that's dying out now. Men don't know how to do that any more . . .* [except Michael Wilding, of course].

I enjoyed doing The Astonished Heart *enormously. It was the first thing I ever did with Noël. We had one long love scene on the sofa which lasted for three days, and Noël and I were glued together like those fish that stick to*

NOEL COWARD · CELIA JOHNSON · MARGARET LEIGHTON (By permission of London Film Productions Ltd.)
in NOEL COWARD'S THE ASTONISHED HEART with JOYCE CAREY · GRAHAM PAYN
Screenplay by NOEL COWARD. Produced by ANTONY DARNBOROUGH. A Directed by TERENCE FISHER and ANTONY DARNBOROUGH.

above, Margaret Leighton.
far right, Gerald Road studio
flat.

rocks. We sat on this damned sofa and I was trying my best, hoping to be all right. 'I'm awfully sorry,' I said to him, 'I'm a dreadful bore. You'll get frightfully bored with me in the space of half an hour.' But he put up with me for three days on that sofa.

And then he used to ask me out occasionally. He had a studio flat in Gerald Road in those days, and I would go to all his big parties. You always saw the Duchess of Kent— Princess Marina—and all the nibs and nobs, and when I first went, I was terrified. But he had this wonderful ability of building you up. I'd just done the two scenes with him on the film, and he said, 'Oh I do want you to meet Margaret Leighton,' and he told some story about me that sounded so fascinating and humorous and funny and gay and jolly— and I'd said nothing of the kind! I just kept thinking that I'd bored him stiff on that sofa for those three days.

He always found out when I was in any trouble, which I constantly was. For eight years I was in permanent trouble, and he did things to help out. He was always on the move, and used to leave an itinerary where he would be. 'I'll be in Bangkok on March 15th, then I shall be . . .' and left a list when he took off from London so that I'd know where to find him when I needed him.

Hugh (Binkie) Beaumont has presented some of the finest plays in the West End of London.

BINKIE BEAUMONT:

I met Noël during Private Lives *at the Phoenix Theatre, and we became firm and lasting friends. In those days I was a young aspiring manager, and Noël gave me invaluable, generous advice, kindness and help. He introduced me to*

CELIA JOHNSON:

everyone one could possibly want to help one's career, but it wasn't really until Tonight at Eight-Thirty *that we worked together. The first time I was connected with him was at the Phoenix Theatre, in* Tonight at Eight-Thirty, *and from then to his last season at the Queen's,* Suite in Three Keys, *I've really done nearly all his plays. And it's the most stimulating experience to work with him. He's quick, he's excitable, but absolutely thrilling and stimulating.*

It never occurred to us, at least it certainly didn't occur to me, that the film Brief Encounter *was going to be—well, I suppose it's become a sort of classic, but we just thought it would be a nice interesting little film. And we were very lucky because it was Noël's script and we had David Lean directing, and then of course there was Trevor Howard, who in those days was hardly known at all. So that it was an amazing sort of happy conglomeration of people and talents. And David Lean having originally been a film cutter has this wonderful eye for cutting.*

I remember Noël sending for me and reading me the play. As you can imagine, I was pretty delighted to be offered such a nice part. A wonderful part. But I really found the whole thing very different to any other film I'd done because being in practically every shot one got to know much more about filming than ever before. And one realised their difficulties as well as one's own. Before, one had always been rather sort of—kept apart from technicians, who I think are always rather frightened of actors. In fact actors are frightened of technicians. So that became fascinating in a way.

We had fun, quite often, doing the station scenes in Lancashire, because it was during wartime, and we had to be away from the coast because it was pre-D-Day and one was allowed to have lights up there on the station. The trains used to come through at night, and in those days they were lovely steam trains, and they screamed in the distance, a high-pitched scream at seeing our lights on the station, and then they'd come hurtling through, all lovely smoke and flame flying behind them. We used to stay up all night in order to hear this and see Scottish expresses go through.

I remember doing the scene with the train hurtling through and trying to get away from the chatting lady and thinking —this is the end for me, I shall finish myself off. And again it had to be done in bits—one bit with the train, one bit with a close-up of just wind and things—and trying to keep it together is difficult, and then coming back into the station waiting-room. And when I see it now, I think, never do that again. That's quite wrong. But that probably happens to everybody doing films, one always thinks one could have done it better, one always thinks, 'never let me catch you doing that again', but you do.

I'm so grateful to Noël for giving me the chance to film because I don't think anybody else would have succeeded in doing so. So I have a lot to thank him for.

Celia Johnson and Trevor Howard in *Brief Encounter* (1946).

144

'Still Life' from
'Tonight at Eight-Thirty'

(Filmed as 'Brief Encounter')
(Taken from Scene Two)

The action takes place in the
refreshment room of Milford Junction
Station. Laura (Gertrude Lawrence) an
ordinary, respectable married housewife,
and Alec (Noël Coward) a married doctor,
have met briefly before while awaiting
their trains for their respective
destinations. They had agreed to meet
again this afternoon - and are now
waiting for their trains home after
their day out.

ALEC: We haven't done anything wrong.

LAURA: Of course we haven't.

ALEC: An accidental meeting - then another
           accidental meeting - then a little
           lunch - then the movies - what could be
           more ordinary? More natural?

LAURA: We're adults, after all.

ALEC: I never see myself as an adult, do you?

LAURA: (Firmly) Yes, I do. I'm a respectable
           married woman with a husband and a home
           and three children.

ALEC: But there must be a part of you, deep
           down inside, that doesn't feel like that
           at all - some little spirit that still
           wants to climb out of the window - that
           still longs to splash about a bit in the
           dangerous sea.

LAURA: Perhaps we none of us ever grow up
           entirely.

ALEC: How awfully nice you are!

LAURA: You said that before.

ALEC: I thought perhaps you hadn't heard.

LAURA: I heard all right.

ALEC: (Gently) I'm respectable too, you know.
           I have a home and a wife and children
           and responsibilities - I also have a lot
           of work to do and a lot of ideals all
           mixed up with it.

LAURA:	What's she like?
ALEC:	Madeleine?
LAURA:	Yes.
ALEC:	Small, dark, rather delicate –
LAURA:	How funny! I should have thought she'd be fair.
ALEC:	And your husband? What's he like?
LAURA:	Medium height, brown hair, kindly, unemotional and not delicate at all.
ALEC:	You said that proudly.
LAURA:	Did I? (She looks down)
ALEC:	What's the matter?
LAURA:	The matter? What could be the matter?
ALEC:	You suddenly went away.
LAURA:	(Brightly) I thought perhaps we were being rather silly.
ALEC:	Why?
LAURA:	Oh, I don't know – we are such complete strangers, really.
ALEC:	It's one thing to close a window, but quite another to slam it down on my fingers.
LAURA:	I'm sorry.
ALEC:	Please come back again.
LAURA:	Is tea bad for one? Worse than coffee, I mean.
ALEC:	If this is a professional interview, my fee is a guinea.
LAURA:	(Laughing) It's nearly time for your train.
ALEC:	I hate to think of it, chugging along, interrupting our tea party.
LAURA:	I really am sorry now.
ALEC:	What for?
LAURA:	For being disagreeable.
ALEC:	I don't think you could be disagreeable.
LAURA:	You said something just now about your work and ideals being mixed up with it – what ideals?
ALEC:	That's a long story.
LAURA:	I suppose all doctors ought to have ideals, really – otherwise I should think the work would be unbearable.
ALEC:	Surely you're not encouraging me to talk shop?

LAURA:	Do you come here every Thursday?
ALEC:	Yes. I come in from Churley, and spend a day in the hospital. Stephen Lynn graduated with me — he's the chief physician here. I take over from him once a week, it gives him a chance to go up to London and me a chance to observe and study the hospital patients.
LAURA:	Is that a great advantage?
ALEC:	Of course. You see I have a special pigeon.
LAURA:	What is it?
ALEC:	Preventive medicine.
LAURA:	Oh, I see.
ALEC:	(<u>Laughing</u>) I'm afraid you don't.
LAURA:	I was trying to be intelligent.
ALEC:	Most good doctors, especially when they're young, have private dreams — that's the best part of them. Sometimes, though, those get over-professionalised and strangulated and — am I boring you?
LAURA:	No — I don't quite understand — but you're not boring me.
ALEC:	What I mean is this — all good doctors must be primarily enthusiasts. They must have, like writers and painters, and priests, a sense of vocation — a deep-rooted, unsentimental desire to do good.
LAURA:	Yes — I see that.
ALEC:	Well, obviously one way of preventing disease is worth fifty ways of curing it — that's where my ideal comes in — preventive medicine isn't anything to do with medicine at all, really — it's concerned with conditions, living conditions and commonsense and hygiene. For instance, my speciality is pneumoconiosis.
LAURA:	Oh, dear!
ALEC:	Don't be alarmed, it's simpler than it sounds — it's nothing but a slow process of fibrosis of the lung due to the inhalation of particles of dust. In the hospital here there are splendid opportunities for observing cures and making notes, because of the coal mines.
LAURA:	You suddenly look much younger.

147

ALEC:	(Brought up short) Do I?
LAURA:	Almost like a little boy.
ALEC:	What made you say that?
LAURA:	(Staring at him) I don't know - yes, I do.
ALEC:	(Gently) Tell me.
LAURA:	(With panic in her voice) Oh, no - I couldn't, really. You were saying about the coal mines -
ALEC:	(Looking into her eyes) Yes - the inhalation of coal dust - that's one specific form of the diseases - it's called anthracosis.
LAURA:	(Hypnotised) What are the others?
ALEC:	Chalicosis - that comes from metal dust - steel works, you know -
LAURA:	Yes, of course. Steel works.
ALEC:	And silicosis - stone dust - that's gold mines.
LAURA:	(Almost in a whisper) I see. (There is the sound of a bell) There's your train.
ALEC:	(Looking down) Yes.
LAURA:	You mustn't miss it.
ALEC:	No.
LAURA:	(Again the panic in her voice) What's the matter?
ALEC:	(With an effort) Nothing - nothing at all.
LAURA:	(Socially) It's been so very nice - I've enjoyed my afternoon enormously.
ALEC:	I'm so glad - so have I. I apologise for boring you with those long medical words -
LAURA:	I feel dull and stupid, not to be able to understand more.
ALEC:	Shall I see you again? (There is the sound of a train approaching)
LAURA:	It's the other platform, isn't it? You'll have to run. Don't worry about me - mine's due in a few minutes.
ALEC:	Shall I see you again?
LAURA:	Of course - perhaps you could come over to Ketchworth one Sunday. It's rather far, I know, but we should be delighted to see you.

ALEC:	(Intensely) Please - please - (The train is heard drawing to a standstill)
LAURA:	What is it?
ALEC:	Next Thursday - the same time -
LAURA:	No - I can't possibly - I -
ALEC:	Please - I ask you most humbly -
LAURA:	You'll miss your train!
ALEC:	All right. (He gets up)
LAURA:	Run -
ALEC:	(Taking her hand) Good-bye.
LAURA:	(Breathlessly) I'll be there.
ALEC:	Thank you, my dear.
	(He goes out at a run, colliding with the ticket inspector, who is on his way in.)
TICKET INSPECTOR:	'Ere - 'ere - take it easy now - take it easy - (Laura sits quite still staring in front of her as the lights fade.)
JOYCE CAREY:	*Sweet Aloes was just closing on Broadway and Noël telephoned me from London to say that Alison Leggat, who was in* Tonight at Eight-Thirty, *was ill, and could I come over to take over all her parts. There were six or seven of them—more were added later—and so they sent them over by special delivery and I learnt them all on the ship back to England, and arrived full of excitement to rehearse a couple of times, and then Gertie Lawrence got ill and they closed the theatre and everybody went away on holiday for three weeks, and I was left in a frenzy of nerves, forgetting all the parts!*

Gertrude Lawrence was at that time facing the bankruptcy courts, and working day and night to pay her debts. She was appearing in the demanding roles of *Tonight at Eight-Thirty* in the evenings, and filming *Rembrandt* during the daytime with Charles Laughton. Not surprisingly she was suffering from nervous exhaustion.

JOYCE CAREY: *But of course later on when it was all back to normal, it was the most wonderful engagement and when we went to New York, it was such a success that the success itself sort of rubbed off on all the company, and we had the most wonderful season there. Thrilling it was.*

Sybil Thorndike and her husband Lewis Casson later toured England with *Fumed Oak* and *Hands Across the Sea*.

SYBIL THORNDIKE: *I rather liked our actual production of it, but we played it differently from the way Noël and Gertie played it. You see Noël wrote bigger than he knew. When he came to produce his own plays, he emphasised the cruelty side, and when we played it, we put the emphasis the other way—we played it more for pity and sympathy than for cruelty, but I don't think we were right, because none of us were as skilled as Noël at playing that sort of comedy.*

Noël and Gertie went with the plays to America, but before the end of their successful run Noël himself collapsed from physical and nervous exhaustion—he was playing nine strenuous roles—and the plays closed on Broadway a month ahead of time. It was his second breakdown in ten years. He was sent to Bermuda to recover, and, on his return to London, retired to Goldenhurst. His doctors advised him not to appear on stage again for at least two years.

above, Jack Wilson and Natasha Paley.
right, Phyllis Monkman.

Noël was now asked by Binkie Beaumont to take over the direction of the Broadway production of Gerald Savory's West End success *George and Margaret*, which had run in London for two years. The New York production was already in rehearsal in Manchester, but the director had resigned after backstage disagreements, and Noël agreed to take over the last week's rehearsal on condition that neither his name nor the name of any other director be displayed in American advertising for the play. Although he altered it slightly for American audiences, he was sceptical of the play's chances in America. As it turned out he was right, for it ran for scarcely two months.

In the wake of his illness and this failure came the news that his father had died. Shortly afterwards Jack Wilson married Russian-born Princess Natasha Paley. For the first time in his life Noël felt very much alone.

SHROUDED IN DEAD SECRECY

Noël stayed on in America to complete a new musical comedy for Peggy Wood and the Viennese singer Fritzi Massary, who came out of retirement to appear in it. The story of *Operette* concerns a Gaiety Girl who achieves stardom overnight. Perhaps it was hoped that by some sympathetic magic the play would follow its own pattern, but . . .

NOËL COWARD:

I remember peering from my box at the Opera House, Manchester, and watching bewildered playgoers rustling the programme and feverishly striking matches in a frantic effort to discover where they were and what was going on.

Musical comedy star Phyllis Monkman was one of the stars at the Alhambra before the First World War and became André Charlot's leading lady in revues at the Comedy. One of the *Co-optimists*, she was Jack Buchanan's partner for over three years in London and Paris. She appeared in *Operette*.

PHYLLIS MONKMAN:

When we opened in Manchester, Noël quite often used to conduct the orchestra. After a few lines, I used to go into a dance and he would pick up the baton, look at me, and wait. So I would wait too. And there we were, both waiting for the cue from one another, sticking it out until neither of us could bear it any longer, and then we'd start together, shrieking with laughter.

When he came back-stage I said, 'Noël, you really ought to be ashamed of yourself, behaving so disgracefully.'

And he said, wagging his finger at me, 'My behaving badly is better than being the oldest soubrette in the business'!

'The Stately Homes of England'
from 'Operette'

Lord Elderley, Lord Borrowmere,
Lord Sickert and Lord Camp,
With every virtue, every grace,
Ah what avails the sceptred race,
Here you see – the four of us
And there are so many more of us
Eldest sons that must succeed.
We know that Caesar conquered Gaul
And how to whack a cricket ball;
Apart from this, our education
Lacks co-ordination.
Though we're young and tentative
And rather rip-representative,
Scions of a noble breed,
We are the products of those homes
    serene and stately
Which only lately seem to have run to
    seed!

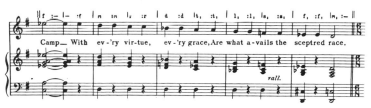

Camp— With ev-'ry vir-tue, ev-'ry grace, Are what a-vails the sceptred race.

rall.

The Stately Homes of England,
How beautiful they stand,
To prove the upper classes
Still have the upper hand;
Though the fact that they have to be
    rebuilt,
And frequently mortgaged to the hilt,
Is inclined to take the gilt
Off the gingerbread,
And certainly damps the fun
Of the eldest son –
But still we won't be beaten,
We'll scrimp and scrape and save,
The playing fields of Eton
Have made us frightfully brave –
And though if the Van Dycks have to go
And we pawn the Bechstein Grand,
We'll stand
By the Stately Homes of England.

E - ton Have made us frightfully brave— And tho' if the Van Dycks have to go And we
sleep there In case they tum-ble down;— But still if they ev - er catch on fire Which, with

OPERETTE

JOHN C. WILSON PRESENTS
OPERETTE BY NOËL COWARD

PRICE 2/6 NET

Vocal Score . 8/-

Dearest Love . . . . 2/- ◆ The Stately Homes of England . . . . . .
Where Are the Songs We Sung . . . . . . 2/- ◆ Countess Mitzi . . . .
Operette . . . . 2/- ◆ Piano Selection . . . .

CHAPPELL
PRINTED IN ENGLAND

748

Beatrice Lillie in *Set to Music*.

NOËL COWARD:

Within a few days of *Operette*'s opening, in March 1938, Noël left London again. Lord Mountbatten, aware that a war was imminent, asked him to travel around the Mediterranean fleet, making a survey of the sort of films the different ranks would like to see on board ship, the films to be supplied by the Royal Naval Film Corporation. As a consequence of this complaints were voiced, and questions asked in Parliament about his being shuttled around by the Royal Navy at public expense.

On his return, Noël set about preparing *Words and Music* for America under the new title *Set to Music*.

In its new form the revue was designed as a vehicle for Beatrice Lillie. An inspired and superbly inventive comedienne on stage, Bea Lillie was equally zany and incorrigible off, and during rehearsals drove Noël and the entire company nearly to distraction with her antics and practical jokes.

If I loathed her with every quivering fibre of my being, which at certain dress rehearsals I have done, I still have to admit that a visit with Bea Lillie is one of the most enchanting things that could happen to anyone.

The first night of *Set to Music* in New York in December 1938 was a brilliant success. Brooks Atkinson wrote in the *New York Times*: 'Whether Noël Coward is Beatrice Lillie's best friend or whether the honours are the other way round is an academic question at best. For the simple fact is that *Set to Music*, which was set to the Music Box last evening, represents both of them at their best. With his familiar prodigality of talents, Mr Coward has written it and staged it, sketches and songs alike, some of it having been retrieved from a revue he wrote for London last season. On the spur of the moment, it seems like the best show he has written. Although Miss Lillie has been synonymous with perfection in comedy for quite a long time, an old admirer might be forgiven for believing that she also is more incandescently witty now than before. For light amusement, written and acted with impeccable taste, this London revue is off the top of the pack.'

'I've been to a marvellous Party'
from 'Set to Music'

Quite for no reason
I'm here for the season
And high as a kite,

Living in error
With Maud at Cap Ferrat
Which couldn't be right.
Everyone's here and frightfully gay,
Nobody cares what people say,
Though the Riviera
Seems really much queerer
Than Rome at its height,
Yesterday night –

I went to a marvellous party
With Nounou and Nada and Nell,
It was in the fresh air,
And we went as we were,
And we stayed as we were
Which was hell.
Poor Grace started singing at midnight
And didn't stop singing till four;
We knew the excitement was bound to
    begin
When Laura got blind on Dubonnet and gin
And scratched her veneer with a Cartier
    pin,
I couldn't have liked it more.

I've been to a marvellous party,
I must say the fun was intense,
We all had to do
What the people we knew
Would be doing a hundred years hence.
Dear Cecil arrived wearing armour,
Some shells and a black feather boa,
Poor Millicent wore a surrealist comb
Made of bits of mosaic from St Peter's
    in Rome,
But the weight was so great that she had
    to go home,
I couldn't have liked it more!

People's behaviour
Away from Belgravia
Would make you aghast;
So much variety
Watching Society
Scampering past.
If you have any mind at all
Gibbon's divine Decline and Fall

```
Seems pretty flimsy,
No more than a whimsy,
By way of contrast
On Saturday last -

I've been to a marvellous party,
We didn't start dinner till ten
And young Bobbie Carr
Did a stunt at the bar
With a lot of extraordinary men;
Dear Baba arrived with a turtle
Which shattered us all to the core,
The Grand Duke was dancing a foxtrot
  with me
When suddenly Cyril screamed
  'Fiddlededee'
And ripped off his trousers and jumped
  in the sea,
I couldn't have liked it more.
```

Cole Lesley first started working for Noël as his Man Friday before the war, and over the years became his private secretary, adviser, administrator and close companion.

COLE LESLEY:

Noël returned to Goldenhurst early in 1939 to begin writing Present Laughter *and* This Happy Breed. *It was the first time that I was really conscious of his tremendous concentration and dedication to his work, and his enormous self-discipline. He has always been self-disciplined in whatever he does. If he had to lose weight, then he was very disciplined about that. He's never drunk much, but could cut it out altogether when he felt like doing so. He still smokes, and I think he always will.*

I was very young when I first came to him, and of course terribly impressed. I thought sometimes that it was a bit exaggerated, being called at half past six in the morning, but I soon realised that he was quite right. Even in the winter he'd be at his writing table by eight at the latest, and work until one o'clock. Absolute application and self-discipline. At eleven o'clock I used to go up with coffee, and if he was working away with a good flow, then I'd put down the coffee tray very quietly and go. Some mornings he'd say, 'Oh, so glad you've come, Coley, I'm having a terrible time. *Let's have some coffee and talk about it.' Which we'd do. Then other times he'd be delighted at what he'd done and say, 'I'm glad you've come, Coley, sit down and I'll read you what I've done.' Great enthusiasm. Things were going well. And that was very exciting.*

Of course he was quite right to work in the mornings, because come lunchtime he'd earned the enjoyment of the rest of the day, and we would then go and see a double-feature movie in Folkestone or Ashford, and go back home. He'd have a drink, early dinner, and retire early to bed to start again early the next day.

And so the image of him as a playboy—all those first nights in London and the long cigarette-holder—was entirely forgotten. No social engagements were accepted until the job was done, and he'd got the idea on paper. He was never diverted until he'd finished the job, and was pleased with it.

NOËL COWARD: *I have an absolutely routine, disciplined mind. When I'm*

Vivien Leigh, Kay Kendall,
Noël, Lauren Bacall.

writing I'm at my desk and hope that by lunchtime some-
thing will have appeared. Sometimes it doesn't until about
ten to one. Sometimes it flows from the word go. You can't
tell. But you can only do it by doing it regularly, as
Maugham always did—he used to go to his little house in
the garden and sit at his desk and wait for something to
happen. When it did, it was summer indoors, and when it
didn't, it was bloody awful.

My advice to aspiring writers is to write, and try where
possible in doing so to use a little critical faculty. Sit down
at the desk and wait until something happens, as Maugham
did. Write. Work, and above all, read everything you can
lay your hands on. All of Shakespeare, all of Shaw, all
Dickens. It's quite enough to feed the brain, and I find
when reading a great classic I nearly always come away
with knowledge and a penny.

The two new plays completed, Noël took another holiday
abroad, this time choosing Scandinavia and Russia. In a
hotel in Leningrad he turned on a tap and found, to his
dismay, tadpoles streaming out instead of water. He sent
for the Hotel Manager.

'In England,' he informed him, 'when we want hot
water, we turn on the tap marked Hot Water. When we
want cold water, we turn on the tap marked Cold Water.
When we want tadpoles, we turn on the tap marked
Tadpoles.'

He returned to England in September 1939 for the
Manchester opening of *Present Laughter* and *This Happy
Breed*, but during rehearsals war broke out. At once he was
given a job in the British Information Service, setting up a
Bureau of Propaganda in Paris, to be operated in con-
junction with the French Ministry of Information, then
being run by Jean Giraudoux. The plays, needless to say,
were suspended.

NOËL COWARD: *We were three days off opening and I had to call the com-*
pany on stage to say that I'd already contracted to do a job in
propaganda in Paris. That was a terrible day. But then
later on in 1942 it was all right, I played in Present
Laughter *and* This Happy Breed *myself.* Present
Laughter *was great fun—and naturally my favourite part*
—it's got all the things I like best in it. I get all the effect—
being there, in the centre of the stage.

In that production, Judy Cornwall played Joanna, but later, in 1947, Moira Lister was cast.

MOIRA LISTER:

I had been doing a year's tour with John Clements and Kay Hammond in The King Maker *and* Marriage à la Mode, *and my agent said, 'There's an audition for* Present Laughter. *They want a rather glamorous lady.' Well I had precisely two pennies to rub together at that time, and I thought I can never look glamorous on this, so I went to my local milliner and said, 'Can you lend me a glamorous hat?' And she lent me this great big black hat, and I wore a plain simple dress.*

Now Fanny Rowe was in the cast of the plays we were doing on tour, and she rang me up on the day of the audition and said, 'Why don't we have lunch today?' And I said, 'Super. But I have to leave early for a three o'clock appointment.' I didn't want to tell her I was going for an audition. We decided to have lunch at the Ivy, but she didn't have any more money than I did, so we agreed to go Dutch. I arrived in my simple black dress, the hat out to here, feeling fantastic, and she arrived in a simple black dress and a mink coat. *She didn't ask, 'Where did you get the hat?' And I didn't ask, 'Where did you get the mink coat?'*

All through lunch we both looked at our watches and said, 'I've got an appointment at three, I must leave promptly,' but neither would say what for. So at twenty to three we both got up. 'Your appointment. My appointment.' We leave the Ivy. I call for a taxi. She calls for a taxi. We both get into our respective taxis and all the way to the Haymarket I see this taxi following me and I think, 'What the devil is Fanny Rowe following me for? She knows I have an appointment. What's she up to?' My taxi gets to the stage door of the Haymarket Theatre and stops, and her taxi stops behind me. We both get out.

'Fanny, what are you doing here?'

'I didn't want to tell you', she said, 'I've got an audition'.

'For Christ's sake, what part are you auditioning for?'

'Joanna'.

'So am I!'

Anyway, I got on the stage, and having just got back from my first trip to Switzerland, I had rather a good tan.

Noël was sitting out front, and he called up to me, 'Where have you come from?'

'I've been ski-ing', I said.

'I see,' he replied. 'I hope you didn't get them up your nose.' But I was too nervous to get the joke.

However, I did the audition and got the part, and when it came to rehearsals I decided to model the part of Joanna on a woman I knew in South Africa, whom I always admired. She was a great beauty and her husband was very rich. Any fellow who came into her net was literally caught. There was nothing obvious about her, though. She was not young, but she had all the physical attributes and this wonderful innocent quality that Marilyn Monroe had. And Joanna was very much like that—a femme fatale *on the make but with a very delicate approach to it, and I think that's what I looked for because she was the only woman I knew who could do this kind of thing—it was the economy with which she made all her conquests that I used as the key-note.*

Noël was fantastic technically. When you're onstage with him you know he is in control therefore you play to him, and you model your performance on what you think is right for him.

We played it in Liverpool. We only had a week out, and then we came in to London. It was my first commercial success, and I was frightened out of my mind of Noël. I couldn't talk to him, I couldn't get near him, I was afraid to speak to him at all. Ten minutes before the curtain went up on the opening night in London he sent for me and I thought, 'Oh well, that's it. I'm no good. I'll be asked to leave.' So I went down to his dressing room, absolutely shaking, and knocked on the door.

'Come in.'

I went in and he said, 'Moira, I'm very pleased with you. You've done a wonderful job on tour. We're opening in ten minutes time and I'd like to give you a little present.'

I was absolutely overcome. I said, 'No. Please. Honestly. It's such an honour working with you. You don't have to do it . . .'

'Don't be silly,' he said, and he went over to his dressing table and picked up a little bottle of perfume. A really tiny bottle, half full. He gave it to me with a magnanimous gesture and said, 'There you are, Moira. That's for you. I have used the other half.'

'Present Laughter'

(Taken from Act Two – Scene One)

Garry Essendine (Noël Coward) is a
famous West End actor. He is arrogant,
knowing and handsome. He is separated
from his wife, and enjoys playing the
field. But he is thrown when the
ravishingly beautiful Joanna (Moira
Lister) sets her cap and plays him at
his own game. Although she is married,
she is having an affair with a close
friend of Garry's in order to gain
access to Garry. Tonight her husband is
out of town, and she has arrived at
Garry's apartment rather late,
determined to succeed. Garry, however,
is too aware of her intentions. Garry
opens the door to Joanna. She is
exquisitely dressed, in her early
thirties. She has a great deal of
assurance and considerable charm.

JOANNA: I can't tell you how relieved I am that
you're in. I've done the most idiotic
thing.

GARRY: Why, what's happened?

JOANNA: I've forgotten my latch-key!

GARRY: Oh, Joanna!

JOANNA: It's no good looking at me like that –
I'm not in the least inefficient as a
rule, this is the first time I've ever
done such a thing in my life. I'm in an
absolute fury. I had to dress in the
most awful rush to dine with Freda and
go to the Toscanini concert and I left
it in my other bag.

GARRY: And I suppose the servants sleep at the
top of the house.

JOANNA:	They do more than sleep, they apparently go off into a coma. I've been battering on the door for nearly half an hour.
GARRY:	Would you like a drink?
JOANNA:	Very much indeed - I'm exhausted. (She takes off her cloak)
GARRY:	(Mixing a drink for her and himself) We must decide what's best to be done.
JOANNA:	I went to a call office and rang up Liz but she must be out because there wasn't a reply.
GARRY:	(Looking at her) You rang up Liz and there wasn't any reply!
JOANNA:	Yes, and as I hadn't any more coppers and the taxi man hadn't either, I came straight here.
GARRY:	Cigarette?
JOANNA:	(Taking one) Thank you - You're looking very whimsical, don't you believe me?
GARRY:	(Lighting her cigarette) Of course I believe you, Joanna. Why on earth shouldn't I?
JOANNA:	I don't know, you always look at me as though you didn't trust me an inch. It's a shame, because I'm so nice really.
GARRY:	(Smiling) I'm sure you are, Joanna.
JOANNA:	I know that voice, Garry, you've used it in every play you've ever been in.
GARRY:	Complete naturalness on the stage is my strong suit.
JOANNA:	You've never liked me really, have you?
GARRY:	No, not particularly.
JOANNA:	I wonder why.
GARRY:	I always had the feeling you were rather tiresome.
JOANNA:	In what way tiresome?
GARRY:	Oh, I don't know. There's a certain arrogance about you, a little too much self-assurance.
JOANNA:	You don't care for competition, I see.
GARRY:	You're lovely-looking, of course, I've always thought that.
JOANNA:	(Smiling) Thank you.
GARRY:	. . . if perhaps a little too aware of it.
JOANNA:	(Doing up her face in the glass from

	her bag) You're being conventionally odious but somehow it doesn't quite ring true. But then you never do quite ring true, do you? I expect it's because you're an actor, they're always apt to be a bit papiermaché.
GARRY:	Just puppets, Joanna dear, creatures of tinsel and sawdust, how clever of you to have noticed it.
JOANNA:	I wish you'd stop being suave just for a minute.
GARRY:	What would you like me to do, fly into a tantrum? Burst into tears?
JOANNA:	(Looking down) I think I should like you to be kind.
GARRY:	Kind?
JOANNA:	Yes. At least kind enough to make an effort to overcome your perfectly obvious prejudice against me.
GARRY:	I'm sorry it's so obvious.
JOANNA:	I'm not quite an idiot, although I must say you always treat me as if I were. I know you resented me marrying Henry, you all did, and I entirely see why you should have, anyhow at first. But after all that's five years ago, and during that time I've done my best not to obtrude myself, not to encroach on any special preserves. My reward has been rather meagre, from you particularly, nothing but artificial politeness and slightly frigid tolerance.
GARRY:	Poor Joanna.
JOANNA:	(Rising) I see my appeal has fallen on stony ground. I'm so sorry.
GARRY:	What is all this? What are you up to?
JOANNA:	I'm not up to anything.
GARRY:	Then sit down again.
JOANNA:	I'd like you to call me a taxi.
GARRY:	Nonsense, there's nothing you'd hate more. You came here for a purpose, didn't you?
JOANNA:	Of course I did. I lost my key, I knew you had a spare room and –
GARRY:	Well?
JOANNA:	I wanted to get to know you a little better.

GARRY:	I see.
JOANNA:	Oh no you don't. I know exactly what you think. Of course I can't altogether blame you. In your position as one of the world's most famous romantic comedians, it's only natural that you should imagine that every woman is anxious to hurl herself at your head. I'm sure, for instance, that you don't believe for a moment that I've lost my latch-key!
GARRY:	You're good - my God, you're good!
JOANNA:	What's the number of the taxi rank? I'll ring up myself.
GARRY:	Sloane 2664.
	(Joanna dials the number and waits a moment)
JOANNA:	Hallo - Hallo . . . Is that Sloane 2664? - Oh, I'm so sorry, it's the wrong number.
	(Garry collapses on to the sofa laughing)
	What are you laughing at?
GARRY:	You, Joanna.
JOANNA:	(Dialling again) You're enjoying yourself enormously, aren't you.
GARRY:	(Jumping up and taking the telephone out of her hand) You win.
JOANNA:	Give me that telephone and don't be so infuriating.
GARRY:	Have another drink?
JOANNA:	No, thank you.
GARRY:	Just one more cigarette?
JOANNA:	No.
GARRY:	Please - I'm sorry.
	(Joanna rises and walks back to the sofa in silence)
JOANNA:	I wish you were really sorry.
GARRY:	(Handing her another cigarette) Maybe I am.
JOANNA:	I could cry now, you know, very effectively, if only I had the technique.
GARRY:	Technique's terribly important.
JOANNA:	Oh dear.
GARRY:	(Lighting her cigarette) Conversation seems to have come to a standstill.

165

JOANNA:	I think perhaps I would like another drink after all, a very small one. You make me feel extraordinarily self-conscious. Of course that's one of your most renowned gifts, isn't it, frightening people?
GARRY:	(Pouring out a drink) You're not going to pretend that I frighten you.
JOANNA:	Freda Lawson's terrified out of her life of you, she told me so the other day.
GARRY:	I can't imagine why, I hardly know her.
JOANNA:	It's personality, I expect, plus a reputation for being - well - (She laughs) - rather ruthless.
GARRY:	(Giving her her drink) Amorously or socially?
JOANNA:	Both.
GARRY:	Well - how are we doing?
JOANNA:	Better, I think.
GARRY:	That's a very pretty dress.
JOANNA:	I wore it for Toscanini.
GARRY:	He frightens people too, when they play wrong notes.
JOANNA:	You look strangely young every now and then. It would be nice to know what you were really like, under all the trappings.
GARRY:	Just a simple boy, stinking with idealism.

Noël left for Paris and took a flat in the Place Vendôme, but the British Press, unaware of his official status, started asking questions about his being supported in Paris by the British taxpayer. Since his activities were connected with Intelligence work a public explanation was out of the question, and obviously he was not permitted to give Press interviews.

I think the reason it was shrouded in absolute dead secrecy was that there was nothing of the least interest to be said about it. I ran a very efficient office and appeared at the office every morning at nine. We read through the monitors of the BBC, discussed the war situation, had lunch—and that went on for about six months. And then I got sick of doing absolutely nothing, and said I must have some leave to go to America for six weeks to get my mind clear. So I went, and then of course—bang—it went. [The fall of France, that is.] *And that was that.*

When I came back, I very nearly landed in Occupied France. Well, I did land, but there was a cordon round the plane so it was all right—I was protected from internment, thank God. But I'd have got up some entertainments, I suppose, even if I'd been interned.

Luckily he was prevented from boarding the train to Paris; it arrived there only twenty-four hours before the Germans did.

Back in England Noël organised the evacuation of the sixty children in the Actors' Orphanage. His farm in Kent having been requisitioned by the Army, he arranged for his mother and aunt to come to New York with him to help to organise homes for the orphan evacuees.

He toured America with shows in aid of the British war effort, during which time he had several meetings with President Roosevelt, 'to discuss Britain's participation in the war, and her prospects of winning it.' He was asked by the Australian and New Zealand Governments to tour their countries with similar shows and broadcasts and to give concerts at training camps in aid of the Red Cross and War Charities.

He went to Australia via China and Japan. The highlight of his visit to Shanghai was a broadcast whose tone, as he later remarked, 'was rather anti-Japanese, and as the Japs were in charge of the City, it was rather awkward'.

Back in London he found that his Gerald Road studio had suffered its share of bomb damage, and he moved to the Savoy. Soon, though, he decided that, as it was two years since he had done any serious writing, and as in any case he had nowhere to live, it would be a good idea

below, outside his Paris flat in the Place Vendome, 1940.
below right, broadcasting in Australia.

Original production of *Blithe Spirit* (Piccadilly Theatre) Margaret Rutherford, Kay Hammond, and Fay Compton.

to spend a week in Wales in search of inspiration. He took Joyce Carey with him, and wrote *Blithe Spirit*.

JOYCE CAREY:

We went to Portmeirion on a Friday. It was May. Saturday was the most beautiful day, so we sat on the beach all day, and Noël constructed the play. He got the names of all the characters, and plotted the story, and I just listened and possibly said once, 'But if you do this, what about that?'

He started writing it the next day, Sunday morning at eight-thirty, and finished it on the following Friday evening at six-thirty, and it came clean off the typewriter, and never had any alterations. Four lines were cut, I think.

'Blithe Spirit'
(Taken from Act One)

Charles Condomine (Cecil Parker) is writing a book, and has asked the local clairvoyant, Madame Arcati, to dinner so that he can study her methods of summoning someone from the past. She and the other guests have now left, and Charles and his second wife, Ruth (Fay Compton), sum up the evening's events. Unknown to them, Elvira (Kay Hammond), Charles's late first wife, has been successfully recalled, and is about to reveal herself.

RUTH: Would you say the evening has been profitable?

CHARLES: Yes – I suppose so.

RUTH:	I must say it was extremely funny at moments.
CHARLES:	Yes – it certainly was.
RUTH:	What's the matter?
CHARLES:	The matter?
RUTH:	Yes – you seem odd somehow – do you feel quite well?
CHARLES:	Perfectly. I think I'll have a drink. (Moves to drinks table and pours whisky-and-soda) Do you want one?
RUTH:	No thank you, dear.
CHARLES:	(Pouring himself a drink) It's rather chilly in this room.
RUTH:	Come over by the fire.
CHARLES:	I don't think I'll make any notes tonight – I'll start fresh in the morning. (Charles turns with glass in hand, sees Elvira and drops his glass on the floor) My God!
RUTH:	Charles!
ELVIRA:	That was very clumsy, Charles dear.
CHARLES:	Elvira! – then it's true – it was you!
ELVIRA:	Of course it was.
RUTH:	(Starts to go to Charles) Charles – darling Charles – what are you talking about?
CHARLES:	(To Elvira) Are you a ghost?
ELVIRA:	(Crosses to fire) I suppose I must be – it's all so confusing.
RUTH:	(Comes closely to Charles, becoming agitated) Charles – what do you keep looking over there for? Look at me – what's happened?
CHARLES:	Don't you see?
RUTH:	See what?
CHARLES:	Elvira.
RUTH:	(Staring at him incredulously) Elvira!
CHARLES:	(With an effort at social grace) Yes – Elvira, dear, this is Ruth – Ruth, this is Elvira. (Ruth tries to take his arm. Charles retreats downstage)
RUTH:	(With forced calmness) Come and sit down, darling.

CHARLES:	Do you mean to say you can't see her?
RUTH:	Listen, Charles - you just sit down quietly by the fire and I'll mix you another drink. Don't worry about the mess on the carpet - Edith can clean it up in the morning. (She takes him by the arm)
CHARLES:	(Breaking away) But you must be able to see her - she's there - look - right in front of you - there -
RUTH:	Are you mad? What's happened to you?
CHARLES:	You can't see her?
RUTH:	If this is a joke, dear, it's gone quite far enough. Sit down, for God's sake, and don't be idiotic.
CHARLES:	(Clutching his head) What am I to do - what the hell am I to do?
ELVIRA:	I think you might at least be a little more pleased to see me - after all, you conjured me up.
CHARLES:	I didn't do any such thing.
ELVIRA:	Nonsense, of course you did. That awful child with the cold came and told me you wanted to see me urgently.
CHARLES:	It was all a mistake - a horrible mistake.
RUTH:	Stop talking like that, Charles - as I told you before, the joke's gone far enough.
CHARLES:	I've gone mad, that's what it is - I've just gone raving mad.
RUTH:	(Pours out brandy and brings it to Charles) Here - drink this.
CHARLES:	(Mechanically - taking it) This is appalling!
RUTH:	Relax.
CHARLES:	How can I relax? I shall never be able to relax again as long as I live.
RUTH:	Drink some brandy.
CHARLES:	(Drinking it at a gulp) There, now - are you satisfied?
RUTH:	Now sit down.
CHARLES:	Why are you so anxious for me to sit down - what good will that do?
RUTH:	I want you to relax - you can't relax standing up.

ELVIRA:	African natives can – they can stand on one leg for hours.
CHARLES:	I don't happen to be an African native.
RUTH:	You don't happen to be a <u>what</u>?
CHARLES:	(<u>Savagely</u>) An African native!
RUTH:	What's that got to do with it?
CHARLES:	It doesn't matter, Ruth – really it doesn't matter – we'll say no more about it.
	(<u>Charles crosses to armchair and sits. Ruth crosses to him</u>)
CHARLES:	See, I've sat down.
RUTH:	Would you like some more brandy?
CHARLES:	Yes, please.
	(<u>Ruth goes to drinks table with glass</u>)
ELVIRA:	Very unwise – you always had a weak head.
CHARLES:	I could drink you under the table.
RUTH:	There's no need to be aggressive, Charles – I'm doing my best to help you.
CHARLES:	I'm sorry.
RUTH:	(<u>Crosses to Charles with brandy</u>) Here – drink this – and then we'll go to bed.
ELVIRA:	Get rid of her, Charles – then we can talk in peace.
CHARLES:	That's a thoroughly immoral suggestion, you ought to be ashamed of yourself.
RUTH:	What is there immoral in that?
CHARLES:	I wasn't talking to you.
RUTH:	Who were you talking to, then?
CHARLES:	Elvira, of course.
RUTH:	To hell with Elvira!
ELVIRA:	There, now – she's getting cross.
CHARLES:	I don't blame her.
RUTH:	What don't you blame her for?
CHARLES:	(<u>Rises and backs downstage a pace</u>) Oh, God!
RUTH:	Now, look here, Charles – I gather you've got some sort of plan behind all this. I'm not quite a fool. I suspected you when we were doing that idiotic seance . . .
CHARLES:	Don't be so silly – what plan could I have?
RUTH:	I don't know – it's probably something

	to do with the characters in your book – how they, or one of them would react to a certain situation – I refuse to be used as a guinea pig unless I'm warned beforehand what it's all about.
CHARLES:	(Moves towards Ruth) Elvira is here, Ruth – she's standing a few yards away from you.
RUTH:	(Sarcastically) Yes, dear, I can see her distinctly – under the piano with a zebra!
CHARLES:	But Ruth . . .
RUTH:	I'm not going to stay here arguing any longer . . .
ELVIRA:	Hurray!
CHARLES:	Shut up!
RUTH:	(Incensed) How dare you speak to me like that!
CHARLES:	Listen, Ruth – please listen –
RUTH:	I will not listen to any more of this nonsense – I'm going up to bed now, I'll leave you to turn out the lights. I shan't be asleep – I'm too upset. So you can come in and say goodnight to me if you feel like it.
ELVIRA:	That's big of her, I must say.
CHARLES:	Be quiet – you're behaving like a guttersnipe.
RUTH:	(Icily) That is all I have to say. Goodnight, Charles. (Ruth walks swiftly out of the room without looking at him again)
CHARLES:	(Follows Ruth to the door) Ruth . . .
ELVIRA:	That was one of the most enjoyable half-hours I've ever spent.
CHARLES:	(Puts down glass on drinks table) Oh, Elvira – how could you!

Sketches by
Anna Zinkeisen

Blithe Spirit.

JOYCE CAREY: Blithe Spirit *opened at the Piccadilly Theatre immediately after it had been written. Margaret Rutherford played Madame Arcati and Fay Compton was Ruth, Cecil Parker was Charles, and of course Kay Hammond played Elvira.*

On the first night there was an enormous bomb crater outside the theatre, and the quite smart audience had to pick its way over it in order to get in, and of course found the best comedy of the war playing inside.

Noël had been asked by an independent film production company, Two Cities, to submit an idea for a film. He was to have complete control over subject, cast and director. Not long afterwards he was lunching with his old friends, Lord and Lady Mountbatten, and learned at first hand of the sinking of the British destroyer H.M.S. *Kelly*, under Mountbatten's command, and from that account came the idea for the film. He wrote a scenario about the sinking of such a ship during wartime, and of the lives and families of the men who went down in her. The film was *In Which We Serve*. It was made with the Royal Navy's permission and Lord Mountbatten's support, took up the next year of Noël's working life, and proved the most difficult production he had ever undertaken.

NOËL COWARD: In Which We Serve *was an offshoot of* Cavalcade, *in a way. I love the Navy, I inherited my affection for it, all my mother's family were Navy. Admirals and Captains. I love anything to do with the Navy. To start with they've got the best manners in the world and I love the sea and Navy discipline, which is very hard. It wouldn't have frightened me because I'm quite disciplined anyway, and I'm used to accepting discipline. I would have loved to have been in the Navy.*

LORD MOUNTBATTEN: *Noël Coward and I met each other in 1924 and we became great friends at once, so much so that he used to come out to the Mediterranean when I was serving in the Fleet out there, and spend much of his summer holidays cruising with the Fleet in my ship. So he got to know the Navy very well, and the Navy got to know him well.*

When he produced Cavalcade *we said it was time he did a* Cavalcade *about the Navy, and I suggested he should do a film. He promised that if one day he had an idea, he would do it. The idea never came.*

Then came the war. I was given command of our newest, latest destroyer flotilla. My own ship was the Kelly. *Noël came on board on several occasions, particularly after we had had various disasters, like having been hit by mines and torpedoes. He talked to the officers, and got to know the story of the ship reasonably well as we went along. After we were sunk in May 1941, in the Battle of Crete, I met him at lunch and he asked me to tell him the story of how we were sunk. I did this and he was obviously very moved. Later on he came to me and said he now had an idea for the Naval film, provided I would agree that it should be about my ship. I was horrified, and of course wouldn't agree at all. He said it must be about a ship he knew something about because he didn't know enough about war at sea.*

'It's got to be genuine, it can't be counterfeit,' he said. 'Otherwise it would be immediately detected.' I agreed, provided that it couldn't be traced back in any way to the Kelly—and above all to me.

This he promised. But he didn't keep his promise. The very first script he showed me had the Captain married to Lady Celia Kinross, living in a large country house with a Rolls-Royce and a driver.

'Noël, this is the limit!' I said. 'This is pointing straight at me!'

He agreed, and so the car was turned into a Ford without a driver and his wife lost her title, and they lived in a small villa. Anyhow, he insisted on going ahead with this particular story and then I made certain other conditions.

'You must definitely make it about more than just the Captain,' I said. 'You must have a Chief Petty Officer, like a Chief Bosun's Mate. You must have a Junior Rating like an Ordinary Seaman. You must have their families, and they must be involved together. But above all, remember that the heroine of the story is the ship, certainly not the Captain or even the other men.' On these conditions I said I would help.

And I did my best to help him, and in fact he produced a film which as far as I was concerned was exactly like life at sea. All the survivors of the Kelly agreed that it was quite staggering to find how true to life the whole film had been.

But when Noël had finished the script, he showed it to the Ministry of Information to obtain the necessary permits to make the film which were required in time of war. The Head of the Film Division read the script and turned it down on the grounds that it was very bad propaganda. Noël saw me and together we went and called on the Minister himself, and this man was there. I asked why it was considered bad propaganda, and he replied, 'Here's a ship that doesn't achieve anything very much, doesn't sink any great ships and gets mined and bombed and torpedoed and finally sunk. Very bad propaganda.'

NOËL COWARD: *Can you imagine it? The Ministry of Information opposing*

174

it on the grounds of a ship sinking in wartime. When else do ships sink so frequently?

'But that's what the war at sea is all about,' Lord Mountbatten said. 'That's what's happening, we're out day and night fighting against all sorts of difficult enemies, against U-boats, against aeroplanes, against E-boats, and many ships and many of my friends are being sunk. That's what the war at sea's all about and it's time the story was told!'

'Well I suppose it can be shown in England,' the Official said, 'but it certainly mustn't be shown to any neutral nations, very bad propaganda, particularly in the United States.'

'I absolutely disagree!' Lord Mountbatten said. 'It's particularly in the United States they want to know what the Navy is doing, what war at sea is like, that's what they want to see.'

LORD MOUNTBATTEN: *By this time I was serving in Combined Operations Headquarters and in close touch with Noël. One day [during shooting] he asked me whether I could possibly get him a destroyer's ship's company from a ship that had recently been damaged, and was being repaired, to come with the clothes they wore when they were at sea, because he had no idea what they wore, and he certainly couldn't have got any active-bodied extras to take the part of a ship's company in the war. So we asked the Second Sea Lord, the Head of Naval Personnel of the Admiralty, and he very kindly sent such a ship's company along for four or five days down to Denham film studios where the film was being made.*

Noël very tactfully asked him to come and visit the shooting. He came down, was very impressed by the men and afterwards Noël said would he like to see some of the rushes. He agreed, and they showed him the scene on the mess deck when the Ordinary Seaman, played by John Mills, had to go and tell the Chief Petty Officer, played by Bernard Miles, that he had a letter from his young wife to say that Bernard Miles' wife had been killed in an air-raid in Plymouth. A very moving scene. The Admiral was very very emotional. 'By jove, Coward,' he said, 'that convinces me you were right to ask for a proper ship's company, real sailors. No actors could possibly have done that.'

Gladys Calthrop was responsible for the film's art direction.

GLADYS CALTHROP: *There was one very bad moment, because we'd had an enormous tank built for the sinking of the ship, and Noël* and I were standing together watching the actors prepare for the sequences which involved their jumping from the sinking ship into it, and Noël said, 'I don't think I like the look of that,' and I said that I didn't like the look of it either.

'Nonsense,' said David Lean, who was directing the film 'It's perfectly all right, it's been tried and it's safe as houses.'

However we stuck our toes in and said, 'No, we must have a rehearsal without the actors,' so they opened all the sluices. Thousands of gallons of water came flooding through, and the entire tank broke into a million pieces. There wasn't a splinter left. That saved a great many lives —including Noël's. He would have been standing on the bridge at the precise moment.

NOËL COWARD:

During filming one day, Gladys Calthrop, whose son Hugo had enlisted in the Navy, came to me and said, 'Could I have a word with you, Noël?'

'Yes of course. What is it?'

'It's about Hugo. I've just heard. He's been killed.'

'Well, there's nothing you can do about it, is there, dear?'

With Gladys Calthrop and David Lean filming *In Which We Serve* (1942).

I knew that if I sympathised for one moment she would have broken up, which she finally did, but not until months later after we'd completed the film. I admired her courage tremendously.

Celia Johnson played Noël's wife in the film:

CELIA JOHNSON: *I think if it hadn't been for Noël I should never have made a film at all. I was living down in the country most of the time, but my husband came home on leave and we were asked to a cocktail party, and Noël was at the same party. I hadn't seen him for a long time, and we did the usual sort of 'darling—darling,' thing.*

'What are you doing at the moment?' I asked him.

'I'm doing the most wonderful film,' he said, and told me about In Which We Serve.

'Why don't you give me a part in it?' I asked, rather brazenly.

He gave me a look of mock disdain, and when he'd recovered himself from my audacity, said, 'Right.'

But the film people didn't want me at all. They said, 'Oh no. Good actress, I daresay, but not photogenic.' In those days you had *to be photogenic. However, Noël wasn't having any of this, and said, 'You're supposed to be camera-men—photograph her!'*

So they shuddered a bit, and we had endless tests. I remember Noël and me reciting The Walrus and the Carpenter *to each other for the test, and it made us laugh. I wasn't a bit nervous in the end, and I found it perfectly fascinating acting with him. And then later on I did three others of his,* This Happy Breed, The Astonished Heart *and* Brief Encounter.

Happy Breed *was rather good, but I don't know that I particularly enjoyed doing it very much, because it was the very early days of colour and it took hours. One used to wait, and wait, and wait. The lighting took so long that I used to get rather depressed because I was playing the part of a woman of seventy, and in those days I wasn't all* that *old. I'd sit in my dressing-room looking at myself in the mirror, thinking, 'That's what you're going to be like any minute now'. It was rather gloomy-making really, but apart from that it was enjoyable, and rather a good film.*

When *This Happy Breed* was produced on American television some years later, Noël had to cut more than half an hour out of the original play. 'It is a distressing experience,' he said, 'and a bitter lesson for an author to find that cutting his work improves it.'

MICHAEL WILDING: *I was dining at the Ivy, and Noël—whom I didn't know then, came up to the table and said, 'Michael, you were just lovely.' He was referring to some dreadful film I'd made at Ealing Studios with John Clements and Michael Rennie about the war, in which we flew aeroplanes, and I thought he was kidding me.*

'Why do you say that?' I asked.

'Because you were an officer and a gentleman,' he replied.

'I'm very pleased to hear it,' I said, 'and surprised, too.'

He offered me the part in In Which We Serve *on the strength of that. I had about four days to do on the film, and he looked at me on the last day and said, 'Michael, dear, you must be the Dean of Juveniles.' I daresay he thought I was too old for the part. However, he added, 'You'll be a great star.'*

'Why?' I asked.

'Because you've personal charm. So have I.'

And then he added, 'But I have talent too. I am very clever indeed. I have this God-given talent, but I don't abuse my talent ever. I work hard at it.'

And he does, too. He works very hard at it, and has done everything that should be done to talent. Not only has he worked very hard, but throughout his lifetime he's done so much for the theatre—I think he's employed more people than any other being in the theatre.

In Which We Serve was the first really important British film about the war, and Noël not only starred as the captain of the doomed ship, but produced the film, co-directed it and wrote the script and the music. It won a special Academy Award.

During the production of the film Noël found himself the subject of adverse newspaper comment as the result of his being served summonses for currency offences. It was alleged that he had kept and spent money in America, in contravention of a law passed in 1939—which he knew nothing about. (The money, incidentally, had been spent on his shows in support of the war effort.) His lawyers advised him that to be found guilty at the Bow Street hearing could involve him in fines of up to £60,000. The newspapers were full of speculation and accusation, but George Bernard Shaw wrote to him saying that there could be no guilt without intention, and since he was unaware of the new laws, having been out of the country when they were passed, he should plead Not Guilty.

A second case followed in which he had to answer a similar charge regarding keeping undeclared dollars in America. He was still further dismayed to find that his business advisers had conducted his affairs so badly that he had to get rid of them.

His career was in jeopardy. He feared a Press scandal might threaten his good relationship with the Admiralty, Lord Mountbatten and the Navy, and the backers of *In Which We Serve*, who had put up £200,000, and there was the further prospect of the heavy fines if the case went against him. But he was only fined a token sum of £200 on the first charge and £1,600 on the second. Thankfully the Press played it down, and he emerged without further attack from them.

BINKIE BEAUMONT:

During the final stage of In Which We Serve *I used to go down to Denham, where Noël had a house. He'd had almost a year at the studio working on the film, and was eager to get back to his first love, the theatre. He talked with great excitement about doing a six-month tour of England in three of his own plays, and I tried to explain to him that conditions were not going to be easy.*

'Nonsense,' he said, 'it'll be much more interesting. People have gone into the provinces and they'll be longing for entertainment. I'd love to do a twenty-six-week tour.'

*So we started off at the Grand Theatre, Blackpool, three First Nights in a row—*Blithe Spirit, Present Laughter *and* This Happy Breed. *Exhausted by the end of the tour, he got jaundice and had to leave the cast, and Dennis Price, who was playing smaller parts, took over and finished the last two weeks while Noël went down to Devon to recover.*

Blithe Spirit CBS T. V. Ford Star Jubilee January 14th 1956. Mildred Natwick, Lauren Bacall, Claudette Colbert, Noël.

Judy Campbell was Noël's leading lady in the original production of *Present Laughter*. She remembers Noël attacking an actress for being particularly slow with her lines. The girl promptly lost her temper. 'If you go on like that I'll throw something at you!' she threatened.

'You might start with my cues,' he snapped.

(Tempers were equally frayed when he rehearsed Claudette Colbert for an American television production of *Blithe Spirit* in January 1956.

'I'm sorry,' said Claudette Colbert apologetically, 'I knew these lines backwards last night.'

'And that's exactly the way you're saying them this morning', Noël replied.)

On November 5th 1941, *Blithe Spirit* opened on Broadway at the Morosco Theatre and ran for eighteen months, with a cast headed by Clifton Webb, Peggy Wood and Mildred Natwick as Madame Arcati.

MARTI STEVENS:
(American musical comedy star):

Noël is the most loyal friend in the world, and in time of trouble he's the first to help or to offer advice. Well, there was this tremendously close attachment between Clifton Webb and his mother Maybell, and as fate would have

'Don't let's be beastly to the Germans' BBC Wartime broadcast, July 1943.

it *Maybell died, and Clifton was distraught. Noël telephoned him at once from Jamaica and said, 'Clifton, dear boy, you must come here for Christmas, and have Helen* [his secretary] *do your packing. Now no nonsense, you're coming for Christmas. Get packed and get cracking.'*

But Clifton could hardly take this in, he was crying so much on the telephone, and Noël suddenly lost patience and said, 'My dear boy, if you go on like this I shall be forced to reverse the charges!'

After he replaced the receiver, Noël announced, 'You realize this makes Clifton the oldest orphan in the world.'

During a Forces Broadcast that Noël did for the BBC he did a number called 'Don't let's be beastly to the Germans', which caused a storm of controversy.

```
We must be kind -
And with an open mind
We must endeavour to find
A way
To let the Germans know that when the
   war is over
They are not the ones who'll have to
   pay.
We must be sweet -
And tactful and discreet
And when they've suffered defeat
We mustn't let
Them feel upset
Or ever get
The feeling that we're cross with them
   or hate them,
Our future policy must be to reinstate
   them.

Don't let's be beastly to the Germans
When our victory is ultimately won,
It was just those nasty Nazis who
   persuaded them to fight
And their Beethoven and Bach are really
   far worse than their bite.

Let's be meek to them -
And turn the other cheek to them
And try to bring out their latent sense
   of fun.
Let's give them full air parity -
And treat the rats with charity,
But don't let's be beastly to the Hun.

We must be just -
```

And win their love and trust
And in addition we must
Be wise,
And ask the conquered lands to join our
  hands to aid them –
That would be a wonderful surprise.
For many years
They've been in floods of tears
Because the poor little dears
Have been so wronged and only longed
To cheat the world,
Deplete the world
And beat
The world to blazes.
That is the moment when we ought to sing
  their praises.

Don't let's be beastly to the Germans
When we've definitely got them on the
  run –
Let us treat them very kindly as we
  would a valued friend –
We might send them out some Bishops as a
  form of lease and lend,
Let's be sweet to them
And day by day repeat to them
That 'sterilization' simply isn't done.
Let's help the dirty swine again
To occupy the Rhine again,
But don't let's be beastly to the Hun.

Don't let's be beastly to the Germans
When the age of peace and plenty has
  begun.
We must send them steel and oil and coal
  and everything they need,
For their peacable intentions can be
  always guaranteed.
Let's employ with them a sort of
  'strength through joy' with them,
They're better than us at honest manly
  fun.
Let's let them feel they're sweet again
  and bomb us all to hell again,
But don't let's be beastly to the Hun.

Don't let's be beastly to the Germans,
For you can't deprive a gangster of his
  gun.
Though they've been a little naughty to
  the Czechs and Poles and Dutch,
But I don't suppose those countries
  really minded very much.

Let's be free with them and share the
  BBC with them,
We mustn't prevent them basking in the
  sun –
Let's soften their defeat again – and
  build their bloody fleet again,
But don't let's be beastly to the Hun.

Although he tried to explain the irony of the lyrics on the radio, he was accused of being pro-German—and left smartly on a planned three-month tour of the Middle East to put on shows for the troops. From Gibraltar to Iraq, in Malta, North Africa and the Near East, he performed in forty hospitals, giving as many as seven concerts in three days.

At one of those hospital concerts in Tripoli he met an old friend, Peter Daubeny.

left, with Norman Hackford at the piano singing for troops in the Arakan, 1944.

PETER DAUBENY:

I was at the Liverpool Repertory Company from the age of seventeen for two years, and it was during that time that I had my first encounter with Noël. I felt from the first time I saw him that he had an extraordinary personality because he made you feel better than you really were. This is some sort of magical gift that he had. And I felt this very much five years later after being for three years right through the North African campaign.

I had been wounded at Salerno and I was in hospital at Tripoli and he came there to entertain the troops. It so happened that I was in a small ward with the Adjutant of the Coldstream Guards, my own regiment. I'd been wounded in the left arm, and he'd lost his right arm. After we'd been there a week, the matron came round and said that Noël Coward was going to entertain the troops.

'The one thing is that you mustn't get out of bed, because you've only been here a week,' she added.

Well, the Adjutant groaned with pleasure at the thought of not having to meet Noël Coward and I was absolutely determined to go to this concert. So as soon as she'd left, I started preparing myself—it took quite a long time getting along because I was completely encumbered by bandages. And when I entered the hall it was like being on board ship. The room seemed to sway about. There were about five hundred people who were all wounded, sitting there, very truculent and ill-at-ease at having been forced into the auditorium. I don't think a lot of them had heard of Noël Coward, and I had a fearful feeling that he wasn't going to make it.

When the curtains parted, and we saw him, there he was —a Desert Rat, as we all were, but this was a Cartier Desert Rat, and he looked absolutely superb. Cool, clean, decent and very dynamic. Well, this didn't enhance him at all in the eyes of the suffering five hundred, but he started off, and it wasn't just the sort of sorcery of his genius that he has on the stage, but his sheer determination, his battering willpower that made that audience absolutely one million per cent with him, and at the end they were choking with emotion. They stood and cheered and cheered. It might have been Maria Callas's first night at La Scala. It was so touching, and they all had to be sent away like little children to bed.

Well, I stayed behind because I wanted to go round and say hello. This was rather difficult because the Brigadier was standing there as a sort of social custodian. It gave him great prestige to be able to say that he was looking after Noël Coward. But I went into Noël's room where he was washing, and when he saw how heavily I was bandaged, he said, 'What's the matter with you?'

'I've lost my arm' I said.

I shall never forget this because I felt that he was much more compassionate than I was, and I think that through the sort of liquid heat and strain, and seeing all these wounded people, and the fact that I knew him slightly . . . he was so deeply moved, I can't tell you.

'Which ward are you in?' he asked.

I said that I was with the Adjutant, and he insisted on taking me back to the ward himself. When we got into the room, there was the sort of antipathy of the Adjutant, but I noticed that almost immediately—he has this power of creating himself through other people—he knew more about

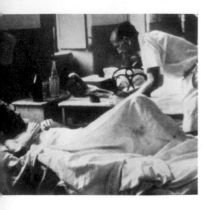

fishing, more about hunting, more about all the sort of social vicissitudes of life, than Bill Gore-Langton did himself, and in a few minutes they were absolutely bosom friends.

That was one of the great encounters I had in the war, and he was doing this to a lot of people, but certainly as an enhancer of the spirit and not a diminisher in any way. I think he's absolutely unique and he helped me enormously to get well.

Ironically, the next time I saw him was when I produced Fallen Angels *at the Ambassadors Theatre, with Hermione Baddeley and Hermione Gingold—and then I encountered another side of him, equally attractive—his wrath!*

HERMIONE GINGOLD:

I was sitting on my terrace quite a long time ago in New York when a telegram arrived from Noël asking whether I would come back to London to play Julia in Fallen Angels, *so I dashed out to get the play and read it. I liked the part of Jane much better, so I cabled Noël: 'Yes, I would very much like to be in* Fallen Angels, *but I want to play Jane.'*

And he cabled back: 'No, no, no. You're being silly because Jane isn't a good part. It's Julia that's the pivot.'

And I cabled back: 'I don't like playing pivots. I'll come if I can play Jane.' And he replied saying: 'All right, but you're a silly cow.'

Darling Peter Daubeny put it on in the West End of London, but Hermione Baddeley and myself thought the play was just a teeny bit old-fashioned, and so we did some pretty tricky things with it. I remember Noël came to Stratford-upon-Avon to see it, and said, 'I don't like this! What are these naughty ladies doing with my play?' And we said, 'Well, you know, people don't really care about two ladies getting drunk any more, if it was two ladies taking dope it wouldn't really be all that bad or frightening—but drink?'

And so when we came to London with the play, Noël came to the first rehearsal and found that we hadn't taken any notice of what he had said, and was naturally angry with us. After all, he had a right to be—he was the author! Peter was rather upset about it, and I said to Noël rather grandly, 'I think we should discuss this in my dressingroom, and not in front of the stagehands.' I can't tell you how brave that was, because we were all terrified of Noël.

However, it opened, and was an enormous success— which was fortunate for us—and we were all forgiven.

We're great friends, Noël and I, and I'm very fond of him. He was a very naughty child, but he grew up to be a very nice, charming and good man.

'KICK THIS BUM OUT OF THE COUNTRY'

After a brief trip to America to make propaganda broadcasts he went to South Africa for a three-month charity concert tour on the invitation of General Smuts. His one-man show raised £20,000 for the Red Cross and Mrs Smuts's Comforts Fund.

'Oh, Mr Coward,' a newspaper reporter rushed up to him, 'Do you have anything to say to *The Star?*'

'Yes,' he replied. 'Twinkle'.

With Norman Hackforth at the piano, he sang his own songs, and included his rewritten version of the lyrics of Cole Porter's 'Let's do it' which was to prove equally popular with audiences years later in cabaret at the Café de Paris in London and the Desert Inn in Las Vegas.

```
              'Let's do It'
      (with apologies to Cole Porter)
Mr Irving Berlin
Often emphasizes sin
In a charming way.
Mr Coward, we know,
Wrote a song or two to show
Sex was here to stay.
Richard Rogers, it's true,
Took a more romantic view
Of that sly biological urge.
But it really was Cole
Who contrived to make the whole
Thing merge.

He said that Belgians and Greeks do it,
Nice young men who sell antiques do it,
Let's do it, let's fall in love.
```

Monkeys whenever you look do it,
Aly Khan and King Farouk do it,
Let's do it, let's fall in love.
Louella Parsons can't - quite - do it
Because she's so highly strung,
Marlene - might do it,
But she looks far too young.
Each man out there shooting crap does
    it,
Davy Crockett in that dreadful cap
    does it,
Let's do it, let's fall in love.

All famous writers in swarms do it,
Somerset and all the Maughams do it,
Let's do it, let's fall in love.
The Brontës felt that they must do it,
Ernest Hemingway could - just do it,
Let's do it, let's fall in love.
E. Allen Poe - ho - ho - ho - did it,
But he did it in verse.
H. Beecher Stowe did it, but she had
    to rehearse.
Tennessee Williams, self-taught does it,
Kinsey with a deafening report does it,
Let's do it, let's fall in love.

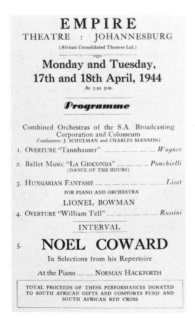

Arrival in Cape Town,
February 1944.

The tour ended in Rhodesia where he received a cable from Lord Mountbatten asking him to fly to his headquarters in Ceylon to entertain the Army in Burma. He afterwards did more troop shows, in India this time, and returned to England a year later, and joined up with Basil Dean's ENSA shows in Versailles and Paris.

If his earlier visit to the hospital in Tripoli had given fresh courage to Peter Daubeny, it incensed the whole of Brooklyn as the result of an account of that visit that he wrote in his little book *Middle East Diary*, wherein he described 'some of the mournful little Brooklyn boys lying there in tears amidst the alien corn with nothing less than a bullet wound in the leg or a fractured arm'.

His criticism caused an outcry in Brooklyn so great as to induce Mayor la Guardia to deprecate on radio Noël's 'attack'. It also resulted in the formation of a 'Prevention of Noël Coward re-entering America' club.

David Niven, Noël's close friend and neighbour in Switzerland, recalls this incident when I asked him for an anecdote about Noël.

DAVID NIVEN:

I racked my brains all night, hoping to say that he was terrible, that he beat his wife, that he drank his bathwater, but I couldn't think of a thing really, so I thought I'd tell you how brave he is—how physically brave.

During the war, Noël went all over the world entertaining the troops, and after a trip to the Middle East he wrote this terrible book called Middle East Diary, *and in it he described going into an American hospital which he said was full of snivelling little boys from Brooklyn. Well this caused an understandable stir in the United States, and the* Stars and Stripes, *which was the American Forces newspaper, had a review of the book and its headline read, 'Kick this bum out of the country'.*

Now, on the day that this 'Kick this bum out of the country' was being read by all the troops in Paris, Noël opened at the Marigny Theatre in Paris with Maurice Chevalier, whom the American soldiers were sure was a collaborator, and with Marlene Dietrich, whom they were convinced was a German spy. And the third was Noël ('Kick this bum out of the country') and I was on leave from my unit up in Holland, and went to this opening.

I went to see Noël before the performance and I said, 'You know, there are about five thousand people out there, and I'm afraid they're all going to kill you. What are you going to do about it?'

So Noël said, 'First I shall calm them, and then I shall sing some of my very excellent songs.'

'Well,' I said, 'I'll stand by the exit door because . . . you know, just in case . . .'

So I went and stood at the back by the exit, and Noël came on to a deathly hush, which he's not used to. A deathly hush. And then he looked at them and said, 'Ladies and Gentlemen, and all you dear, dear snivelling little boys from Brooklyn . . .' And they fell down and absolutely loved it.

Now I've known him for thirty-five years, and I know this about him, that if and when I finally do it, I kill my mother-in-law or I rape a nun, and I'm in the cooler for ever, when everybody else sees fit to disown me, Noël will come and see me every day.

Dorothy Dickson, the American musical comedy star, came to England in the twenties with her dancing partner and husband, Carl Hyson. She became the talk of the town, and was greatly admired. She starred in *Sally*, *Tip-Toes*, *Peggy-Ann* and *The Cabaret Girl*, played Peter Pan twice, and in the thirties appeared in many shows including Ivor Novello's *Careless Rapture* and *Crest of the Wave*.

She became a great friend of Novello, and the lucky recipient of coveted invitations to visit his house, 'Red Roofs'. She combined beauty and wit, and some of her most famous quips were made on the stage. While appearing in *Careless Rapture*, dancing with Wally Crisham, she sped past him on stage during a performance as he was about to take her in his arms and lift her up.

'Where are you going?' he hissed in the loudest stage-whisper, dashing after her, with the music in pursuit of them both.

'Red Roofs,' she replied. 'You coming?'

On another occasion she was in a wartime troop show. The opera singer who preceded her at the end of the first half sang aria after aria, and each time she finished an aria, Dottie and Wally Crisham prepared to go on, and each time they did so, the singer added yet another song from her repertoire. When the final moment came for her to make her bow, she walked down to the footlights and announced, 'And now a little Mozart . . .'

To which an exasperated Dottie added drily, '. . . goes a *long* way'.

DOROTHY DICKSON:

When we came back to England, from three months doing troop shows for ENSA across North Africa, there was Bea Lillie, myself, Vivien Leigh and Leslie Henson. I realised that the best thing to do in London for my war effort was to have a Stage Door Canteen for troops of all nation-alities.

So when I came over I got hold of financiers and members of Parliament. Our American Ambassador said he'd pre-pare a building—a bombed-out building, which we finally got in Piccadilly—for the occasion.

I worked very hard at this project, got very depressed, and then thought, if I can get top names from the theatre and so forth, people will be enthusiastic. So I thought, Noël! That's the thing. I'll give them Noël Coward and they'll all come along. So I asked him to lunch and told him about it, and he seemed rather keen on the idea, but I later got a message from him saying no, he was too tired. He simply couldn't do anything more.

This naturally depressed me, but finally after talking to masses of people, we organised a meeting of the prospective financiers, Government representatives and theatre people. There were about two hundred all together. I've never had such stage fright in my life. I couldn't go in— I had to walk round the block twice before I could muster up the courage.

When I finally got inside, the first person I saw was Noël Coward.

'What are you doing here?' I asked.

He went down on one knee and said, 'Darling, I was wrong and you were right. I will come here, entertain on the stage; I'll go to the committee, I'll play the piano. I'll do anything you like.'

And I rather had a tear in my eye. I shall never forget that.

In May 1945 he appeared at the Cambridge Theatre at a Gala Variety Concert in aid of war funds, with Josephine Baker and Cedric Hardwick.

By now his new revue, *Sigh No More*, was ready, and opened at the Piccadilly Theatre. It starred Cyril Ritchard, Madge Elliot, Graham Payn and Joyce Grenfell.

JOYCE GRENFELL:

I was doing a tour of India, and a cable came from Noël saying he was planning a revue for the midsummer of 1945, and would I be in it. Of course I cabled back saying that I would love to, and I started writing numbers with Richard Addinsell [who had composed Warsaw Concerto, among a great many other brilliant pieces for the theatre and films] *for me to do in the show. Noël produced me in a number called 'Du Maurier' which Richard and I wrote together, and it was a wonderful experience because he took such enormous trouble. I had to play an eighteen-ninety lady in a very very tight dress designed by Gladys Calthrop with long black gloves and a sort of eighteen-nineties fringe. That was twenty-five years ago, and I remember almost every gesture Noël taught me—the hands, the position, everything.*

I also did a song of his called 'That is the end of the news', disguised as a schoolgirl with pigtails, all my make-up off, a shiny face and a terrible grin.

Joyce Grenfell singing 'That is the End of the News' from *Sigh No More*.

'That is the end of the News'
from 'Sigh No More'

We are told very loudly and often
To lift up our hearts,
We are told that good humour will soften
Fate's cruellest darts.
So however bad our domestic troubles
    must be
We just shake with amusement and sing
    with glee.

Heighho, Mum's had those pains again,
Granny's in bed with her varicose veins
    again,
Everyone's gay because dear cousin
    Florrie
Was run down on Saturday night by a
    lorry,
We're so thrilled, Elsie's in trouble,
That hernia she had has turned out to
    be double,
When Albert fell down all
The steps of the Town Hall
He got three bad cuts and a bruise,
We're delighted
To be able to say
We're unable to pay
Off our debts,
We're excited
Because Percy's got mange
And we've run up a bill at the vet's.
Three cheers! Ernie's got boils again,
Everything's covered in ointment and
    oils again,
Now he's had seven
So God's in His heaven
And that is the end of the news.

GRAHAM PAYN:

I first met Noël in 1932 when I was a boy soprano aged fourteen. I'd done concerts, broadcasts and a couple of records, but when I auditioned for Words and Music *I realised that there wasn't much call for a boy soprano in revue, and my mother advised me to do everything at once, so I sang 'Nearer my God to Thee' and did a tap-dance at the same time. This extraordinary exhibition so intrigued Noël that he gave me the job on the spot. But I didn't work for him again until 1945—thirteen years later!*

He wrote 'Matelot' for me, and another song called 'Wait a bit, Joe', both of which were very good songs.

He came into my dressing-room one night and said, 'I think a little more charm in that number wouldn't hurt.'

190

So I thought, 'All right', and bounced on to the stage and did the lot. He came flying through the pass-door and reproached me, 'I said a little more charm wouldn't hurt—I didn't ask you to be Mary Rose *on skates!'*

'Matelot'

from 'Sigh No More'

Matelot, Matelot,
Where you go
My thoughts go with you,
Matelot, Matelot,
When you go down to the sea
As you gaze from afar
On the evening star
Wherever you may roam,
You will remember the light
Through the winter night
That guides you safely home.
Though you find
Womenkind
To be frail,
One love cannot fail, my son,
Till our days are done,
Matelot, Matelot
Where you go
My thoughts go with you,
Matelot, Matelot,
When you go down to the sea.
Jean Louis Dominic Pierre Bouchon
Journeyed the wide world over,
Lips that he kissed
Could not resist
This loving roving rover.
Jean Louis Dominic, right or wrong,
Ever pursued a new love,
Till in his brain
There beat a strain
He knew
To be his true love
Matelot, Matelot,
Where you go
My heart goes with you,
Matelot, Matelot,
Where you go down to the sea.
For a year and a day
You may sail away
And have no thought of me,
Yet through the wind and the spray
You will hear me say,
No love was ever free.
You will sigh
When horizons are clear,

above, Graham Payn singing 'Matelot' from *Sigh No More* (1945).
below, Graham Payn.

Something that is dear
To me
Cannot let me be.
Matelot, Matelot,
Where you go
My heart goes with you,
Matelot, Matelot,
When you go down to the sea.

above, with Mary Martin in
Jamaica.
right, Drury Lane Theatre being
restored after bomb damage.

With the coming of peace, Noël felt that the public, after
being saturated with wartime bombing and misery for so
long, would prefer something gentle, soothing and
nostalgic. With that in mind he wrote *Pacific 1860*. He set
the love story on a tropical island in the 1860s, a location
inspired by his love for Jamaica. It concerned the visit of
a prima donna, played by Mary Martin, who falls in love
with a young man (Graham Payn); his Victorian family,
however, will have nothing to do with a woman who has
been on the stage.

The show was presented by Prince Littler on December
19th 1946 in the newly restored Drury Lane Theatre, but
the musical, with its sparkling dialogue and enchanting
score, a cast that included Maidie Andrews and Sylvia
Cecil, beautiful sets and costumes, opened in the midst of
the worst winter England had known for years. Snow fell
heavily and lay deep, there were constant lighting and fuel
cuts (the box office had to sell tickets by candlelight), and
the theatre could not be properly warmed. Also there
was something indefinably wrong with the kind of show

it was. The net result was that it failed to succeed.

This setback was underlined by the runaway success of the next musical to open at that theatre—*Oklahoma!* Noël saw the change in the public taste for musicals and decided that he must make a fight to regain his rightful place in the West End.

Meanwhile, however, he turned to his next commitment, which was to direct a revival of *Present Laughter* in

Mary Martin in *Pacific 1860*.
Graham Payn extreme left.

which he also played his original role. It opened at the Haymarket in April 1947, and in June he returned to America to witness Tallulah Bankhead's triumph in *Private Lives*, which opened in Bridgeport, Connecticut and ran for over a year on a national tour before opening at New York's Plymouth Theatre on October 4th 1948.

'I played it for an entire summer in Chicago,' Tallulah Bankhead wrote in her autobiography, 'while racked with neuritis, and for an entire season in New York. I played it in summer theatres, in Shrine mosques, in school auditoriums, in a blizzard in Minneapolis, in a coma in Westport. I played it in Passaic, in Flatbush, in Pueblo, in Cedar Rapids, in Peoria, in the Bronx, in Joplin, in "thunder, lightning and in rain" (Macbeth), in towns known but to God and Rand McNally. Unless my abacus is out of order I impersonated Amanda—a Riviera doxy of a bigamous turn —for over two hundred weeks, hither and yon, as well as in Montgomery, Alabama, flying the Confederate flag.'

Still in America, he directed a coast-to-coast revival of *Tonight at Eight-Thirty*, with Gertrude Lawrence and Graham Payn. It opened in New York in February 1948, but Graham contracted flu and the play came off after three weeks at the National Theatre.

GRAHAM PAYN: *We had had a lovely success in it on the coast, but I lost my voice—not soprano this time, but lyric baritone. Anyway, I lost it, and Noël went on for me. That was the last time he ever played with Gertrude Lawrence, which was very sad indeed.* [She died of cancer four years later, on September 6th 1952].

Graham Payn and Gertrude Lawrence.
right, in Jamaica.

After *Tonight at Eight-Thirty* closed, Noël returned to Jamaica, where he rented Ian Flemings' house, 'Goldeneye' to write the second half of his autobiography. Noël re-christened the house Golden Eye, Nose and Throat.

NOËL COWARD: *It was not strictly speaking a very comfortable house. I used to call it bed-and-board because the beds were so hard, but it was Ian who first of all persuaded me to go there, and he rented it to me for three months. The rent was extremely high.*

If he had built it on the angle to the right, he would have had a full view of all the sunsets. But he built it flat, facing the sea, and therefore didn't get the sunsets. And the window sills were too high, so that you sat in that lovely big room with the window sill just about to your eye-level and you got an admirable view of the sky, and nothing else.

Ian married Lady Ann Rothermere whilst I was there. It was her third marriage. The wedding was an entirely hysterical occasion. It took place in the parochial hall in

Port Maria and Annie was very nervous. She had on an eau-de-nil silk dress, and she shook so much that it fluttered. I can't think why she should have been so terrified, but she was. The principal official of the ceremony spoke very close to them, which I don't think they cared for, so they had to turn their faces away when they said, 'I do. I do.' After the ceremony Coley and I were so unnerved by the whole experience that I tied a shoe on to my own car and drove home.

Noël so fell in love with Jamaica that he decided to buy a piece of land there, and build himself a house. He chose a spot just outside Port Maria, right on the sea, and called the house 'Blue Harbour'. He later decided to build

another little house just for himself, at the top of the mountain behind Blue Harbour. When his friends visit they stay in the first house, and he goes up to the other one where he does his writing. He goes to Jamaica every winter, and returns to Switzerland in the spring, so he has the best of both worlds.

While in Jamaica in 1951, he was saddened to hear of the deaths of two close friends: C. B. Cochran, in January, and Ivor Novello two months later.

He was still working as hard as ever. There was his book of short stories, *Star Quality*, and then he undertook to play the French version of *Present Laughter*, called *Joyeux Chagrin*, in Paris. This was followed by a new West End musical, *Ace of Clubs*, but it failed dismally, even though it starred Pat Kirkwood, and featured one of his best songs, 'Chase me Charlie'. The latter was a duet written for two cats, which the BBC considered to be in something less than the best of taste. When they insisted that the words 'bound to give in' be replaced by 'waiting for you' before they would broadcast it, Noël retorted: 'Apparently the BBC thinks that the idea of a cat giving in is more likely to create immoral thoughts in listeners' minds than the idea of a cat waiting to achieve its object.'

'Chase me, Charlie'
from Ace of Clubs

When it's late
And the world is sleeping,
Our little black cat,
No bigger than that,
Has a date
Which she's keen on keeping.
No use dissuading her,
She's serenading her – beau
In the garden below,
She sings, 'Oh, won't you –

Chase me, Charlie,
Chase me, Charlie,
Ovor the garden wall?
I'd like to wander for miles and miles
Out on the tiles with you.
Chase me, Charlie,
Chase me, Charlie,
Don't be afraid to fall,
Love in the moonlight can be sublime,
Now's the time,
Charlie, I'm
Bound to give in if you'll only climb
Over the garden wall.

below left, Ace of Clubs.
below, Ivor Novello.
below right, with Hollywood
Reporter columnist Radie
Harris.

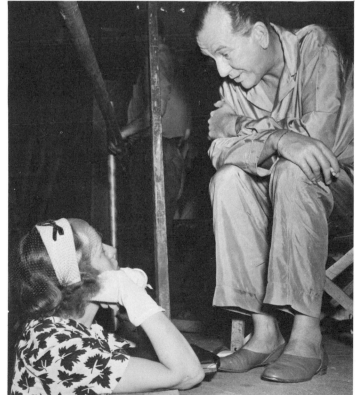

His next play, *Peace in Our Time*, was another flop. It also suffered at the hands of the critics, provoking Noël to retort, 'I could learn from Gielgud, from Olivier, from Somerset Maugham, from the public. Never from the critics.'

COLE LESLEY: *Of course that was a very bad patch that Noël went through. On the whole the critics were beastly, but what impressed me was something that people don't know about, and that is that when any of these enterprises were over, they were done with as far as he was concerned, and he was filled with enthusiasm for the next thing. He's always had this forward-looking attitude for the next thing, and the feeling that it was going to be wonderful. He never looked over his shoulder at any of his failures or disappointments.*

NOËL COWARD: *My feelings about critical attacks have never been very strong because I've been in the theatre too long. Only occasionally could I pick up a hint—but only from a good critic, like Agate. He once or twice said something or other that made me think, but as a general rule, as I only played a three-month season at a time, we were always sold out for the three months before we opened, so it didn't matter what the critics said anyway.*

I'm so terribly, terribly sorry for critics. They have to go to the damned theatre every night, and see all sorts and kinds of nonsense, and I think their senses—if you'll forgive the phrase—get dulled. And I think that they suddenly will spring a surprise on you, and you come out with a rave and a long scream. And then very often the play closes. You can't tell. You can't tell.

Some of Hollywood's gossip writers claimed many of the stars as their friends, but the relationship was often bound by the stars' fear of the journalists' powerful pen. But Radie Harris, the gossip columnist for *The Hollywood Reporter*, is genuinely devoted to the theatre and films, and as a result builds up rather than knocks down images. She had thus become a friend of such stars as the late Vivien Leigh and Noël himself.

RADIE HARRIS: *One of Noël's most enviable traits is that he can always ad-lib a perfect retort when most of us mortals think of what we should have said after we arrive home. Noël learned of the suicide of an actor he knew, who, to understate it, was not overly bright.*

'How did he kill himself?' Noël wanted to know.
'He shot his brains out,' came the answer.
Whereupon Noël commented, 'He must have been a marvellous shot!'

Another dreary and not-so-good actor was continually threatening to kill himself. When finally a friend reported to Noël, 'Have you heard? He tried to commit suicide. He put his head in the oven.'

Noël replied, 'Don't tell me he didn't succeed.'

When Noël was coming out of the stage-door of a theatre in the West End, where he had gone to congratulate the actors on their performances, there was the usual cluster of gallery girls waiting outside, and one of the regulars approached him and asked, 'How did you like the play, Mr Coward?'

'I liked the acting enormously,' he replied, tactfully avoiding comment on the play which he didn't care for.

'I didn't even like the acting,' said the distaff critic, and then added, 'But who am I to argue with a self-appointed genius?'

'Precisely, my dear, who indeed,' replied Noël as he climbed into his waiting limousine.

Now came a change in his fortunes, in the shape of the London premiere of his new comedy, *Relative Values*. It was the first of his works in four years to score the kind of success to which he had been so accustomed. It opened at the Savoy, with the late Dame Gladys Cooper leading a brilliant cast.

GLADYS COOPER:

I was in California at the time where I was doing films, and Binkie Beaumont wrote, 'I'm going to do a play of Noël's. Will you come and do it?' So I cabled back saying, 'Yes', without reading the script. He then sent me the script, and on the way to London I stopped in Jamaica and read it.

'Why are they putting this play on?' I thought, 'It's not awfully funny.' But after all, who was I to know? It was Noël and Hugh Beaumont. They're a successful management. So there it is. That's how I came to do it. It was a very long play. I was on the stage the whole time—never stopped talking.

When I arrived back in England, I had dinner with Binkie and I said, 'You know, that first scene of mine isn't very funny. It's too wordy.' Binkie's very good to be with, because he's a master of—not intrigue—tact. I don't know how he does it, but he does it beautifully.

So he said, 'Darling, it's perfectly all right. Noël will cut it, or change it. Leave it to me.'

The week before we went into rehearsal we all went, the whole cast that is, to have tea with Noël at his Gerald Road studio to discuss the play, and as we were leaving Noël waved his finger at us and said, 'Now then, darlings, no books next Monday.'

I said, 'What do you mean? Learn this part in a week and come word perfect? No. No, I'm much too old a dog to learn those new tricks. Certainly not.' I like to hold my book until the last minute. It's not my way of learning. I like to hold on to my book and learn as I go along.

Came the Monday when rehearsals began, some did struggle who had shorter parts, but I didn't attempt to. I had the feeling that Noël was sitting out front, bored stiff with us all. He was only waiting for us to really get at it without our books in our hands, and when I did get the book out of my hand to learn the lines, Noël used to underline every word that I'd cut out, and of course the scene that I'd spoken to Binkie about wasn't cut at all. It was absolutely awful. I don't know why I ever spoke to him again after all those rehearsals.

NOËL COWARD:

I can't judge actors walking about with books in their hands, so I have a reading of the play, and then in somewhere around ten days I expect them to learn it absolutely by heart like a parrot.

I never mind about the meaning, nor about the motive, or about any of those things—that's bullshit. I can tell them about all that when we get to rehearsal. Just to know it. It's absolutely impossible to play a comedy unless you know it inside out. Everything goes—and timing's the most important thing in comedy. If you hesitate over one line, you kill the whole scene, so therefore you have to know—through your tentacles—*just where to stop—or where to go on.*

What fascinates me about acting is when a beautiful talented actress can come on the stage and give a performance that makes your blood curdle with excitement and pleasure, yet she can make such a cracking pig of herself over where her dressing-room is or some such triviality, for which you hate her.

Intelligent actors never do that, but then they're seldom as good as the unintelligent ones. Acting is an instinct. A gift that is often given to people who are very silly as people. But as they come on to the stage, up goes the temperature.

GLADYS COOPER:

We went away on tour with Relative Values. *It was long, too long, and Noël got obstinate about it. But we got a long way away from London where he couldn't get at us because he was just starting himself to do this one-man show in cabaret for the first time, and he was very busy on that so we were left alone. Then suddenly, when we were up North somewhere, Binkie arrived with the script and all the cuts one wanted and said: 'Noël says take over. Make the cuts. Do it yourself.' That was wonderful about Noël.*

Obstinate, you see. But he had faith in one, and it made me very proud that he thought I could take over and do it, which I did. I made the cuts and came back very happy.

When we were touring with the play, we had a very enterprising publicity lady who was always sending round the local newspaper photographers to photograph us. Well, I photograph very badly in stage make-up because I use rather a dark make-up and it isn't good for cameras. The most hideous photographs of me were always appearing in the local papers after we'd opened.

One particularly revolting picture came out, and I got the usual sort of anonymous letters saying, 'You old hag, why don't you go back to America.' So come the dress rehearsal of the play in London, Noël and Binkie were in my dressing-room, and our publicity lady came in and said, 'Oh, the evening paper would like to photograph you.'

'Send her away,' I said. 'I wouldn't dream of it.'

Noël was very surprised and said, 'Why are you being so hostile? What's all this about?'

So I told him the story, and they both fell about, roaring with laughter.

The next night when we opened, I had flowers from Noël with a note saying, 'Why don't you go back to America, you old hag, and take my play with you!'

And ever since then I've been his hag. If I ring him up I say, 'Tell Sir Noël it's Dame Hag on the telephone.'

Gladys Cooper (Felicity) Renee Hill (Maid) seated, Simon Lack (Peter) Richard Leech (Crestwell) Ralph Michael (Don Lucas) in *Relative Values*.

'Relative Values'

(Taken from Act Three)

The Earl of Marshwood — Nigel (Ralph Michael) — has decided to marry a rather flashy Hollywood film-star, Miranda Frayle. His mother, Felicity, Countess of Marshwood (Gladys Cooper), is sceptical about the alliance — but not half as much as her maid Moxie (Angela Baddeley), who reveals that the star is her younger sister, whom she hasn't seen for twenty years. She refuses to stay on in the house under the circumstances, but Miranda, finding Felicity insufferable, goes off instead with her old flame Don Lucas, who has followed her from Hollywood.

(Miranda sweeps out. Don, after an embarrassed look at Felicity, follows her.)

FELICITY: Poor Miranda! She's been on edge all the morning.

NIGEL: This is all your doing, Mother. I hope you're satisfied. You engineered the whole thing. You deliberately drove her into the arms of that lout.

FELICITY: I did not. She's been in and out of his arms like a jack-in-the-box ever since he set foot in the house.

NIGEL: You've behaved abominably and I'm ashamed of you.

FELICITY: And I'm most bitterly ashamed of you. You, a Peer of the Realm and a member of White's, allowing the woman you love to be whisked away from under your nose without a protest! I can hardly believe it.

NIGEL: Of all the hypocritical nonsense! You wanted to get rid of Miranda and you succeeded. You're absolutely delighted!

FELICITY: And you? Are you going to stand there and pretend that you're heartbroken? You seem to forget that I'm your mother, dear. I brought you into the world, in the middle of Ascot week, and I know you through and through. You never really loved Miranda, any more than you really loved any of the others. Of course I'm delighted. We're all delighted. And now, for heaven's sake

202

	let's go - we're terribly late, the last bell went ages ago.
	(Moxie enters, in her hat and coat) Ah, there you are, Moxie! I couldn't think what had happened to you!
MOXIE:	I've come to say goodbye, my Lady.
FELICITY:	Rubbish! Take off your hat and don't be so silly.
MOXIE:	But, my Lady . . .
FELICITY:	Do as I tell you, and for Heaven's sake give me some money for the collection. There's nothing more to worry about. I haven't time to go on about it now, but Crestwell will explain . . . Come along, everybody! (Moxie gives Felicity a coin) Thank you. Give Moxie a glass of sherry, she looks as if she's going to fall down. Come, Nigel, it's your first Sunday at home and you must try to look as if nothing had happened. After all, when you analyse it, nothing much has, has it? (Felicity sweeps out through the french windows - Peter follows her) (Nigel is about to go too, but he suddenly sees Moxie's expression)
NIGEL:	Cheer up, Moxie! Everything's all right, now. (He pats her on the shoulder affectionately, and goes out after the others)
MOXIE:	(Tremulously, as he goes) Thank you, my Lord. Thank you ever so much . . . (She sinks down on a chair and rummages in her bag for her handkerchief)

Noël's cabaret season came about when, after the failure of his last three expensive musicals, he found himself sadly short of money. He therefore accepted a nightly engagement at the Café de Paris in London in order to recover himself. He scored a tremendous success, finding in these appearances a new outlet as a raconteur and singer of his own music—numbers such as 'A Room with a View', and 'Nina'.

'Nina'

from 'Sigh No More'

Senorita Nina
From Argentina
Knew all the answers,

Although her relatives and friends were
    perfect dancers,
She swore she'd never dance a step until
    she died.
She said, 'I've seen too many movies
And all they prove is
Too idiotic,
They all insist that South America's
    exotic
Whereas it couldn't be more boring if it
    tried.'
She added firmly that she hated
The sound of soft guitars beside a still
    lagoon,
She also positively stated
That she could not abide a Southern
    moon,
She said with most refreshing candour
That she thought Carmen Miranda
Was subversive propaganda
And should rapidly be shot,
She said she didn't care a jot if people
    quoted her or not!
She refused to begin the beguine
When they requested it,
And she made an embarrassing scene
If anyone suggested it
For she detested it.
Though no one ever could be keener
Than little Nina
On quite a number of very eligible men
    who did the Rhumba
When they proposed to her she simply
    left them flat.
She said that love should be impulsive
But not convulsive,
And syncopation
Had a discouraging effect on procreation
And that she'd rather read a book –
and that was that!

Noël's next play was *Quadrille*, written as a vehicle for Lynn
Fontanne and Alfred Lunt to play in London, and Cecil
Beaton was asked to design the sets.

CECIL BEATON:

*I had long been an admirer of Sir Noël. In fact I remember
when I was at Cambridge, one night I was on top of a bus
going to see a play of his called* The Queen was in the
Parlour, *and I thought, really, this is worth growing up
for. I loved everything that he wrote and copied out sentences
and thought he was the most remarkable pattern of the new*

playwright. And all through his long career I had enormous admiration for Gladys Calthrop who designed for him. She was a great support and a great designer. But when she felt that she didn't want to do another production just then, and Quadrille *came my way, I was in transports.*

As soon as I started working with Noël I felt, I hope he doesn't mind my saying it, that perhaps the visual sense isn't his strongest point. In fact he's so talented that there are certain sides that really don't exist for him. I think that comfort is one. He doesn't really care at all about comfort. He doesn't mind what he eats—except humble pie, of course. But still, I respected his judgment because he's nothing if not a professional. And as soon as we started working together it was a question of really doing the best for the play, and I've never had a happier experience in the theatre.

Everyone was so pleased with the play and the Lunts' marvellous performances, and everyone was so charming to one another—no bites—and any suggestions taken at face value.

We opened in Manchester—got wonderful notices, but I think my greatest admiration for Noël came on the first night in London.

We had three charity previews, which really don't give you any sort of impression of how the audience like the thing. And then suddenly on the first night, after this marvellous tour, it really died the death. And I felt so appalled because one becomes very closely associated with the whole business. I suffered terribly, but I wondered what on earth Noël was feeling as he sat up there in the box and just that silence instead of the customary reaction.

I remember backstage some very tiresome little journalist girl rushing up to him at a most busy moment and saying, 'Mr Coward, how did you react to the non-reception that you got tonight?'

And Noël, with the most wonderful smile on his face, said, 'I thought they were the best audience that I've really ever come across in my life. I'm so grateful to them.'

I respected him so much for being able to put on that show.

NOËL COWARD:

The only really desperate thing with Quadrille *was that Lynn had a bustle, and she'd been sitting on the sofa, and a cushion caught on the bustle. She was playing a scene with Joyce Carey, and as she got up, the cushion stuck to her bustle, and bobbled up and down as she moved. There was a slight titter from the audience.*

Joyce, who was in a frenzy, tried to get at it, and pursued Lynn, who evaded her. Lynn didn't like being touched, and Joyce chased her right round the stage, and finally had to make her exit. Lynn was left to do a little dance by herself with the cushion bobbing up and down, and she said to me afterwards, 'You know, that scene's never got so many laughs.'

They loved it, the audience. But we never dared tell her.

'Quadrille'
(Taken from Act Three)

The scene is set in the sitting-room of the Marchioness of Heronden – Serena – in Belgrave Square (it is 1874). Serena (Lynn Fontanne) has discovered her husband Hubert's infidelity, and has fallen in love with Axel, the husband of her husband's mistress. Hubert is about to leave for a six-month African safari, and Lady Harriet Ripley (Joyce Carey) has come to tea specifically to tell Serena that Hubert is to be escorted by his new mistress. This information has been passed on to her by her gossipy manicurist, Miss Francis. This clears the field for Serena's escapade with Axel . . .

SERENA:	Would you like some more tea?
HARRIET:	No, thank you. (After a slight pause) Will you mind Hubert going to Africa?
SERENA:	We must ask Miss Francis, she will be bound to know.

left, Cecil Beaton's set design
for *Quadrille*.
right, Lynn Fontanne in
Quadrille.

HARRIET:	No, but seriously, do you?
SERENA:	Of course not.
HARRIET:	It was rather a sudden decision, wasn't it?
SERENA:	I believe that he has had the idea in his mind for some time. I am sure that it will do him a great deal of good. Take him out of himself.
HARRIET:	It will also take him out of harm's way.
SERENA:	Harm's way?
HARRIET:	It is no use pretending that you don't know what I mean.
SERENA:	I am not pretending. I haven't the least idea what you mean.
HARRIET:	(With a little laugh) Really, Serena!
SERENA:	What are you hinting at, Harriet?
HARRIET:	Hubert has a new 'friend'.
SERENA:	That doesn't surprise me. He's naturally gregarious.
HARRIET:	This one is brunette and very vivacious. I am told that she has a charming singing voice – untrained, you know, but absolutely true.

SERENA:	Hubert often pretends to have an ear for music, but he hasn't really, so it won't matter much whether her voice is true or not.
HARRIET:	Do you seriously mean to tell me that you know nothing about Hubert and this Mrs Mallory?
SERENA:	(Sharply) Mrs what?
HARRIET:	Mallory. She is Irish, so is her husband. Apparently they are rather rolling stones, always travelling about the world. Charles Barrington met them in Egypt last year. I don't think he formed a very favourable impression of them.
SERENA:	Why?
HARRIET:	It seems that he, Mr Mallory, is none too scrupulous over money matters.
SERENA:	And the wife? Is she unscrupulous too?
HARRIET:	Very, I believe.
SERENA:	Oh, poor Hubert!
HARRIET:	That's what I meant when I said that the trip to Africa would take him out of harm's way.
SERENA:	I see it all now.
HARRIET:	Is he leaving soon?
SERENA:	Yes, at the end of the month.
HARRIET:	That should be a great relief to you.
SERENA:	(Laughing) It is! Oh, it is!
HARRIET:	Why are you laughing?
SERENA:	Because I feel gay. I've felt gay all day.
HARRIET:	You're certainly in a very strange mood.
SERENA:	Hubert said that only a little while ago. I was listening to a hurdy-gurdy playing in the Square and all at once everything seemed to be vibrant and sweet and full of furtive excitements.
HARRIET:	Furtive excitements? What do you mean?
SERENA:	If he'd come into the room a moment later he would probably have discovered me hopping about the floor kicking my legs in the air like a ballet dancer.
HARRIET:	(Slightly scandalised) Serena!
SERENA:	How do I look, Harriet? Tell me - be a mirror and tell me true. From where you

are sitting can you see any crow's feet,
any wrinkles?

HARRIET: How absurd you are. Of course I can't.

SERENA: But if I bend closer, there - like that.
(She bends towards Harriet). Now - how
do I look?

HARRIET: Candidly, my dear, you look unbalanced.

SERENA: That doesn't matter. It is the texture
that counts. My skin is still soft, is
it not? Soft enough, at any rate.

HARRIET: (Sternly) Soft enough for what, Serena?

SERENA: Soft enough to compensate a little for
the hardness of my character.

HARRIET: What rubbish you talk.

SERENA: Do you think there is still time? Do you
think it isn't too late?

HARRIET: Something must have happened to make you
behave like this. What is it?

SERENA: The hurdy-gurdy, perhaps; or the sudden
vision I had of poor Hubert filing away
so diligently at his chains.

HARRIET: Chains?

SERENA: The stubborn romantic, the eternal
troubadour, still eager to sing his
lilting ballads to anyone who will
listen. Oh, how dull I have been to
him! And how cruel! Have some bread and
butter.

HARRIET: I don't want any bread and butter. I only
want to know what has happened to you.

SERENA: Nothing, Harriet, I promise you.
Nothing at all.

HARRIET: But why should you suddenly accuse
yourself of being cruel to Hubert,
when you know perfectly well that but
for your amazing patience and tolerance
your married life would have broken up
years ago?

SERENA: Would the world have come to an end if
it had?

HARRIET: No. The world wouldn't have come to an
end, but it might have laughed at you,
and that would have been intolerable to
your pride.

SERENA: How right you are, Harriet. And what a
terrible indictment!

HARRIET: Indictment?

SERENA:	Yes - oh, dear me, yes! To deny the spring of the year for fear of mockery! What a fool I have been.
HARRIET:	Spring of the year, indeed! What nonsense! Hubert is a middle-aged philanderer and old enough to know better.
SERENA:	Charm is independent of age. He will always have charm.
HARRIET:	(Searchingly) Do you still love him?
SERENA:	(With a smile) Yes. I think that for the first time, I love him enough.
HARRIET:	And what can you possibly mean by that?
SERENA:	What a becoming hat, Harriet. Is it new?
HARRIET:	There are moments when I could willingly slap you, Serena.
SERENA:	Dear Harriet. Are you quite sure you won't have some more tea?
HARRIET:	You infuriate me, and what is more, you do it deliberately.
SERENA:	Just half a cup?
HARRIET:	(Rising) No thank you. I have to go.
SERENA:	Tell me more about Mrs Mallory.
HARRIET:	I've told you all I know.
SERENA:	Tell me other things, then. Tell me more about Miss Francis. She fascinates me. I see her suddenly in a new light; a refined, suburban truffle-pig, burrowing her way into her client's confidences, unearthing their sad little secrets, polishing them up to a nice shine, and then selling them round the town.
HARRIET:	Miss Francis is a perfectly respectable, hard-working woman, and she earns her living honestly.
SERENA:	(With finality) Goodbye, Harriet.
HARRIET:	(Startled) Serena! What do you mean?
SERENA:	You said you were going, and I said goodbye. What is there odd about that?
HARRIET:	You said it so abruptly.
SERENA:	I wish I could make amends.
HARRIET:	What for?
SERENA:	For being so - so unsatisfactory. We have been friends for so many, many years, and I have given you so little. Dear Harriet!

HARRIET:	Good heavens! There are tears in your eyes!
SERENA:	(Smiling) I know.
HARRIET:	You are unhappy about something. I knew it!
SERENA:	No, no. On the contrary, I am very happy indeed. (She unpins a brooch from her gown) I want you to have this. (She holds it out to her)
HARRIET:	(Astounded) Serena!
SERENA:	It belonged to my great-great-great-grand-mother. I believe she was very skittish.
HARRIET:	But why do you suddenly wish to give it to me?
SERENA:	To remember me by.
HARRIET:	Are you going away?
SERENA:	Yes. The seven-fifteen from Cannon Street. Alford is meeting me at Deal with the dog-cart. I am devoted to Alford, but he is getting dreadfully old. It's very sad, is it not, when people get dreadfully old - so soon? Please take the brooch.
HARRIET:	(Taking it) It's exquisite - I hardly know what to say. (She kisses her) Thank you, Serena - I shall treasure it always.
SERENA:	That's what I wanted you to say.
HARRIET:	You're sure that you're quite well? That there's nothing wrong?
SERENA:	Quite, quite sure.
HARRIET:	(Still puzzled) Goodbye, my dear.
SERENA:	Goodbye, Harriet. (Harriet goes out) (Serena stands looking after her for a moment, then she goes over to the bell-rope and pulls it.) (The hurdy-gurdy starts to play again a few streets away. Serena smiles and begins to waltz slowly round the room) (Catchpole, the Butler, enters)
CATCHPOLE:	You rang, milady?
SERENA:	(Stopping her dance) Yes, Catchpole. Has his lordship gone to the club?
CATCHPOLE:	He left a few minutes ago milady.

211

SERENA:	(Producing from her bag the letter she was writing at the beginning of the scene) Will you give him this when he comes in tonight? I shall be gone, and it is rather urgent.
CATCHPOLE:	(Taking it) Very good, milady. Will that be all?
SERENA:	Yes, Catchpole. That will be all. (Catchpole goes out and closes the door behind him) (Serena begins to dance again as the lights begin to fade on the scene)

Noël now agreed to play in Shaw's *The Apple Cart*, with Margaret Leighton as his co-star. 'I was bewitched by the play,' he said, 'because it's really an extremely good play. It's overwritten, like all Shaw, but I wish everyone had seen me in it. Lots of people approved. It's a fine play, except that it reaches its climax half the way through. Shaw's terribly difficult to play.'

MARGARET LEIGHTON: *My own part was relatively small. I only had one act in it. But Noël was absolutely splendid in it, and he knew it all backwards before rehearsals began—but this is one of his prerogatives, and I think in a sense, and certainly in Shaw, I would agree with him, because Shaw writes like a musical score, so that you can safely learn the notes before you start. We had a super time in that.*

As King Magnus in *The Apple Cart* with Margaret Leighton as Orinthia, Haymarket Theatre, London, May 1953.

During the London run of *The Apple Cart* Noël was doing his second season at the Café de Paris.

He used to go tootling off at night after the show to sing and I was having this lovely affair at the time which caused a great scandal [with Laurence Harvey, whom she subsequently married]. *Noël used to sing, 'Let's do it', but he used to make up his own lyrics and bring in all the names of the celebrities who came to the Café de Paris and when I used to go with Larry he would sing, 'Actors in Shakespeare do it'.*

When Hermione Gingold made *her* first appearance in cabaret at the Café de Paris, Noël went to see her.

HERMIONE GINGOLD: *His visit was the most frightening thing of all because Noël wags his finger and you never know whether he's saying, 'You are very bad' or 'You are very good', because it's the same finger wagging.*

212

However, when I heard he was in front, I was panic-stricken and I thought, 'I don't know if I can go on with this,' and then the most beautiful bouquet of flowers arrived in my dressing-room from Noël. It was absolutely lovely, and wrapped in cellophane, and I said, 'Well this I have got to open before I go on because it's so beautiful,' and I didn't want the flowers to die. So I opened it, and out flew a wasp. A large wasp which started to attack me! I was sure that Noël had put it there. I was so frightened of it chasing me round the room that I quite forgot to be nervous.

When Noël came round afterwards and I told him about the wasp, he absolutely denied having put it in the bouquet, but I still think he did. [He had no doubt remembered her performance in *Fallen Angels*.]

Noël had now finished *After the Ball*, his musical adaptation of Oscar Wilde's *Lady Windermere's Fan*. Although it was expertly directed by Robert Helpmann, and had enchanting music and lyrics, it flopped.

ROBERT HELPMANN:

You would have thought that a play of Wilde's with music by Noël Coward should be marvellous but I suddenly realised at the first rehearsal it was like having two funny people at a dinner party. Everything that Noël sent up Wilde was sentimental about, and everything that Wilde sent up Noël was sentimental about. It was two different points of view and it didn't work. It could never have worked.

It was at Ivor Novello's the first time I met Noël and I was doing an impersonation of Mary Ellis singing 'Glamorous Night' dressed up in one of Ivor's bedspreads, and Noël thought it was an absolute scream. I was a great one for doing party tricks in those days, impersonations of Margaret Rawlings and other leading ladies. But I never actually worked with Noël until he suddenly asked me to do After the Ball. *I think he'd seen some of the opera productions I'd done, and he just rang up out of the blue and said he was going to Jamaica, that I could have* carte blanche, *so I went down to see him in the country, and he played some of the music.*

'Absolute carte blanche, *dear boy. Absolutely . . .'*

Well! When he went off, talk of carte blanche! *He'd already cast it, selected the orchestrator and done everything.*

Then when he arrived back we were at Bristol. I'll never forget, it was a nightmare. I'd suggested cutting a rather difficult number one of the cast had to sing—the number would have made Kirsten Flagstad *boggle—and he replaced it with a comedy scene, but the actress fought like* a stag to keep the singing number in. However, it was cut and she was so nervous that she missed the first laugh. Noël and I were in the box—and she missed the second laugh, and she missed the third laugh, and Noël finally said, 'Come along with me,' and we rushed down the back of the circle, and I was saying, 'I'm the director, Noël, you're not to speak to anybody till after the performance.' As we got right down, I said, 'It's very difficult to get a laugh when you're nervous.'

And he turned to me and said, 'She couldn't get a laugh if she pulled a kipper out of her —' And with that we just both collapsed. And he never went around to see her. By the time we got back to the box, she was off the stage, and the audience were going 'Ha, ha, ha, ha', and Noël said, 'She's just pulled it out.'

That's why I've got a cigarette box in my drawing-room with a kipper drawn on it. He gave it to me on the first night.

Unfortunately she went from bad to worse, and got rather tricky during the tour, and Noël cracked, 'Trouble with her, she was dropped on her head when she was forty.'

He'd get in a fever of nerves, but he was so funny with it, we'd get home and absolutely roll about.

But a very odd thing about Noël—I don't know why, but twice in my life I've had complicated emotional problems— serious ones, and each time he's suddenly arrived. And I discussed it with him, and both times he advised me—both times correctly. It was very curious.

below, Vanessa Lee (Lady Windermere) and Mary Ellis (Mrs Erlynne) in *After the Ball* (1954).
right, in Las Vegas.

'Sweet Day'
from 'After the Ball'

Sweet day, remain for me
Clear in my memory,
When my heart's chilled by the snows of
  December,
Let me remember –
Let me remember,
Sweet day
That seems to be
Made up of dreams for me,
But when they've faded away
Let me remember today.

No melancholy dream,
No shadow of my heart,
No transitory gleam
Of danger in the sky,
Why should such happiness fill me today,
Why must such loveliness fade away,
Why must these magic moments fly
Just as the leaves of summer fall and
  die?

No melancholy dream,
No shadow on my heart,
Expecting that I know perfection cannot
  stay,
This has not been in vain,
This I will not betray,
When summer comes again
I shall remember . . .

The only remaining member of his family was his mother. But she was now ninety-one years old, and in July 1954 she died. He was deeply devoted to her, and her death was a great loss to him. He now appreciated the importance of close friends more than ever before. He spent his holiday that year in the South of France with his old friend Somerset Maugham.

After his fourth successful appearance at the Café de Paris he accepted a cabaret engagement at the Desert Inn Las Vegas for forty thousand dollars a week which he badly needed to pay his English back taxes.

MICHAEL WILDING:

I saw his opening night, his proud first night in Las Vegas. He wanted me to go, so I flew out with Joseph Cotten and his wife. And there was Noël. Terribly nervous, but of course splendid. He was excellent at it. Afterwards we went back-stage to see him, and he said, 'Michael, where were you? Why weren't you here?'

He had wanted me to be there all through rehearsals as

well! No one thinks of him as being nervous, or needing moral support. But he certainly wanted it.

He took no breaths at all when he sang, or so it seemed, at any rate. He breathed out all the time, never in once—he took no breaths at all—how he lived . . .?

'Put your hand on my stomach,' he said, and then sang 'Mad Dogs and Englishmen', it seemed from the top of his head, because there wasn't a single breath.

Radie Harris also flew over for his Las Vegas supper club début:

RADIE HARRIS:

I made the special trip out from New York to see him, and in his dressing-room before the show I told him that one of his favourite composers, David Rose, was at a ringside table. Noël was ecstatic because he's mad about David Rose's 'Holiday for Strings'. So as soon as his first show was over, Noël asked where David was sitting, and came round and stood at the back of him with his hands over David's eyes, and hummed through the entire chorus of 'Holiday for Strings'. The only mistake he made was that the man to whom he was singing was not *David Rose. He'd gone to the wrong table.*

With Jane Powell and Zsa Zsa Gabor in Las Vegas.

Later *Quadrille* opened on Broadway; the Lunts were still in it, and Alfred Lunt was directing. Although American earnings kept the wolf from the door, it did not entirely relieve Noël's English tax burden. The severe losses of *Pacific 1860*, *Ace of Clubs* and *After the Ball* left him with a bank overdraft of £19,000, making it impossible for him to run his three houses in Kent, London and Jamaica. He was advised to give up British domicile and take up permanent residence abroad, forcing him to choose between the England he loved, and saving money for his old age.

COUP AND RECOUP

as Roland Hesketh-Baggott,
Around the World in Eighty Days.

NOËL COWARD:

Noël sold his Gerald Road studio flat, and Goldenhurst in Kent, and, since Bermuda offered greater tax concessions than Jamaica, he moved into a house on the former island, Spithead Lodge in Warwick, once owned by Eugene O'Neill.

Here he stayed for two years, although he kept on Blue Harbour in Jamaica, and later returned there.

He accepted several film roles, among them Michael Todd's production of *Around the World in Eighty Days*. He played Roland Hesketh-Baggott, manager of a London employment agency, and he wrote his own dialogue.

One of the reasons I accepted the part was that, having seen Oklahoma! *I thought that if Todd-AO could make acres of green corn look so lovely, it could do the same for me. I was fascinated to see that the script described my role as 'superior and ineffably smug'. It was clearly type-casting.*

This was followed by three coast-to-coast American television specials for CBS—*Together with Music*, with Mary Martin, *Blithe Spirit*, with Claudette Colbert and Lauren Bacall, and *This Happy Breed*, with Edna Best.

In a supreme effort to recover his British losses, he revised a play of his that had been produced in America five years before, *Island Fling*. Retitled *South Sea Bubble*, and with Vivien Leigh playing the lead it was put on in the West End. Noël had put everything he knew into it, and his labours paid off. It was a roaring success.

Vivien Leigh and Ian Hunter in *South Sea Bubble*.

'South Sea Bubble'
(Taken from Act Three)

The action is set on the verandah of Government House on an island, a British possession, in the Pacific. Lady Alexandra – Sandra (Vivien Leigh) – has been out until late the night before with Hali Alani, one of the island's young native politicians. He has made an amorous pass at her in a drunken scene at his home, and in order to get away from him, she hit him over the head with a bottle. The following morning she is breakfasting with her husband George, the Governor, and Boffin, a novelist friend visiting from England.

GEORGE:	I wonder who the devil did it?
SANDRA:	(Absently) Did what?
GEORGE:	Tried to murder Hali, of course.
SANDRA:	Murder? Really, George, aren't you being a little melodramatic?
GEORGE:	Well, he had his head bashed in with a bottle.
SANDRA:	Probably only in fun.
GEORGE:	Was he drunk at Mitzi's party?
SANDRA:	Of course he wasn't. He behaved exquisitely. There's a certain old-world courtesy about Hali that I find most engaging. Didn't you notice it at dinner, Boffin?
BOFFIN:	I was too riveted by Admiral Turling's conversation to notice anything else.

	I had no idea sailors' lives were so monotonous. As far as I could gather he had Mrs Turling in every port.
GEORGE:	I don't altogether trust that old-world courtesy. I suspect that underneath it he is a horse of quite a different colour.
SANDRA:	Do you mean a dark-coloured horse or a coloured dark horse?
GEORGE:	It's nothing to joke about. This business might lead to a lot of trouble - bad trouble.
SANDRA:	I don't see any reason to make such a terrible issue of it. It's all quite obvious to me.
GEORGE:	Oh it is, is it?
SANDRA:	Of course.
GEORGE:	Perhaps you'll explain then, if you know so much about it.
SANDRA:	I don't know anything. But I can make a pretty shrewd guess.
BOFFIN:	So can I.
SANDRA:	(Shooting him a quick look) What do you mean by that?
BOFFIN:	Exactly what you mean, dear, I suspect.
GEORGE:	If either of you have any ideas that might shed a little light on the situation I should be very pleased to hear them.
SANDRA:	Well, my theory is that he had a woman out there with him in the beach house and that they had a row, and she fetched him a nice wallop with the bottle and took his car and drove home.
GEORGE:	Why was the car abandoned in a ditch?
BOFFIN:	(Looking at Sandra) Perhaps she didn't drive very well. Or perhaps she was drunk - what do you think, Sandra?
SANDRA:	I couldn't agree with you more. I can visualise the whole thing. She was probably one of those almond-eyed half-caste women, very sinuous and clattering with cheap jewellery.
GEORGE:	How did she get there? It's a long way away and quite isolated.
SANDRA:	I expect he'd sent her over earlier in the day and she was waiting for him there, crouching in the shadows with her

	eyes gleaming like half-moons.
BOFFIN:	Half-caste half-moon.
SANDRA:	Perhaps it was a sort of show down. She might have had a child by him, and . . .
GEORGE:	One of those strong swimmers, no doubt.
SANDRA:	It's all very fine for you to jeer, but I bet I'm right.
GEORGE:	You say Hali dropped you off here at approximately twelve forty-five?
SANDRA:	No, it was Bob who said that. Don't you remember he kept adding up all the times –
GEORGE:	Be that as it may, Hali did drop you here after the party, didn't he?
SANDRA:	Of course. I couldn't very well have walked, could I? It's miles.
GEORGE:	You'd be willing to swear to that in a court of law?
SANDRA:	You always have to swear to everything in a court of law on account of them rushing at you with that little Bible.
GEORGE:	Do you remember which sentry was on duty at the door last night?
SANDRA:	(After an imperceptible pause) Distinctly. The very tall thin one with the enormous Adam's apple.
GEORGE:	Did you say good night to him?
SANDRA:	No. I didn't want to wake him.
GEORGE:	Wake him! You mean he was asleep?
SANDRA:	Fast asleep. And I for one don't blame him. Having to stand there hour after hour with nothing to look at but that awful old banyan tree. It's enough to give one the creeps.
GEORGE:	Are you telling me that the sentry on duty outside Government House was fast asleep?
SANDRA:	If you say anything about it I shall never forgive you. I should hate to get the poor boy into trouble.
GEORGE:	You are telling me the truth, Sandra, aren't you?
SANDRA:	George, whatever is the matter with you? You're behaving exactly like one of those Agatha Christie detective inspectors with pin-stripe suits and bowler hats.

GEORGE:	Are you or are you not telling me the truth?
SANDRA:	Of course I am. Why on earth shouldn't I?
GEORGE:	You left the party with Hali. He drove you back here . . .
SANDRA:	Far too fast. We nearly killed two chickens and we missed the lamp standard at the crossroads by inches.
GEORGE:	And he wasn't drunk?
SANDRA:	No. He just likes driving like a maniac.
GEORGE:	He dropped you here and went on by himself?
SANDRA:	He flashed off down the drive like a streak with the exhaust full out. I wonder you didn't hear it, it was enough to wake the dead.
GEORGE:	But it didn't wake the sentry?
SANDRA:	(After a slight pause) No - he just gave a little grunt and turned over.
GEORGE:	Was he lying down?
SANDRA:	No - just sort of leaning, and he didn't exactly turn over, he just changed his position.
GEORGE:	You didn't go with Hali?
SANDRA:	(Shocked) George!
GEORGE:	It wasn't you who was with him at the beach house?
BOFFIN:	Clattering with cheap jewellery?
GEORGE:	Shut up, Boffin.
SANDRA:	(With dignity) I think, George, that this inquisition has gone far enough.
GEORGE:	You haven't answered my question.
SANDRA:	It didn't deserve an answer. No man with the faintest sensitivity or perception would have asked it.
GEORGE:	Now look here, Sandra -
SANDRA:	(Mowing him down) I'm willing to forgive you for being a little crotchety and difficult in the mornings. That's only to be expected, because you eat far too much and take no exercise whatever. I should like to remind you that this is a very hot and livery climate, far, far removed from the bracing, invigorating breezes of Huddersfield.

GEORGE:	I haven't set foot in Huddersfield for fifteen years.
SANDRA:	That in itself is a shameful admission and only proves how dismally ambition and the lust for power has corrupted you. A man who will ruthlessly abandon his own birthplace and cold-shoulder his childhood playmates merely for political advancement – the man who would do these things – the man who would so complacently betray his ideals, is most certainly not the man I married. Where – I ask you – is the man I married?
GEORGE:	Standing directly in front of you, my love, and stop talking nonsense.
SANDRA:	I am willing to forgive you for your curious behaviour this morning because it is my considered opinion that you are far from well.
GEORGE:	Sandra . . .
SANDRA:	Doctor Crosbie said only the other day, when you were gorging those Bombay mangoes at lunch, that you were insulting your metabolism.
GEORGE:	My metabolism, Sandra, has nothing whatever to do with the subject under discussion.
SANDRA:	Of course, if you wish to insult your metabolism from morning till night, that's entirely your own affair. But for you to insult me with your base insinuations and lascivious innuendoes in front of poor Boffin, who has come all the way out here to relax and bask in this glorious climate –
GEORGE:	You said just now that it was hot and livery.
SANDRA:	I'm going to my room. I have a great deal to do this morning, so I shall not see you again until luncheon, by which time I hope that you will have recovered your manners
GEORGE:	(Firmly) Once and for all, Sandra, did you or did you not go with Hali Alani to his beach house last night and bash him over the head with a bottle?
SANDRA:	Certainly I did. And if you don't stop bellowing at me I'll do the same to you. Come, Boffin – (She sweeps away, with Boffin in tow)

Noël's next play, *Nude with Violin*, both starred and was directed by John Gielgud. Before it opened in Dublin, Noël went to see a dress-rehearsal and found that Gielgud had concentrated so much on directing the play that his own performance had been neglected. He offered to help him by directing the scenes in which he appeared.

JOHN GIELGUD:

We had rehearsed and opened in Ireland, but on his arrival in Dublin from Bermuda Noël was warned that to land in England itself would involve him in a £25,000 surtax debt.

Kathleen Harrison, Patience Collier and I opened it in London on November 7th 1956, at the Globe Theatre, but I had to leave the cast after seven months to fulfil a Stratford-upon-Avon commitment, and Michael Wilding took over the role.

MICHAEL WILDING:

I wasn't very good in it, and I don't think Noël liked me much in it either. I didn't apply myself. Noël was there during most of the rehearsals when I took over. I remember one day in the middle of a scene, this scream rent the air, 'No, no, no, no, no!'

Noël came flying down the aisle to the foot of the stage. 'What—what's wrong?' I asked anxiously.

'You mooooved!' he said.

'Where—where did I move—I only moved about two inches.'

'You don't move at all on that line!'

'All right, Noël, I won't,' I replied meekly. And I didn't.

But when I was in it, the business simply shot up—I believe I broke the theatre's record. But it was really because of an American lawyer's convention that had arrived in London—three thousand of them, with their wives, and they all came to see the play. They didn't come to see me, they came to see a Noël Coward play. As the result of those packed houses a producer gave me a rather good job in America—but I never told him about the convention.

MARGARET LEIGHTON: *I saw Noël in it too, in New York. I went to see it with Adlai Stevenson, no less.*

MICHAEL WILDING: *Who was better in it? Noël or me?*

MARGARET LEIGHTON: (Tactfully) *You were more attractive.*

MICHAEL WILDING: *It was a very difficult part to learn, there were four languages to speak and Noël writes dialogue for himself, and it's hard to copy him—which is boring for others, but to do it your own way doesn't suit the dialogue quite so well.*

I played it for about six months and was followed in it by Robert Helpmann. I remember going in to say goodbye to the company, and nipped into my old dressing-room. There was Bobby, ready to go on—made up like a dago, with an ear-ring in his ear!

MARGARET LEIGHTON: *My favourite thing that happened was one night when Michael and I asked Noël to come to dinner, and we suggested a well-known West End fish restaurant.*

'I've never heard of it,' Noël said, and I replied. 'It's basically a step up on Wheelers.'

'Is one step enough?' he asked tartly. Anyhow, we went, and there wasn't a soul there. There were a lot of waitresses in white coats.

'This looks very sinister,' Noël said, 'I don't like those matrons wandering about, it's like a hospital.' And then the head waiter came up and said, 'Oh, Mr Wilding, we have two woodcock left—we've saved them specially.' Yet there wasn't anyone else in the place. So Michael insisted that Noël and I should have the woodcock, and he gallantly ordered salmon for himself.

Well, Noël couldn't get his knife through it, but tried the best he could to tackle it. The head waiter came hovering back and said, 'Ah, Mr Coward—I do hope, sir, that you found no shot in it.'

'No, no,' said Noël, 'it died a natural death.'

'*Trouble is,*' *he added, digging his knife into it,* '*there's too much wood, and not enough cock.*'

The part of Sebastien in *Nude with Violin* was first written for Noël himself; the play was then altered to suit Yvonne Arnaud as a French maid, but Noël changed it once again as a vehicle for Gielgud.

Kathleen Harrison, who was cast for the role of Cherry-May Waterton, a rather strident ex-chorus girl, was more accustomed to playing gentle, sympathetic parts. During rehearsals, when Noël told her to make the character harder, she replied, 'But if I do, the audience won't like me.'

'You could cut up a baby on the stage and they'll still love you,' he retorted.

ROBERT HELPMANN:

I was asked to take over from John Gielgud in Nude with Violin *but I couldn't because I was still at the Old Vic, then Michael Wilding went in, and then Binkie said would I take over from him. So I went over and had tea with Noël in Philadelphia and he said,* '*I've written in new things.*' *I looked at the script, and he'd written in some Chinese dialogue. There were already four languages to learn as it was, and now Chinese! So I said,* '*Noël, dear, it's difficult enough.*'

'*Bobby, remember,*' *he replied,* '*that one night, the lonely little Chinaman sitting in the front.*'

So I said, '*Oh Noël!*'

Several times in the play he answered the telephone in these various foreign languages, and each time one of the cast would ask who it was, and there was a funny line; for the Chinaman he said, '*The physical training instructor from the Shanghai Y.M.C.A.*'

'*You've got to learn the Chinese properly. Remember that little lonely Chinaman . . .*' *he kept saying.*

But that night he came on, picked up the telephone and said, '*Chu Chin Chow. Hong Kong. Anna May Wong.*' *Never said a word of Chinese! And I went round and said,* '*You really are too much,*' *and he replied,* '*It's all right, there was no Chinaman in front tonight.*'

I rehearsed to myself, learning the lines in Noël's voice, an imitation of him, then did it in my own voice of course. It's an absolute definite rhythm. We had a dress rehearsal preview. And when it came to a laugh line I tested it out by saying it in Noël's voice and it always worked, so I knew the rhythm—but naturally it would have been fatal for me to have impersonated him on the stage, but it was certainly a way of getting the laughs.

He's as difficult to learn as Bernard Shaw, because he

puts everything so rightly that if you get a word wrong you can't substitute words for Noël's lines. If you dry you can't substitute—you're lost—even Shakespeare you can substitute, you can sometimes make up a Shakespearean line in rhythm, but you can't Noël—you've got to keep it on the nose.

John Gielgud made one of his marvellous bricks during rehearsals. I said I wouldn't play it if I was just put in by a stage manager, and John was at Stratford, so he said he would come up and rehearse me for a week. But he never said a word to me at all—he gave notes to the cast who'd been playing it for two years till they nearly went out of their minds and he never corrected me once. He'd say, 'Try it lying down.' I'd lie down. He said, 'Stand up.' I stood up. 'Sit over there. Move over there.' And then he'd say to the others, 'You see, he can do it. He's a dancer. He's trained to do it. You can't do it.'

The final rehearsal before I opened, he walked down and said, 'I think you're absolutely marvellous, Bobby, the way you've done it in the time. It's absolutely extraordinary. Of course I could never have played it like that. You see, I'm a straight actor.'

And I said, 'I've been waiting for that one the whole week.'

'Oh my God,' he said, 'I didn't mean that . . .'

It was a huge success in Australia. It opened in Melbourne and Sydney, Brisbane and New Zealand, and ran for over a year altogether. I said to Williamsons that the chorus girl should be played by a woman called Fifi Banvard—she was an old musical comedy actress—and they said, 'Oh I think she's dead.' But she wasn't. She is now. She played it and was absolutely marvellous because she was an old chorus girl. When I was a little boy my mother and father were mad about a woman called Mini Love who played in The Pink Lady *and she'd been retired for years, and I found her. She came back and played Zena Dare's part—Zena took over from Joyce Carey in London when I played it—finally Mini went on to play the mother in* My Fair Lady *in Australia—she's dead now, too.*

By chance I invented some business which happened by accident, and I took a recording of the production and played it to Noël when I got back and he said, 'And what *did you do there?'*

'Well, when I was serving the drink to the Countess,' I said, 'I jumped over her fur and kicked it so it finished up on my shoulders.' And he said, 'You would, you clever little thing.'

I don't think Noël frightens people, I think they want to

please him so much that they get thrown sometimes. His standards are tremendously high and I think everybody thinks if they fall below that it's very bad.

above, Robert Helpmann in *Nude With Violin*.
above right, John Gielgud.

'Nude with Violin'
(Taken from Act One)

The action of the play takes place in the Paris studio of Paul Sorodin, a rich and famous artist, who has just died. He has left no will and his wife, Isobel (Joyce Carey), from whom he has been separated for twenty-five years, has returned to claim the estate, bringing with her their children, Jane and Colin. Colin's wife Pamela is also present, as is Jacob Friedland, art-dealer and family friend.
The family wish to make some financial allowance to the indispensable butler, Sebastien (John Gielgud), who has served Sorodin for the past twenty years.

SEBASTIEN: You were about to say, madame –?

ISOBEL: I was about to say that, in consideration of your services to my late husband, Mr Friedland and I have

	decided to offer you the choice of a sum of money to be paid in the near future – or – or a small pension. Which would you prefer?
SEBASTIEN:	Without wishing to be discourteous, neither, madame.
PAMELA:	Well, really!
SEBASTIEN:	Please believe me when I say how profoundly I appreciate your kindness and consideration. To you, Miss Jane, and you, Mr Friedland, I must also express my gratitude. I happened to be listening outside the door just now when the matter was being discussed.
COLIN:	Typical! Exactly what I should have expected.
JANE:	(Amused) That was disgraceful of you, Sebastien.
SEBASTIEN:	You will understand therefore how much it pains me, in the face of such spontaneous generosity, to be the bearer of what I fear will be most disturbing news.
JACOB:	Disturbing news! What do you mean?
SEBASTIEN:	Although Mr Sorodin left no will, he did leave a letter.
JACOB:	Letter?
SEBASTIEN:	A personal letter addressed to me. It was written in the early hours of the morning of January 1st of this year, and was witnessed by Marie-Céleste and the head waiter from the 'Grâce à Dieu'. He had organised the catering.
COLIN:	Catering?
SEBASTIEN:	We had given a little party. Nothing grandiose, you understand, just a small gathering of intimate friends, quite informal.
JACOB:	(Obviously disturbed) Never mind about that. What's all this leading up to?
COLIN:	Blackmail. I can smell it a mile off.
JACOB:	Where is this letter?
SEBASTIEN:	In a strong-box in the Royal Bank of Canada. But I have a copy of it.
JACOB:	(Authoritatively) Let me see it, please.
SEBASTIEN:	No, monsieur. That would be a betrayal of confidence. Also it is very long and contains many irrelevancies of a

	personal nature. I am, however, perfectly prepared to read you any extracts that are pertinent to the present circumstances.
JACOB:	What is the meaning of this? What are you up to?
SEBASTIEN:	I'm not up to anything. I'm merely embarrassed, for reasons that will be only too apparent later on.
JACOB:	Come to the point, please. Read the letter.
SEBASTIEN:	(Looking at Isobel) Have I madame's permission?
ISOBEL:	(Agitated) I suppose so - Jacob - what am I to say?
JACOB:	(To Sebastien) You have madame's permission to proceed.
COLIN:	There's something fishy about this.
JANE:	Shut up, Colin.
JACOB:	(Impatiently) Go on.
SEBASTIEN:	(With a slight shrug) Very well. Actually I would have preferred to read it to you or to your lawyer in private, Monsieur Friedland. However, if you insist, I have no choice. Just a moment.
	(In tense silence he produces a wad of papers from his inner pocket, glances through them, extracts a typewritten letter and places the rest carefully back in his pocket. He clears his throat and looks at everyone with a slight smile) Ready?
COLIN:	For God's sake get on with it.
SEBASTIEN	(Reading) 'My dear Sebastien. In case the validity of this personal letter to you should ever be questioned, I will begin it by stating that I am sane and healthy and in full possession of my faculties -' (He looks up) Actually he had a slight head cold at the time.
JACOB:	Never mind about that - go on.
JANE:	The news in your letter must be very bad, Sebastien, you're obviously enjoying yourself.
SEBASTIEN:	Not exactly bad, Miss Jane. Shall we say - startling?

229

JACOB:	(Almost shouting) Read it!
SEBASTIEN:	(Continuing to read) 'In the event of my demise, I have decided to leave no will and testament, for the simple reason that always having spent any money I earned the moment I received it and frequently before I received it, I have nothing to leave to anyone beyond a few personal effects. In recognition of your loyal service to me since July 13th, 1946, I should have liked to have bequeathed you a handsome emolument, or at least to have repaid the two hundred and seventy thousand francs I owe you. However, you will doubtless be able to recover this paltry sum from that stingy old bastard Jacob Friedland.' (He looks up and smiles deprecatingly)
JACOB:	(Grimly) Continue.
SEBASTIEN:	'The whole of my estate will inevitably revert to my loving wife as a just and fitting recompense for the monumental lack of understanding she has lavished on me since we first met on Armistice night 1918, when, owing to an excess of patriotism and inferior Sauterne, she consented to join her life to mine.'
COLIN:	(Protectively) Mother, I really think --
ISOBEL:	Hush, Colin. I would like to hear the rest of the letter.
JACOB:	Perhaps it would be advisable, Isobel, for you to return to the hotel with Pamela and Jane. I can deal with this.
ISOBEL:	No, Jacob. My husband's insults, even from beyond the grave, are powerless to hurt me.
COLIN:	Good for you, Mother.
JACOB:	Whatever you wish, my dear. (To Sebastien) Go on.
SEBASTIEN:	(Reading) 'I am well aware that, thanks to Mr Friedland's unscrupulous business acumen, my canvases have achieved a commercial value grossly out of proportion to their merits. In fairness to him, however, I must state that I have reaped considerable financial benefit from his quite remarkable capacity for deceiving the public. My wife and family, also thanks to him, have received over the years a fair

percentage of the profits, although I consider this sop to the laws of matrimony unnecessary as my wife has always enjoyed a more than adequate income of her own' - (He looks up) there now comes a rather long dissertation on the iniquities of the marriage and divorce laws. It is actually irrelevant to the present situation but quite amusing in a bawdy way. Mr Sorodin had a rich and varied vocabulary, as you may remember. Would you like me to read it or skip to the more important part of the letter, the clou, as we say in France?

JACOB: (Tersely) Skip it and go on.

SEBASTIEN: Very well. (He reads in a barely distinguishable undertone) - 'bla bla bla - Canon Law - bla bla bla - self-centred, sanctimonious hypocrites - bla bla bla - bloody impertinence - bla bla bla -' Ah, here we are. 'In consideration of the fact that when this letter is ultimately made public I shall be in my grave, I feel it to be only fair that the world of Art, to which I owe so much, should receive from me one final and unequivocal statement, which is that, with the exception of a water-colour of a dog executed at Broadstairs when I was eleven years old, I have never painted a picture of any sort or kind in the whole course of my life.' (Isobel gives a slight cry, puts her hand to her throat and chokes)

(Curtain)

Ballet dancer and choreographer Anton Dolin, was director of the London Festival Ballet Company in 1959, and for its tenth anniversary he asked Noël to compose the music for a new ballet. In due course Noël invited him over to hear the score

ANTON DOLIN: *I got to the airport in Bermuda, and a Press photographer asked whether she might take a photograph of me with Noël. I went through Customs, and said to Noël, who had come to the airport to meet me, 'I'm afraid I've let you in for a photograph.' He looked at me for a moment, and said, 'I'd've been pretty well annoyed if you hadn't. What do you think I've come all this way to meet you for? It's a long bicycle ride.'*

He played some of the music to me on the piano in his

drawing-room, and it turned out to be exactly what I'd hoped for. Charming, light and lyrical. The ballet was done eventually in London, and though I can't say the critics cared for it much, it filled the Royal Festival Hall every time it was performed for at least two or three seasons. They loved it in Israel, they loved it in Barcelona and they loved it in South America.

Perhaps if it had been a more serious work it might have lived longer in the repertoire of any ballet company, but it was what Noël wanted.

It was called London Morning, *and its setting was outside Buckingham Palace.*

Actually, it had a rather drastic influence on the Palace. The sentries at that time were outside the Palace gates, and part of the ballet involved good-humoured American tourists arriving in London, and together with naughty children coming up from their schools, rather annoying the sentries, parodying what the real sentries had to endure. About four weeks later the sentries outside the actual Palace railings were moved inside the gates.

With the beginning of the sixties there bourgeoned a new school of playwrights in the English theatre, including John Osborne, Harold Pinter, Arnold Wesker, John Arden, Sheila Delaney and many others. As the new and exciting *Oklahoma!* had brought with it a change in audience's tastes for musicals, the 'kitchen sink' now took its firm grip on the theatre-going public, leaving Noël, whose romantic and sophisticated style was inimitably set, out in the cold. Further evidence of the audiences change in taste came with the failure of *Look after Lulu*, Noël's adaptation from the Feydeau farce *Occupe-toi d'Amélie*, starring Vivien Leigh.

Noël decided to sell his Bermuda home, and, for tax reasons, settle in Switzerland. He bought an enchanting villa on the edge of a tiny village called Les Avants, on the slopes above mountains and at the far end of Lake Geneva. The house is set into the hillside, surrounded on three sides by snow-capped mountains where a funicular clangs its way to the top; a girls' school stands below, and beyond lies the lake.

Fortunately he was continuously in demand for film appearances, and over the next few years he made in swift succession *Our Man in Havana*, an adaptation of the Graham Greene novel, directed by Carol Reed, in which he played an MI5 high-up who recruits Alec Guinness as an unwilling spy; *Surprise Package* with Yul Brynner; *Paris When it Sizzles* with Audrey Hepburn and William Holden, and *The Italian Job* with Michael Caine.

NOËL COWARD:

(Talking about his new career as a film actor) *I think it's very very valuable to have been a theatre actor, because of a sense of timing. But I find it terribly tedious making movies. For one reason only—the rest of it I enjoy very much, but the tedious thing is that you play a scene for the first time and the entire staff—convulsions! So then you do it another time for the sound, and then you do it again because the lighting hasn't been quite right, or something's gone wrong, and by the time you get to the actual take, they're all going about yawning and looking away, and wishing they weren't there. That is not encouraging for light comedy. That's what I don't like about filming.*

far left, with Vivien Leigh. *left*, in *Our Man in Havana*. With Michael Caine in *The Italian Job*. *right*, in *Paris when it Sizzles* (1963).

He had now completed his first novel, *Pomp and Circumstance* and began revising the play *Waiting in the Wings*, soon to open in the West End. I asked him how he found

the comparison between writing books and plays, and the concentration and time involved in both.

NOËL COWARD: *Well, I need much longer for books. A book takes months and months and months. A play, if all goes well, takes only a comparatively short time. A few days.*

CHARLES CASTLE: *But a great many playwrights sweat for months over their plays.*

NOËL COWARD: *I've been in the theatre all my life and it makes a great difference. I don't have to worry as an amateur playwright would about getting people on and off the stage. I've been brought up on that, so I know. For instance, something subtle like a bell ringing and someone saying, 'That must be for me.' And then they go off; and it's for them. It's not difficult.*

CHARLES CASTLE: *And the technique of writing comedy?*

NOËL COWARD: *The technique of writing comedy is absolutely indefinable because you can be very surprised by a line which you don't think is funny at all—you get a belly laugh. And a line that you've been planning to rock the house with—dead silence. That often happens with comedy.*

I've never had any ambition to do anything other than be in the theatre. Perhaps in surgery, though. A doctor maybe. Or a surgeon. I've seen almost every major operation there is—I love watching operations. It might have something to do with the fact that people fascinate me most of anything in life.

SEIZED WITH EXCITEMENT

Waiting in the Wings was now complete, and Sybil Thorndike was asked to play the leading part.

SYBIL THORNDIKE: *I'd just finished a play, and was sitting at home thinking, 'Now I'm going to have a little bit of peace,' when Peggy Webster and Noël came in with this play and said, 'We want you to do it.' Of course I was thrilled to be asked, and said, 'Of course I'll do it.' Mind you, I hadn't read it yet, but I knew that it would be something—and I was absolutely delighted at being asked.*

It was a beautiful piece of characterisation, and so tender. That's where Noël is so wonderful—he's got this infinite tenderness. I think it was his devotion to old people that made him so desperately sorry for all those old girls in that home [the play concerns a home for retired actresses]. *Oh, I loved that play, it's the most lovely modern play I've played. It was modern with a beautiful shape—not like some of the modern plays you see today that have no beginning and no end—but that was his musicianship. All his plays have perfect shape.*

Mind you, it had that same cruelty that The Vortex *had. My scene with my son was a very cruel scene really, but awfully funny.*

On the day before the opening, Marie Löhr, who had gone to early morning mass, slipped on the steps as she left the church and broke her arm. She opened on the first night, all the same, but with her arm in a sling.

'It just goes to prove,' said Noël philosophically, 'that good deeds never go unpunished.'

Of course when Noël was in front we were all seized with, no, not nerves—but excitement; I used to be frightfully excited when I knew he was in front. And every blessed time he was there I dried up. I always had one bad dry when Noël was in front. And he came round after the first performance I gave and said, 'Fluffy Damesy!'

And 'Fluffy Damesy' has been my name that has stuck to me from Noël. He always begins letters or telegrams, 'Darling Fluffy', which is a shame, because I'm not a fluffy actress. But always when he was in front, I fluffed. Wasn't it terrible?

NOËL COWARD: *Waiting in the Wings depressed me really. I thought it was very well played, but it was a very depressing subject and it used rather to get me down.*

Sybil Thorndike and Marie Lohr in *Waiting in the Wings* (Graham Payn on left).

'Waiting in the Wings'
(Taken from Act Two)

'The Wings' is a small charity home for retired actresses, subscribed to by public funds, and controlled by a committee of leading actors and actresses. The occupants are keen to have a solarium, but at a cost of £2,500 are doubtful that the committee will agree. Perry (Graham Payn), an intermediary between the committee and the home, has devised the scheme whereby Zelda Fenwick (Jessica Dunning), a journalist, should visit 'The Wings' in order to write an article on the home and to make a television appeal for funds for the solarium. However, journalists are officially forbidden access. Lotta (Sybil Thorndike) and May Davenport (Marie Löhr) don't see eye to eye. They, and Cora, May, Estelle and Deirdre, four of the other retired actresses, are present when the journalist arrives.

PERRY: Lotta, I don't think you've met Miss Starkey.

ZELDA: (Advancing) Hallo - how are you?

LOTTA: (Shaking hands and staring at her) Miss Starkey?

ZELDA: Yes. I came down with Perry. We're old friends.

LOTTA: Is Starkey your private name?

ZELDA: Private name? I -

LOTTA: You're Zelda Fenwick, aren't you - the one who writes the 'People are News' column in the Sunday Clarion?

ZELDA: (After a pause) Yes. Yes I am.

MISS ARCHIE: Oh Lord - that's torn it!

MAY: (Rising) Is this true, Perry?

PERRY: (Guiltily) Yes. Perfectly true.

LOTTA: (To Zelda) I saw you on television a few weeks ago. (She turns to Perry) I think, Perry, that it would have been far more polite and considerate if you had introduced Miss Fenwick by her proper name.

PERRY: (Miserably) I'll explain it later. I'll explain it all later.

LOTTA: I'm sure that no explanation is in the least necessary. It's merely a little confusing, that's all.

MAY: I beg to differ. A great deal of explanation is necessary. (To Zelda) May I ask, Miss Fenwick, if you are here in a professional capacity?

ZELDA: (With spirit) I am always in a professional capacity, Miss Davenport. That is an essential part of my job.

MAY: Is the committee aware of your visit to us?

ZELDA: No. And, if I may say so, I rather resent your tone. I am not answerable

	to you for my actions or to your committee.
PERRY:	Just a minute - please let me explain.
MAY:	(In rich tones) Be quiet, Perry.
LOTTA:	(With considerable authority) It seems to me that the situation is being rather over-dramatised. (May starts to interrupt but Lotta silences her) No, May. I'm afraid I must insist on speaking. I would like Miss Fenwick clearly to understand that we are delighted to welcome her here. We have, as a rule, very few visitors. I am sure, however, that Miss Fenwick herself will be the first to realise that it will place us all in a most humiliating position if she mentions either 'The Wings' itself or any of its occupants in her newspaper. In the first place it would be a breach of the rules of this - (She smiles) - this rather 'specialised' charity, and in the second place I am sure that, even in her professional capacity, she would not wish either to betray our confidence or abuse our hospitality. I am right, aren't I? Miss Fenwick?
ZELDA:	(Awkwardly) Well - er - as a matter of fact -
LOTTA:	You will promise, won't you, even if you had it in mind to write a story about us, not to write it? Our own professional careers are long ago over and done with, some of our names may still be remembered by a few people but those get fewer and fewer as the years go by. We are quite content, living out our days in this most agreeable backwater. The last thing we want any more is publicity. It would shed too harsh a light on us, show up all our lines and wrinkles, betray to the world how old and tired we are. That would be an unkind thing to do. We are still actresses in our hearts, we still have our little vanities and prides. We'd like to be remembered as we were, not as we are. You will give us your promise, won't you?
ZELDA:	I appreciate what you say, Miss Bainbridge. But I'm afraid I must be

honest with you. My editor's been trying to get a story on this place for years. I know you'll understand that it isn't only in the theatre that the job must come first. I can't promise not to write about 'The Wings' but I can promise to do all I can to help. I'd already arranged with Perry that if he let me come here I would make a personal appeal on television for your solarium.

CORA:	Solarium - good God! Are we to sell our souls to get that damned solarium!
LOTTA:	Oh, Cora - please -
MAY:	I'm ashamed of you, Perry. Mortally, mortally ashamed.
MISS ARCHIE:	Here, steady on. It's no good flying off the handle to Perry. He only did it for the best.
ESTELLE:	(Wailing) It's all my fault - I was the one who suggested it in the first place.
DEIRDRE:	(Rising dramatically) Shame on you, Miss Whatever-your-name-is! Shame on you for worming your way in here like a wolf in sheep's clothing and talking to us as sweet as honey while all the time you were gouging out the secrets of our hearts for your shoddy catchpenny newspaper. Shame on you, I say! And may the Holy Mother of God forgive you for making a mock of a houseful of poor defenceless old women who are only asking to be left in peace and quiet. The devil's curse on you for being a double-faced, scheming hypocrite! Write what you like and be damned to to you! I've said my say. (She sits down again)
LOTTA:	You certainly have, Deirdre. And I for one would like to throttle you.
ZELDA:	I can't stand any more of this. Are you coming, Perry?
PERRY:	(Wretchedly) No. I'm staying here.
ZELDA:	(Curtly) Goodbye, everybody. I'm sorry to have caused such a hullabaloo. (She marches out)
MAY:	(In stentorian tones) The whole thing is an outrage - an outrage!
CORA:	For heaven's sake calm down, May.
MAY:	The committee must be warned

```
immediately, pressure must be brought to
bear.
Personally I think a great deal of fuss
is being made about nothing. What does
it really matter whether she writes
about us or not?
We shall be publicly degraded.
Nonsense! She'll probably write a lot of
sentimental rubbish which will embarrass
us for a little until we forget it and
everyone else does too. Let's go in to
tea and talk about something else.
I really am sorry. I did it for the
best, honestly I did.
I'm sure you did, Perry, but, if you
will forgive my saying so, it was an
error in taste.
          (She sweeps out, the others follow,
     all talking at once)
```

Occupied with his film commitments, Noël had done little writing in the past two years, but now spent the winter of 1960 at Blue Harbour in Jamaica where he wrote *Sail Away*, his first musical since *Ace of Clubs*. The title was taken from the hit number in *Ace of Clubs*.

It opened on Broadway in October 1961, where it ran for five months, and transferred to the Savoy Theatre in London in June 1962 where it ran for the remainder of the year.

(When, years later, Noël went to the film preview of *The Lion in Winter* with Margalo Gillmore, who had appeared in the Broadway production of *Sail Away*, he was exasperated by the long slow bells that toll interminably at the beginning of the picture.

'If it strikes *twelve*,' he warned, 'I'll turn into a pumpkin.'

'If you do,' Margalo promised, 'I'll ride home in you.')

Elaine Stritch played the lead in *Sail Away* on Broadway and in the West End. She later co-starred in *Company* in both America and England, and she spoke to me after a matinée performance of *Company* at Her Majesty's.

With Judy Garland at *Sail Away* opening night party in Boston (August 1961).

ELAINE STRITCH:

In Sail Away *I had to have a little dog on a lead, on board a ship. I was staying at the Savoy Hotel, and when Noël auditioned dogs for the part, I went into the theatre right next door—'This I've got to see,' I thought. So that morning he was sitting in the second row, in pin-striped shirt and cuff-links all done up, looking very elegant, and a little Dickens-type character from the kennels brought on the dogs. And these dogs started to do their tricks. Somersaults,*

240

dancing, jumping through hoops, the lot. *Practically doing 'Swanee' with hats and canes. And I could see Noël saying to himself, 'Oh Christ!' And on and on they went—it was like a Russian circus act. And in the play all I had to do was have a little mutt on a lead.*

And there on the side of the stage sat a little dog with a rope round its neck, doing nothing, just sitting there.

'What's the dog's name?' Noël asked pointing to the quiet one.

'Oh, that's Suzie Mr Coward,' said the trainer enthusiastically, 'she'll be out in a minute, and when she gets on stage under those lights, you'll really see something!'

But Noël replied, 'Any animal who's smart enough not to want to go into the theatre is smart enough to play the lead.' And that dog Suzie got the part. He gave her to me afterwards as a present.

CHARLES CASTLE:

If you had any criticism to make of Noël at all, what would it be?

ELAINE STRITCH:

I say this guardedly, because I love him, respect him as a friend, and admire his talent—but the truth is that he is an extremely impatient man, and rather stubborn. He likes to have his way, professionally, and generally gets it. But the trouble is that he's usually right, so you don't mind so much. But he should never work with bad actors. He's impatient enough with the good ones, but he won't tolerate bad acting, or lack of talent. I think any talented person is impatient with no-talent. It wastes their time, and it wastes their talent. And one thing about Noël is that he doesn't waste. The secret of Noël Coward is his success as a human being. He is kind, generous, helpful to friends in need, gives more than anyone I know—but he never wastes.

Elaine Stritch learning Italian in *Sail Away*.

'Useless useful phrases'
(from 'Sail Away')

```
When the tower of Babel fell
It caused a lot of unnecessary Hell.
Personal 'rapport'
Became a complicated bore
And a lot more difficult than it had
    been before,
When the tower of Babel fell.

The Chinks and the Japs
And the Finns and Lapps
Were reduced to a helpless stammer,
And the ancient Greeks
Took at least six weeks
```

To learn their Latin grammar.
The gutteral wheeze
Of the Portuguese
Filled the brains of the Danes
With horror,
And verbs, not lust,
Caused the final bust
In Sodom and Gomorrah.

If it hadn't been for that
Bloody building falling flat
I would not have had to learn Italiano
And keep muttering 'Si, si'
And 'Mi chiamano Mimi'
Like an aging Metropolitan soprano!

I should not have had to look
At that ghastly little book
Till my brain becomes as soft as
  mayonnaise is,
Messrs Hugo and Berlitz
Must have torn themselves to bits
Dreaming up so many useless useful
  phrases.

Pray tell me the time,
It is six,
It is seven,
It's half past eleven,
It's twenty to two,
I want thirteen stamps,
Does your child have convulsions?
Please bring me some rhubarb,
I need a shampoo.

How much is that hat?
I desire some red stockings,
My mother is married,
These boots are too small;
My Aunt has a cold,
Shall we go to the opera?
This meat is disgusting,
Is this the town hall?

My cousin is deaf,
Kindly bring me a hatchet,
Pray pass me the pepper,
What pretty cretonne.
What time is the train?
Is it late,
Is it early,
It's running on schedule,
It's here,
It has gone.

I've written six letters,
I've written <u>no</u> letters,
Pray fetch me a horse,
I have need of a groom;
This isn't my passport,
This isn't my hatbox,
Please show me the way
To Napoleon's tomb.

The weather is cooler,
The weather is hotter,
Pray fasten my corsets,
Please bring me my cloak;
I've lost my umbrella,
I'm in a great hurry,
I'm going,
I'm staying,
D'you mind if I smoke?

This mutton is tough,
There's a mouse in my bedroom,
This egg is delicious,
This soup is too thick;
Please bring me a trout,
What an excellent pudding,
Pray hand me my gloves,
I'm going to be sick!

On remarking to Noël about the regularity with which old friends seemed to die, David Niven said, 'Every time they come for weekends, I wonder whether I'll see them again.'

'I'm lucky if mine last through luncheon,' Noël replied.

We filmed Terence Rattigan in his suite at Claridges. He had just then been knighted for his contribution to the theatre, and had returned to live in England after many years abroad.

TERENCE RATTIGAN:

Somebody in New York came to me with the idea of making The Sleeping Prince *into a Broadway musical.*

It was a play that I'd written for the Coronation in 1953, and that Laurence Olivier and Vivien Leigh played. And then later it was turned into a film under the title of The Prince and the Showgirl *with Larry and Marilyn Monroe—which was rather a startling combination.*

I wasn't too keen on the idea of a musical, except that I said that if they could persuade Noël Coward to do the lyrics and the music then I would agree, but under no other circumstances, and to my amazement and joy he said, yes, he would do it—and indeed he did.

I didn't, however see it, because it was at a period when I was rather ill, in fact very ill.

Noël came to see me, and told me all about the show [now called The Girl who came to Supper], *recited me the lyrics, and played me some of the music. And then they opened in New York, where it was quite a success. It would have run much longer if it hadn't been so very expensive to run, but it got good notices, and his part of it was acclaimed as it should have been.*

He came to see me in bed again and again. He's a marvellous sick-visitor, Noël. Not many people know that about him; what a very kind man he is. It's a thing that I myself find awfully difficult, a duty that I sometimes perform, but I'm afraid I make it seem like a duty, whereas Noël always makes it seem a pleasure, and manages to make one feel better again.

Tessie O'Shea and Dan Siretta
in *The Girl who came to Supper.*

'London'
from 'The Girl who came to Supper'

I was born and bred in London,
It's the only city I know,
Though it's foggy and cold and wet
I'd be willing to take a bet
That there ain't no other place I'd
    want to go.

London - is a little bit of all right,
Nobody can deny that's true,
Bow Bells - Big Ben,
Up to the heath and down again
And if you should visit the monkeys in
    the zoo
Bring a banana,
Feed the ducks in Battersea Park
Or take a trip to Kew,

244

It only costs a tanner there and back,
Watch our lads in the Palace Yard
Troop the Colour and Change the Guard
And don't forget your brolly and your
    mac;
And I'd like to mention
London - is a place where you can call
    right
Round and have a cosy cup of tea,
If you're fed right up and got your
    tail right down
London town
Is a wonderful place to be.

Noël now began to plan the production of *High Spirits*, the musical version of *Blithe Spirit*, the music and lyrics were by Hugh Martin and Timothy Gray, and Noël himself was to direct. It ran for eight months on Broadway, with Bea Lillie playing Madame Arcati, and Tammy Grimes, Elvira. In London a new cast was headed by Cicely Courtneidge and American musical comedy star Marti Stevens.

Fenella Fielding had originally been cast for the part of Elvira for the London production, but because of differences with the author had left the company before it opened in London. Noël at once contacted Marti Stevens.

MARTI STEVENS:

It was a Sunday night, and I was at Dorothy Dickson's flat. The telephone rang. It was Noël.

'Darling, would you do me a great, great favour?' he asked.

'Of course, sweetheart. What?'

'Do you think you could open cold in High Spirits *in Oxford in ten days time?'*

I was absolutely stunned. I said I'd call him right back. I'd always wanted to work for him and now came the chance. I'd auditioned for a part in New York, but being American, I couldn't possibly get a work permit in London.

However, I rang my friend and dresser Mrs Finlay, who knows me better than anyone, and asked what she thought. 'You could try,' she said, and I rang Noël who said, 'Fine. Be at the Savoy tomorrow morning at ten and read it.' So I read it, and got the part. I had three wonderful sessions with him which was exciting beyond belief.

But Noël was taken ill, and he'd been committed to direct Edith Evans in the National Theatre's revival of *Hay Fever* at the same time, and so Timothy Gray and Graham Payn took over the direction of *High Spirits*.

MARTI STEVENS: *We opened in Oxford and then came the first night in Manchester.*

I made my first entrance on a twelve-foot-high platform, holding a microphone. My first line was, 'Good evening, Charles,' through the microphone, and then I had to sweep on to the stage on this flying cable. Well, as I said, 'Good evening, Charles,' the microphone, which apparently had a short that had landed a guitarist in the last show in hospital, gave me a shock which went straight down the steel attachment to the flying-harness, down my neck, and knocked me off the twelve-foot platform. I swung to the left of the stage, to the right of the stage, and was dropped unceremoniously in the centre of the stage on my behind.

In the interval Noël came to my dressing-room, and wagged his finger at me. 'I'm very proud of you,' he said. 'You managed to play the first act of my little comedy tonight with all the Chinese flair and light-hearted brilliance of Lady Macbeth.'

Cicely Courtneidge played Madame Arcati.

CICELY COURTNEIDGE: *Noël always said he wanted to write something for me, and when* High Spirits *came along, he asked me to do it. Well, we were led to believe that it was a hit in America, and I knew that Bea Lillie had made a personal success in it. I thought it was a wonderful part and I loved the play, but it wasn't until the rehearsals began that I realised that Noël himself hadn't written the music and the lyrics, and that it hadn't been such a success in America either. Then came the news that Noël wasn't going to direct, and I was miserable. He said, 'But Cis, Timothy Gray is wonderful— he's a wonderful director.' But I wanted Noël to direct the show. In the end there were three directors—Timothy Gray, Graham Payn and Noël, who came along in between directing Edith Evans in* Hay Fever. *Everybody was going mad towards the end and it got out of hand, so I lost my confidence. I couldn't do a thing, and I honestly didn't want to open in it.*

I'm a great admirer of Noël's, I have tremendous admiration for him. I think he's the cleverest man of our generation —a wonderful man, with great humour, but he's cruel. He's cruel as hell, and I'm no good when people are cruel to me. That's my only criticism of Noël. I don't think it's necessary to be like that, and when he was cruel to me I couldn't be funny on the stage any more. I can't work like that. I said to him, 'Noël, I want to go. I can't be funny. I'll never be funny again in this part.'

'One day,' I said, 'when you're not in the theatre, you

come home and have a drink and I'll tell you why it's no good. Because you break people's hearts. You've got these wonderful ideas, and you're stubborn because you want it your way. You upset people, and I don't admire it.'

When we opened in Manchester, Edith Evans opened in the same week in Hay Fever. When my husband and I were lunching together, she used to come up to our table and say, 'Well, how are you getting on?' And she would be in floods of tears.

'Nothing will make me work for him again,' she cried. 'I've got enough money. I've got a home. Why should I be insulted?'

Yet if he walked in here now he'd be so charming and we'd all adore him. Everyone does adore him—me included—but he's hell to work with, and I never want to do anything else with him. I'd have to be starving, I really would. Yet if he were to ask me to go and do something for him at a charity or something like that, I'd be delighted to

Cicely Courtneidge
as Madame Arcati

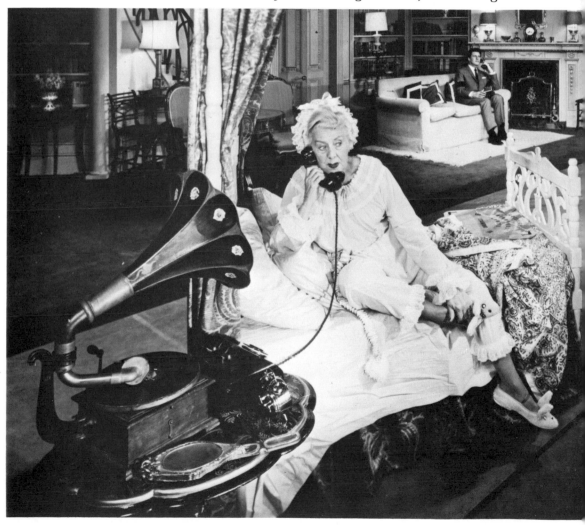

do so. I'd be thrilled to meet him socially or ask him to come and have dinner, and just be together quietly with him. I'd love that. We did have supper together and we talked until the early hours, and Noël was Noël. We laughed a lot, and I listened to all the wonderful things he had to say. He was so kind and gentle, and I thought, 'Oh, Noël, if only you could have been like this during High Spirits.'

During the London run of *High Spirits* the National Theatre's revival of *Hay Fever* opened at the Old Vic, with Edith Evans playing Judith Bliss. Although considered by some too old for the part she gave a magnificent performance, but not before she and Noël had quarrelled on tour.

One night in Manchester she lost her confidence, couldn't remember her lines and refused to go on. Noël, angered by her behaviour, went to see her, words were exchanged, and after his visit, she went on . . .

MARTI STEVENS:

Members of the cast of Hay Fever *told us that they took it in turns to prompt her with the lines, and one hilarious evening when the whole cast, Maggie Smith, Robert Stephens, Robert Lang and the others were on stage, the scene ground to a halt. Dame Edith had to say the lines in order to give the cue for somebody's entrance, and prompting came three times from the wings. None of them could tell her it was for her. She was doing a lot of stage 'business' stroking a cushion anxiously, and finally announced adamantly, 'I won't say it. It's not my turn!'*

EDITH EVANS:

You see, I'm an absolute rebel about one thing. I cannot and will not learn my part before I come to rehearsal. I justify myself by that—I know what Noël means when he says he expects everyone to be word perfect on the first day of rehearsal, that when you've got the words, you can get on with the staging, and the meaning, but I can't get on until I know how I am going to say them.

I'm not quite sure how I learn my parts. I've tried to figure it out recently. Do I learn by the sound of the words? I certainly don't learn by the look of them on the page. If Noël wants you to learn it all and then come knowing the words and begin to act, I don't do that because I don't know how I'm going to say them. For instance that thing of having a postcard in front of the line—once you've taken the postcard away, I don't know what the line is any more! It has to be alive *if it has to be somebody saying it. It has to have meaning. And that's what our quarrel was about.*

All the same I enjoyed Hay Fever *tremendously. I felt— it's one of his qualities—I felt it had been written now—*

and it was written a long time ago. I felt it was written for me, *because she was a delicious silly woman, and I loved playing her.*

One always likes seeing Noël, and hearing of his successes. He's a wily old bird [at this Dame Edith's voice rises, and her eyes gleam]. *He can get into two or three little words, just dripped out, such a witty comment on the situation. He doesn't waste words. It's a style of his own, but it certainly is going on. It goes on through today. It isn't dated, as so many good writers are. He has this extraordinary quality of being up to date.*

Now I think it would be quite safe to say that almost anywhere in the world today where they have knowledge of the theatre, mention the name Noël and they would know at once that one meant Noël Coward. He has got an absolutely really truly world-wide reputation. I think it is fair to say that he is one of the greatest contributors to the theatrical scene, because his music is good and delicious, and his plays are witty and they are varied, and they still go on—and don't date, they're playing them all over the place.

Yes, I like the old boy very much. Oh, I must stop calling him old boy. I'm years *older than he is!*

'Why must the show go on?'

```
The world for some years
Has been sodden with tears
On behalf of the acting profession,
Each star playing a part
Seems to expect the Purple Heart,
It's unorthodox
To be born in a box
But it needn't become an obsession.
Let's hope we have no worse to plague us
Than two shows a night at Las Vegas.
When I think of physicians
And mathematicians
Who don't earn a quarter the dough,
When I look at the faces
Of people in Macy's
There's one thing I'm burning to know:

Why must the show go on?
It can't be all that indispensable,
To me it really isn't sensible,
On the whole,
To play a leading role
While fighting those tears you can't
   control,
Why kick up your legs
When draining the dregs
```

Of sorrow's bitter cup?
Because you have read
Some idiot has said,
'The curtain must go up!'
I'd like to know why a star takes bows
Having just returned from burying her
    spouse.
Having boop-a-doopers,
Go home and dry your tears,
Gallant old troupers,
You've bored us all for years
And when you're so blue,
Wet through
And thoroughly woebegone,
Why must the show go on?
Oh Mammy!
Why must the show go on?

A SONG AT TWILIGHT

Noël's next film role was in Otto Preminger's *Bunny Lake is Missing*, with Laurence Olivier, Martita Hunt and Anna Massey. He played Carol Lynley's seedy landlord, clad in shapeless filthy clothes. Apologising for his appearance, he announced, 'You'd really think I was a modern young actor on his way to rehearsal.'

In 1966 he was taken seriously ill while on holiday in the isolated Seychelles Islands. What with surgical operations and seeing specialists in far-flung places, he was out of circulation for over six months, but insisted on honouring a promise to appear again in London. This he did in a new programme he had written called *Suite in Three Keys*, which consisted of one full-length and two one-act plays. He played the lead with Irene Worth and Lilli Palmer.

We filmed Lilli Palmer in the drawing-room of Noël's Swiss villa:

LILLI PALMER:

In this room we started rehearsing because Noël wasn't well at the time, so Irene Worth and I came down here, and we started the play in the girls' school right underneath Noël's house—where, as he always puts it, 'hundreds of brown bloomers flash past'. This girls' school has a little theatre— and that's where we started rehearsing. After the first two weeks we went to London. A week later, when Irene and I felt we still needed another week's rehearsal, Noël announced that as far as he was concerned he was ready for the audience. We were aghast.

'We don't know our lines,' we insisted.

'But I do,' he replied. Well, it was easy for him, he'd written them.

However, we opened. I was trembling from head to foot

above, with Laurence Olivier in Otto Preminger's film *Bunny Lake is Missing* 1965.
above right, with Marlene Dietrich and HRH Princess Margaret.
above far right, with Lilli Palmer in A Song at Twilight from *Suite in Three Keys*.

and breaking out in sweat because for me it was double jeopardy, English not being my first language, and comedy being such a national thing. You can cry in any language, but comedy . . .? Yet I needn't have worried, because Noël is the supreme master of the art of comedy. He handed the cues to me on a platter. All I needed to do was to take them, and I must say all through the play it was marvellous because he's such a wonderful professional. He gives you what's yours, and takes what's his, which is an actor's idea of heaven.

Noël had still not recovered from his illness and had to take a lot of antibiotics during the run. Occasionally he dried up, I suppose because of the antibiotics, and that was very funny, because there was a dinner party in the play, right downstage at the footlights. I enjoyed it very much—chocolate pudding, simulated beefsteak and salad, but he used to dry up right behind the salad—but nobody used to notice, and he would whisper, 'What's my line?' And I used to be aghast and give it to him—and later he grew bolder and said, 'What?' And I used to give it to him again, and the audience never noticed behind all that salad.

NOËL COWARD:

There was one moment in Suite in Three Keys *when a bit of lettuce got on to Lilli's tooth during the scene, which I tried to make her see, and I gestured to my own teeth with my forefinger, and she looked at me as if I'd gone barmy. And then I did it again—and she gave me another quizzical look, so I went into a great act, but she paid absolutely no attention at all—and it was still there when she took her curtain call.*

252

'Suite in Three Keys'
'A Song at Twilight'
(Taken from Act One)

The action passes in Sir Hugo Latymer's private hotel suite in Switzerland. Sir Hugo (Noël Coward), an elderly writer of considerable eminence, is visited by Carlotta (Lilli Palmer), an actress with whom he had a love affair eighteen years before. She has given no reason for her wish to see Sir Hugo. The latter's wife has tactfully left them to dine out, and Sir Hugo is about to find out the reason for Carlotta's visit. They have just completed the first course.

HUGO:	Why did you come here, Carlotta?
CARLOTTA:	I told you. I'm having a course of injections at Professor Boromelli's clinique.
HUGO:	(Frowning) Professor Boromelli!
CARLOTTA:	Yes. Do you know him?
HUCO:	I know of him.
CARLOTTA:	You look disapproving.
HUGO:	His reputation is rather dubious.
CARLOTTA:	In what way?
HUGO:	The general concensus of opinion is that he's a quack.
CARLOTTA:	Quack or no quack he's an old duck.
HUGO:	Don't be foolish, Carlotta.
CARLOTTA:	There's no need to stamp on my little

253

	joke as though it were a cockroach.
HUGO:	Well? (He smiles a faintly strained smile) I'm still waiting to hear the reason that induced you suddenly to make this, shall we say, rather tardy reappearance in my life? It must be a fairly strong one.
CARLOTTA:	Not so very strong really. It's only actually an irrelevant little favour. Irrelevant to you I mean, but important to me.
HUGO:	What is it?
CARLOTTA:	Prepare yourself for a tiny shock.
HUGO:	(With a note of impatience) I'm quite prepared. Go on.
CARLOTTA:	I, too, have written an autobiography.
HUGO:	(Raising his eyebrows) Have you? How interesting.
CARLOTTA:	There's a distinct chill in your voice.
HUGO:	I'm sorry. I was unaware of it.
CARLOTTA:	It is to be published in the autumn.
HUGO:	Congratulations. Who by?
CARLOTTA:	Doubleday in New York and Heinemann in London.
HUGO:	(Concealing surprise) Excellent.
CARLOTTA:	(With a trace of irony) I'm so glad you approve.
HUGO:	And have you written it all yourself? Or have you employed what I believe is described as a 'ghost writer'?
CARLOTTA:	No, Hugo. I have written every word of it myself.
HUGO:	Well done.
CARLOTTA:	On an electric typewriter. You really should try one. It's a godsend.
HUGO:	I have no need of it. Hilde does my typing for me.
CARLOTTA:	Of course, yes - I'd forgotten. Then you can give her one for a birthday present.
HUGO:	(After a slight pause) I suppose you want me to write an introductory preface.
CARLOTTA:	No. I've already done that myself.
HUGO:	(With a tinge of irritation) What is it, then? What is it that you want of me?
CARLOTTA:	Permission to publish your letters.

HUGO:	(Startled) Letters? What letters?
CARLOTTA:	The letters you wrote to me when we were lovers. I've kept them all.
HUGO:	Whatever letters I wrote to you at that time were private. They concerned no one but you and me.
CARLOTTA:	I agree. But that was a long time ago. Before we'd either of us become celebrated enough to write our memoirs.
HUGO:	I cannot feel that you, Carlotta, have even yet achieved that particular distinction.
CARLOTTA:	(Unruffled) Doubleday and Heinemann do.
HUGO:	I believe that some years ago Mrs Patrick Campbell made a similar request to Mr George Bernard Shaw and his reply was, 'Certainly not. I have no intention of playing the horse to your Lady Godiva.'
CARLOTTA:	How unkind.
HUGO:	It would ill become me to attempt to improve on Mr George Bernard Shaw.
CARLOTTA:	(Helping herself to some more salad) You mean you refuse?
HUGO:	Certainly. I most emphatically refuse.
CARLOTTA:	I thought you would.
HUGO	In that case surely it was a waste of time to take the trouble to ask me?
CARLOTTA:	I just took a chance. After all, life can be full of surprises sometimes, can't it?
HUGO:	If your forthcoming autobiography is to be peppered with that sort of bromide it cannot fail to achieve the bestseller list.
CARLOTTA:	You can turn nasty quickly, can't you? You were quite cosy and relaxed a moment ago.
HUGO:	I am completely horrified by your suggestion. It's in the worst possible taste.
CARLOTTA:	Never mind. Let's have some more champagne. (She takes the bottle out of the bucket and pours herself some. She holds it up to him enquiringly)
HUGO:	Not for me, thank you.
CARLOTTA:	There's quite a lot left.

HUGO:	Finish it by all means.
CARLOTTA:	Professor Boromelli will be furious.
HUGO:	I gather he doesn't insist on any particular regime. What sort of injections does he give you?
CARLOTTA:	(Enjoying her steak) Oh it's a formula of his own. Hormones and things.
HUGO:	The same kind of treatment as Niehans?
CARLOTTA:	Oh no, quite different. Niehans injects living cells from an unborn ewe, and as long as he doesn't pick a non U Ewe it works like a charm.
HUGO:	Have you been to him as well?
CARLOTTA:	Oh yes, ages ago. He's an old duck too.
HUGO:	You seem to regard Switzerland as a sort of barnyard.
CARLOTTA:	(Raising her glass to him) Quack quack!
HUGO:	(Crossly) Don't be so childish.
CARLOTTA:	(Laughing) You used to enjoy my jokes when you and I were young, love, and all the world was new.
HUGO:	Flippancy in a girl of twenty-one can be quite attractive, in a woman of more mature years it is liable to be embarrassing.
CARLOTTA:	Like a bad temper in a pompous old gentleman –
	(Felix re-enters, wheeling a table on which is a chocolate soufflé)
CARLOTTA:	(Continued) – Perfect timing, Felix. I congratulate you.
FELIX:	Thank you, madame. (He deftly removes the empty plates to the movable table, places clean ones before them and proceeds to serve the soufflé.)
CARLOTTA:	(After a longish pause) The lake's like glass tonight. There'll be a moon presently.
HUGO:	How clever of you to know.
CARLOTTA:	There was a moon last night. I just put two and two together. (To Felix) Sir Hugo tells me you are half Austrian and half Italian, Felix.
FELIX:	That is correct, madame.
CARLOTTA:	Which half do you like best?
HUGO:	Please, Carlotta –

FELIX:	I find the two perfectly satisfactory, madame. (He smiles)
CARLOTTA:	I expect both the waltz and the tarantella come quite naturally to you.
HUGO:	(Testily) That will be all for the moment, Felix. Please bring the coffee immediately.
FELIX:	Subito, signore! (He bows, smiles at Carlotta, and leaves)
HUGO:	I hate familiarity with servants.
CARLOTTA:	Oh, eat up your soufflé for God's sake and stop being so disagreeable.
HUGO:	(Outraged) How dare you speak to me like that!
CARLOTTA:	Dare? Really Hugo. What have I to fear from you?
HUGO:	I consider your rudeness insufferable.
CARLOTTA:	And I consider your pomposity insufferable.
HUGO:	(Icily) I should like to remind you that you are my guest.
CARLOTTA:	Of course I am. Don't be so silly.
HUGO	And as such I have the right to demand from you at least a semblance of good manners.
CARLOTTA:	'Semblance of good manners'! Talk about clichés. That's a clanger if ever I heard one.
HUGO:	(Quivering with rage) Once and for all, Carlotta –
CARLOTTA:	For heaven's sake calm down. Your wife told me earlier on that it was bad for you to over-excite yourself. You'll have a fit in a minute if you don't stop gibbering.
HUGO:	(Beside himself, shouting) I am not gibbering! (There is silence for a moment. Carlotta continues to eat her soufflé. (Hugo rises majestically) (With superb control) I think, Carlotta, that as we really haven't very much more to say to each other, it would be considerate of you to leave as soon as you've finished eating. As I told you, I have been rather ill recently and it is my habit to retire early. I also feel that I have reached an age when I no

257

	longer have to tolerate being spoken to as you spoke just now.
CARLOTTA:	If you are determined to decline so rapidly you'll reach an age when nobody will be able to speak to you at all.
HUGO:	I am sorry if I appear to be discourteous, but after all, it was you who forced us both into this – this rather unprofitable meeting. I have done my best to receive you kindly and make the evening a pleasant one. That I have failed is only too obvious. I am sorry also that I was unable to accede to your request. I am sure, after you have given yourself time to think it over, that you will realise how impertinent it was.
CARLOTTA:	Why impertinent?
HUGO:	Not having read your book I have naturally no way of judging whether it is good, bad or indifferent. I am perfectly aware, however, that whatever its merits, the inclusion of private letters from a man in my position, would enhance its value considerably. The impertinence I think lies in your assuming for a moment that I should grant you permission to publish them. We met and parted many years ago. Since then we have neither of us communicated with each other. You have pursued your career, I have pursued mine. Mine, if I may say so without undue arrogance, has been eminently successful. Yours, perhaps less so. Doesn't it strike you as impertinent that, after so long a silence you should suddenly ask me to provide you with my name as a stepping-stone?
CARLOTTA:	(<u>Looking at him thoughtfully</u>) Am I to be allowed a cup of coffee before I leave?
HUGO:	Of course. He will bring it in a moment.
CARLOTTA:	Poor Hugo.
HUGO:	I am in no need of your commiseration.
CARLOTTA:	Think carefully and you may not be quite so sure.
HUGO:	I haven't the faintest idea what you are implying nor, I must frankly admit, am I particularly interested.

CARLOTTA:	I am implying that a man who is capable of refusing a request as gracelessly and contemptuously as you have done can be neither happy nor secure.
HUGO:	Happy and secure? My dear Carlotta, I salute the facility with which you have picked up the glib, sentimental jargon of American women's magazines.
CARLOTTA:	Look out, Hugo. You're riding for a fall. Your high horse may suddenly buck and throw you. (Felix enters with the coffee)
FELIX:	Coffee – m'sieur?
HUGO:	For madame only. You can put it over here and take away the dinner table.
FELIX:	Very good, sir.
CARLOTTA:	You're afraid of not sleeping?
HUGO:	(Coldly) I never drink coffee in the evening.
CARLOTTA:	What about a nice cup of cocoa? Inelegant but soothing.
FELIX:	That will be all, m'sieur?
HUGO:	Yes, thank you.
FELIX:	Goodnight sir – madame.
CARLOTTA:	Goodnight Felix. The dinner was delicious and the service impeccable.
FELIX:	(Shooting a quizzical glance at Hugo's stony face) Madame is most kind. A votre service, M'sieur. (He bows and wheels the table out of the room).
HUGO:	(Pouring out a cup of coffee) Do you take sugar?
CARLOTTA:	Yes please, a little. How long have I got before the curfew sounds?
HUGO:	(Ignoring this) Here's your coffee.
CARLOTTA:	The letters really are very good, Hugo. It's disappointing that you won't allow me to use them. They are love letters of course, up to a point, and brilliantly written. The more ardent passages are exquisitely phrased, although they do give the impression that they were commissioned by your head rather than dictated by your heart.
HUGO:	I have no wish to discuss the matter any further.
CARLOTTA:	It seems a pity that posterity should

	be deprived of such an illuminating example of your earlier work.
HUGO:	I really am very tired Carlotta. I feel that my age entitles me to ask you to leave me alone now. Perhaps we may meet and talk again within the next few days.
CARLOTTA:	My wrap is in your bedroom. Hilde put it there. May I fetch it?
HUGO:	By all means.

<u>(Carlotta goes into the bedroom. Hugo lights a cigarette and then immediately stubs it out again. He is obviously seething with irritation. He opens the table drawer, takes two white tablets out of a bottle and crunches them)</u>
<u>(Carlotta returns)</u>

CARLOTTA:	Goodnight, Hugo. I'm sorry the evening has ended so . . . so uncosily.
HUGO:	So am I, Carlotta. So am I.
CARLOTTA:	(<u>Turning, on her way to the door</u>) To revert for a moment to the unfortunate subject of the letters. You may have them if you like. They are of no further use to me.
HUGO:	That is most generous of you.
CARLOTTA:	I'm afraid I can't let you have the others, though. That would be betraying a sacred promise.
HUGO:	Others? What others?
CARLOTTA:	Your letters to Perry.
HUGO:	(<u>Visibly shaken</u>) My letters to Perry! What do you mean?
CARLOTTA:	Perry Sheldon. I happened to be with him when he died.
HUGO:	What do you know about Perry Sheldon?
CARLOTTA:	Among other things, that he was the only true love of your life. Goodnight, Hugo. Sleep well.

<u>(Curtain as Carlotta turns upstage, exiting through the door.</u>)

After the publication of a book of short stories, *Bon Voyage*, and a volume of verses called *Not yet the Dodo*, Noël appeared in another film, *Boom*, with Elizabeth Taylor and Richard Burton, adapted by Tennessee Williams from his own play *The milk train doesn't stop here any more*, and directed by Joseph Losey.

RICHARD BURTON:

Oddly enough, though both Elizabeth and myself have

known Noël for many years, we only worked with him four years ago, in Sardinia, in Boom. Noël played a part that was originally written for a lady but was quickly transferred to accommodate Noël, and of course he played it absolutely superbly.

I was particularly fascinated to see what would happen when two major figures in the world of theatre and film confronted each other head-on. It was fascinating to see the particular kind of fencing that went on between these two dynamic characters. The major scene was a night shot, as I remember, when I wasn't working, and normally I would have stayed at home and read, or slept the night through, but I was so fascinated that I stayed on the set right through the night to watch their performances. Noël thought I was terribly professional, being prepared to stay up for so long when I wasn't asked to work, but I enjoyed watching him work tremendously.

With Elizabeth Taylor in *Boom*.

About two or three years ago Noël, Elizabeth and I were going to a Royal wedding. That is to say, not entirely a Royal wedding; the couple involved were not Royal [they were Sharon Cazalet and Simon Hornby] but Royalty attended the wedding—the Queen Mother, and Princess Margaret. It was an exquisite occasion, held in Kent, and naturally because of the great friendship Elizabeth and the bride had, and because Royalty were going to be there, Noël insisted that I should put on top hat and tails. I didn't possess such garments, but I borrowed *some from a friend, and was dressing at the hotel when Noël arrived. I couldn't get the collar button fixed, and I cursed and bawled and shouted, insisting how ridiculous it was that I of all people should have to dress up in such clothes. I was terribly angry and red-faced, and Noël sat there implacably and said, 'You are without any question the man I dislike most in the world—with the possible exception of the man who saved my life during the war.' And with veins standing out of my forehead, I said, 'Crimean?'*

'No!' he said tartly, 'Roses!'

At the wedding itself, we sat down and drank champagne in this lovely garden, after the Queen Mother and Princess Margaret had left, and out through the French windows came a few assorted Lords and a Duke and many Honourables, and Noël looked up, looking, as someone once said of him, like a very handsome tortoise, and said, 'Here comes the riff-raff.'

An example of the enchantment of being in the company of Noël Coward is perhaps slightly illustrated by a post-Christmas Day party at our house in Switzerland to which came Noël, who lives quite nearby, and David Niven, who also lives nearby, and perhaps twenty other people. At this little hangover party, the subject turned to aberrations—mental aberrations—and everyone had a contribution to make.

Lorn Loraine.

David Niven said that he for a fact knew of a man who could become excited—sexually—if he sat naked in a cake. This then prompted Noël to give us a lecture—lasting, I would say, roughly two and a half hours—on the particular kind of cake one should sit in for this particular stimulation. I cannot repeat of course verbatim exactly what was said, but I can only say that I was very ill for about two days because I laughed so much. I mean the choice, the delicate choice, as to whether the cake should have icing or whether it should be chocolate mousse was of enormous importance!

In November 1967 Lorn Loraine, Noël's London representative and adviser for forty-seven years, died at the age of seventy-three, severing one of Noël's last close links with England, and of his closest companions leaving only Cole Lesley and Graham Payn.

Noël's seventieth birthday celebrations began late in 1969 when the theatrical profession regaled him with excerpts from his best known works, at a charity midnight matinée in London at the Phoenix Theatre.

MERLE OBERON:

The last time I was in London was for Noël's seventieth birthday. I was his 'date'. It was the most thrilling experience of my life.

When we went into the Box, everyone stood up and started to applaud—Princess Margaret started it—and I tried to back away, because it was so marvellous for him, that moment. I certainly had tears in my eyes; I don't know how he was feeling! And then I thought the most thrilling thing was after the interval, when the curtain went up. There on stage was every actress and actor throughout the years who had been in every play and in every movie of his, all sitting grouped round the stage as though they were at a party. I said to him under my breath, 'You must be dying,' and he replied, 'I'm a stretcher case.'

His knighthood was announced in the 1970 New Year's Honours list.

NOËL COWARD:

It was most charmingly done. I sat next to the Queen at a private luncheon, and she said, 'If I offered you a knighthood, would you accept it?'

And I said, 'Of course, Ma'am, I should be very honoured and very touched.' I bent down to kiss her hand, disappearing from view, and Princess Margaret, who was at the other end of the table, thought I'd disappeared entirely.

The knighthood itself was charmingly done. I was waiting in a pen with a lot of elderly gentlemen and a very young man came in in order to instruct us what to do, and he said, 'Now look, you see this chair? You take a firm grip on the back of the chair, you then swing your left leg out which brings your right knee into the right position for Her Majesty to give you the accolade.'

top, with Cole Lesley and Graham Payn.
above, Merle Oberon.

And I said, 'If I grip the back of the chair and swing my leg right out I shall fall flat on my face, and I think, having had all these years of making entrances and exits and things in the theatre, if you'll just show me where the chair is, I'll manage to work my way towards it and get there.' Which indeed I did; it was quite, quite simple.

But to be serious, I loved being knighted. It was for my services to the theatre, which have been considerable and it's nice to know that Royalty have recognised it.

Getting a knighthood is like getting a peerage or a delicious meal or anything wholly agreeable. But the thing that's exciting is the career. The rare occasions when you know beyond a shadow of a doubt that you are doing it really well. That is very exciting.

LORD MOUNTBATTEN:

As President of the United World Colleges, I organised the Charity Gala at the Festival Hall in November 1970. I'd got Frank Sinatra and Bob Hope, and I asked Noël if he would come over and introduce them. He accepted, and then I heard in the papers that his health was bad, and I got hold of him and said, 'Look, if you don't feel up to it, just let me know and I'll get somebody else.'

'Not a bit of it,' he said, 'I won't let you down. I'll get there even if I'm taken across Westminster Bridge in an ambulance.'

And that's just what happened. He was taken across Westminster Bridge in an ambulance, but instead of turning left to the Festival Hall, he turned right to St Thomas's Hospital. I went to see him in the hospital— he was terribly upset, and he said, 'I'm really miserable at having let you down.'

'Noël, you haven't let me down at all,' I replied, 'I got Grace Kelly to take your place, and she's much *prettier than you are.'*

'The Party's Over Now'

```
To stay out,
And dance about,
Because we've nothing else to do,
Though every night
We start out bright
And finish with a row,
We've been so bored,
Thank the Lord
That the party's over now!

Night is over, dawn is breaking,
Everywhere the town is waking.
Just as we're on our way to sleep,
Lovers meet and dance
A little,
```

Snatching from romance
A little
Souvenir of happiness to keep.
The music of an hour ago
Was just a sort of 'let's pretend',
The melodies that charmed us so
At last are ended.

The party's over now,
The dawn is drawing very nigh,
The candles glitter,
The starlight leaves the sky.
It's time for little boys and girls
To hurry home to bed,
For there's a new day
Waiting just ahead.
Life is sweet
But time is fleet,
Beneath the magic of the moon,
Dancing time
May seem sublime

But it is ended all too soon,
The thrill has gone,
To linger on
Would spoil it anyhow,
Let's creep away from the day
For the party's over now.

It was the last day of filming Sir Noël's biography in Switzerland and we were ready to shoot the final sequence of the film. The camera was focused on The Master whose final comment was on his life's work.

Sum it up? Well, now comes the terrible decision as to whether to be corny or not. The answer is one word. Love.
To know that you are among people whom you love, and who love you. That has made all the successes wonderful—much more wonderful than they'd have been anyway, and I don't think there's anything more to be said after that. That's it.

INDEX

Entries in italics are the names of plays, films, etc.; numbers in italics indicate illustrations.